excellence in
Public Sector
Procurement

How to how to control costs and add value

excellence in

Public Sector Procurement

How to how to control costs and add value

Stuart Emmett and Paul Wright

ISBN 1-903-499-66-6
978-1-903499-66-5

Printed and bound in the United Kingdom by
4edge Ltd, 7a Eldon Way Industrial Estate, Hockley, Essex, SS5 4AD.

Contents

Introduction

This book adds another title to the "Excellence in" range on Procurement, Warehousing, Freight Transport, Supplier Management and Supply Chain Management.

Why then a title covering just public sector procurement? There are many general books covering Procurement but there are not many that solely cover the public sector.

Yet this sector spends colossal amounts of taxpayer's money on goods and services; in the UK, the NHS is one of the largest organisations in the world, and the world's seventh largest employer (ref: The Economist, October 2011).

The public sector also has its own peculiarities and differences from the private sector, for example, the EU Procurement Rules that guide and direct how purchasing must be undertaken.

At regional and local level there are additional priorities, which are often subject to political oversight. In addition there are opportunities to use Procurement as a tool for wider objectives.

Regulation can constrain and limit procurement best practice; such tensions will be explored in the book. However the main thrust of the book, will be the requirement to work working within the existing European rules and guidelines.

Whilst the approaches and practices identified in this book should have applicability in many, if not most countries, there are some aspects to be considered when moving out of the English or EU contexts, and we indicate some of these in the Appendices.

In writing this book, we have endeavoured not to include anything that if used, would be injurious or cause financial loss to the user. It must be appreciated that legislation, rules and regulations change. The user is therefore strongly recommended before applying or using any of the contents, to check and verify their own organisation's policy/requirements. No liability will be accepted by the authors for the use of any of the contents.

The public sector in the UK is undergoing significant changes as a result of the increased attention focused on public finances resulting from the new government and the global downturn. These changes are continuing during the production of the book, and so cannot be fully captured. One change worth noting is that the Office of Government

Commerce (OGC) has been incorporated into the Cabinet Office. As a result the numerous OGC documents referred to in this book can be found in the National Archives rather than the OGC website, which is no longer being updated.

It can also happen in a lifetime of learning and meeting people, that the original source of an idea or information has been forgotten. If we have omitted in this book to give anyone due credit, we apologise and hope they will make contact so we can correct the error in future editions.

Due to the involvement of Government and the ensuing changes made to legislation and departmental names/websites, we have maintained an up to date blog at www. pawablog.blogspot. Here you will find, as well as updates, topical discussions and comments on public sector procurement.

This book is intended for:
*   Professional managers in all public sector procurement and supply roles and positions.
*   Suppliers in the private sector who need to understand the public sector
*   Academics such as lecturers or students studying business topics like procurement, purchasing and the supply chain
*   Students of professional institutes such as the Chartered Institute of Purchasing and Supply, The Chartered Institute of Logistics and Transport, Institute of Supply Management and others.

About the authors

Stuart Emmett

After spending over 30 years in commercial private sector service industries, working in the UK and in Nigeria, I then moved in Training. This was associated with the, then, Institute of Logistics and Distribution Management (now the Chartered Institute of Logistics and Transport).

After being a Director of Training for nine years, then chose to become a freelance independant mentor/coach, trainer and consultant. This built on my past operational and strategic experience and my particular interest in the "people issues" of management processes. Trading under the name of Learn and Change Limited, I now enjoy working all over the UK and on five other continents, principally in Africa and the Middle East, but also in the Far East and North and South America.

Additional to undertaking training, I have been involved with one to one coaching/ mentoring, consulting, writing, assessing and examining for professional institutes' qualifications. This has included being Chief Examiner on the Graduate Diploma of the Chartered Institute of Procurement and Supply and as an external university examiner for an MSc in Procurement and Logistics.

My previous publications include *Supply Chain in 90 minutes* (2005), *Excellence in Warehouse Management* (2005), *Excellence in Supply Chain Management* (2008), *Excellence in Freight Transport* (2009), and a series of seven *Business Improvement Toolkits* (2008) with individual titles on motivation, learning, personal development, customer service, communications, systems thinking and teams. The following books were written with others; *Excellence in Inventory Management* (2007, co-written with David Granville), *Excellence in Services Procurement* (2010 co-written with Barry Crocker and David Moore), *Green Supply Chains; An Action Manifesto* (2010, co-written with Vivek Sood). *Excellence in Maintenance Management (2011)* with Paul Wheelhouse, and the following were all written with Barry Crocker: *The Relationship Driven Supply Chain* (2006), *Excellence in Procurement* (2008), *Excellence in Supplier Management* (2009), and *Excellence in Global Supply Chain Management* (2010).

I would like to publically thank all the authors I have worked with on the above titles; it is always good to exchange ideas and to share experiences. This has continued in this book written with Paul.

I can be contacted at stuart@learnandchange.com or by visiting www.learnandchange.com. I do welcome any comments.

Paul Wright

One day in the mid-1990s, I was asked a question by a manager looking to recruit new people for his team; had I ever thought about Purchasing? The honest answer was no. Like many people in many organisations up until that point I had thought that purchasing just happened, and was not that important. Over the next few months the scales fell from my eyes, to the extent that I have spent the following years either Buying, Training or consulting in Buying, and generally evangelising about the importance of buying and its contribution to the success of organisations.

Originally I was a Physicist, completing a PhD at the University of Leeds before joining Chemical industry multinational ICI. There I had the opportunity to work in a number of functions, including doing some selling, marketing, new business development and project management, before joining the Contracts Management Group.

I left to establish PAWA Consulting in 1998, and have since carried out a range of assignments covering purchasing, supply chain management, marketing and innovation. In the UK I work mostly in the public sector, with clients including Regional Development Agencies, Cluster groups, Councils and other publically funded bodies. I regularly spend time training in Europe, the Middle and Far East. Clients include engineering, chemicals, oil & gas companies, and bodies involved in major sporting events.

Projects in 2010 included studying the supply chains of major sporting events, tender evaluation for UKTI, a study of the linkage between trade and innovation in the chemicals industry for the OECD, and evaluation of a project on printable electronics. Hopefully this proves that procurement is not a narrow based activity.

This is my first book, and I would like to thank Stuart for his help and support and for collaborating in writing it. It draws on my experience of both winning work from public sector clients, and working with them to deliver high quality projects and value for money.

You can find out more about PAWA Consulting at www.pawa.co.uk

I also have a blog at www.pawablog.blogspot, where I shall be happy to discuss any and all issues raised by this book, and to host debates on the content. Any legislation changes, corrections or addendums will also be published on the blog before incorporation into any future editions.

1. Procurement Objectives

Procurement Evolution and the Supply Chain

Procurement is steadily evolving – the following changes and stages can be identified as it develops from a purely transactional process into one delivering extra value to organisations:

- Stage one: Product/services centred procurement that was concerned with tangible products and outcomes
- Stage two: Process centred procurement that has moved beyond stage one into process measurement
- Stage three: Relational procurement that has expanded into purchaser/ supplier relationships
- Stage four: Performance centred procurement that focuses on best product/ service management and integrates relationships, processes and outcomes, which are jointly resourced with suppliers. (Some in the Public Sector have a number of issues here, as having joint resourced relationships can be seen to be in conflict with audit trails and legislation).

Suppliers and the supply chain

Public procurement is following the general trend and encompassing more than simple acquisition. In stages three and four we can see a move to incorporate and recognise the wider supply chain. The Public Sector through the Office of Government Commerce defines supply chain management as the *"coordination of all parties involved in delivering the combination of inputs, outputs or outcomes that will meet a specified Public Sector requirement"* **(Supply Chain Management in Public Sector Procurement – a Guide, in OGC, June 2006)**

This definition is reminiscent of an input/process/output model, as shown overleaf:

1

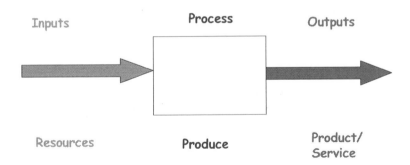

Whilst we will use this model later when discussing Key Performance Indicators, the OGC definition also has the important addition of *the coordination of all parties involved* in delivering a specified Public Sector requirement. This may not be restricted simply to the supplier and buyer. In all Public Sector activities there are a range of stakeholders and interested parties, including the media, which means a wider range of issues may be considered than in private sector procurement.

Procurement and Suppliers are however critical inputs in Supply Chain management – the process, which integrates, coordinates and controls the movement of goods, materials, services and information from a supplier, through to a customer to the final consumer/user. In the case of Public Procurement, this often means us – the public.

The essential point here is that the supply chain links all the activities between suppliers and customers to the consumer in a timely manner. Supply chains therefore involve all of the activities of buying/procurement, making/manufacturing, moving/distributing, and selling/marketing; however and importantly, ownership of these activities is not the issue.

The philosophy of Supply Chain Management is therefore to view all these processes as being related holistically so as to:

- Integrate, co-ordinate and control,
- the movement of materials, services, inventory and information,
- from suppliers through an organisation to meet all the customer(s) and the ultimate consumer/user requirements,
- in a timely manner

A diagrammatic view follows, where it will be seen that the flows of products and the flows of information are represented by ideas, order creation, and cash/orders:

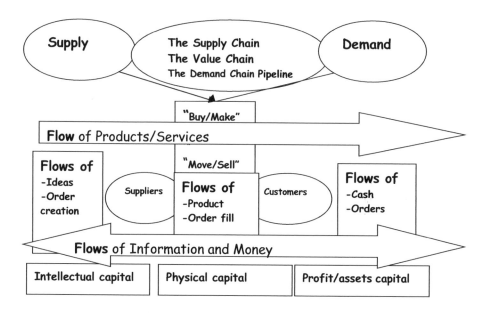

In this diagram:

- The demand chain represents the creation of demand, for example, marketing and selling.
- The supply chain represents fulfilment, for example, procurement and buying, production and making with distribution and moving.
- The value chain represents performance, for example, financial measures and capital in both the internal value chain and the "extensions" upstream and downstream to the value chains of:
  - the upstream first level suppliers
  - the first level suppliers supplier and so on, upstream
  - the downstream customers
  - the downstream users and final consumers

The Supply Chain Philosophy is about networks

Each organisation has not one supply chain, but many, as it deals with different suppliers and has different customers or groups of customers for each of its activities. For each individual, finished product or service, whilst some of the buying, making, moving and selling processes may be identical or very similar, the total supply chain for each product will be different and will involve often a complex network. This goes, for example, far beyond the first supplier and includes the supplier's supplier, then that supplier's supplier and so on.

The supply chain is therefore effectively a large network of many and varied supplier/customer players.

To continue the evolution in Procurement, then all of the activities of Buying-Making-Moving/Delivery and Selling (that take place in business operational functions such as Procurement, Production, Distribution, Services and Marketing) must be integrated through all of the strategic, tactical and operational levels in organisations, for example to:

- Acquire and procure what the organization needs, by spending money externally, to satisfy the needs, of internal customers/users or external consumers
- Follow up on the performance of suppliers
- Provide information and services to internal customers
- Liaise, integrate and coordinate the internal supply chain

Procurement and the internal offer

In many organisations Procurement is recognised as:
- Poviding both value for money and cost reductions
- Taking a whole/holistic views over the longer term
- Using a more integrative process approach
- Building internal and external relationships
- Coordinating with suppliers so as to meet the requirements of the users/customers/consumers
- Helping the organisation achieve its broader goals

Many organisations however, actually operate their procurement activities sub-optimally and in a silo. As a result suppliers, organisations and internal processes are not integrated in any meaningful way. Such issues have been fully covered in the book *Excellence in Supplier Management* (Crocker and Emmett, 2009). What must be clearly avoided is finding there are many internal departments or users who are buying directly from suppliers with little or no procurement department involvement.

4

Procurement should therefore be part of the organisational strategy that involves aspects such as value, risk, cost, diversity, environment, service etc. and recognise that these are all involved in a complex series of trade offs that attempts to optimise the "whole" supply chain.

In the Public Sector, procurement can be seen as bureaucratic, hidebound, inflexible and slow to react. However these criticisms, which in places have some truth behind them, do not take into account the fact that Public Sector Procurement processes have developed to balance a series of competing objectives, such as value for money and market development, in ways that ensure fairness and opportunity for any and all suppliers.

Strategic and Organisational Procurement

Organisational strategy

Procurement Strategy should link to the overall organisational strategy, rather than being developed in a standalone manner. The following points can be noted on the links and connections between strategies:

- Strategy is long term, broad in scope and can be determined at organisational, department or functional levels
- Strategy is best applied by establishing a mission or goals, assessing the organisation, assessing the environment, identifying strategic options, implementing strategy to achieve the chosen option(s)
- Continuous improvement will be needed to continue gain best value in times of dynamic change in markets, shortened product life cycles, tighter budgets and a more demanding public.

Organisational strategy is therefore a concept which provides a unifying theme for all its activities by asking three basic questions:

- What is the mission: what will we do and for whom will we do it?
- What objectives do we want to achieve, what are the goals?
- How will we manage the activities to achieve the chosen objectives?

In the Public Sector these questions have many more dimensions than the private sector primary focus on making profits.

Strategic management of procurement

A strategic management of procurement needs to include the following tasks:

- Reviewing existing suppliers, determining potential supply risks for the organisation and the current spend levels
- Examining existing activities to see if they can be outsourced (both in terms of market capability and political acceptability)
- Developing strategic alliances, collaborations and partnerships with other private sector bodies as well as with suppliers
- Developing strategic objectives and performance criteria
- Development of appropriate sourcing strategies to ensure legal compliance and delivery of the strategy

The strategic management of procurement will need to be related to both the strategy and needs of the organisation. For example, local Public Sector authorities need to demonstrate public accountability, and have interests in developing the local marketplace, as well as ensuring value for money, quality of delivery and legal compliance. Additionally there is an overriding and potentially counteracting requirement to follow EU procurement directives.

Taking a more strategic view of procurement involves the following differences:

Operational procurement	Strategic procurement
Transactional order placers	Value added facilitators
Short term	Long term
Cost focus	Customer/user focus
Internal view	External views
Performance statistics	Benchmarking
Technical processes	Business process

Procurement objectives and the Five Rights

In examining the objectives of the procurement process, let us make the important point that these objectives do not necessarily involve only one functional department in an organisation. Just as the organisation's objectives and strategies cover a number of departments, so most departments should have a role in delivering the procurement strategy and objectives.

The classic definition of the procurement process is the Five Rights:

"Securing supplies, materials, and services of the right quality in the right quantity at the right time from the right place (source) at the right cost"

It should be appreciated that the Five Rights, (quality, quantity, time, place and price) are interrelated. The value however is in ensuring that all aspects have been considered and given an appropriate priority based on the organisation's strategy and needs.

These requirements are not those of the procurement department but those of the whole organisation; the procurement department is an internal service provider that works towards meeting the overall objective(s). Another aim for procurement is:

"To obtain bought in goods/services at the lowest acquisition cost."

The total acquisition cost (TAC) concept emphasises that more than the cost price is involved: for example, delivery performance, stock levels needed, product quality etc. This is covered in the Right Price below. In general tendering processes the supplier is selected either according to the Lowest Price, or the Most Economically Advantageous Tender (MEAT). The MEAT approach has the best chance of ensuring that all of the Five Rights are achieved.

So let's look at each of the Five Rights, and again, it should be appreciated that these Five Rights apply for the whole organisation. Additionally, as we will explain later, the Five Rights are important when determining the Key Performance Indicators for the procurement process.

The Right Quality

Quality is the degree of level of excellence as perceived by the customer; it may also be viewed as the product or service being "fit for purpose" and also "performing right first time every time". These involve such aspects as:

- Meeting requirements
- Fitness for purpose
- Minimum variance
- Elimination of waste
- Continuous improvement culture

The right quality should be agreed by the buyer with their internal customer, who may be an internal contact rather than the end consumer. Whilst the customer may be restricted by design, performance or safety factors, the buyer may be restricted by costs and the desire for market competition.

From the buyers' perspective, the quality agreed must allow for and facilitate fair competition between suppliers. The agreed definition of quality will then become part of the specification, and one of the criteria by which suppliers are evaluated.

The Right Quantity

The right quantity to be ordered by the buyer and being sold by the supplier, will attempt to balance the requirements of both parties. If taking a wider procurement/supply chain management view, then possibly collaboration or partnership methods may be used to better balance the requirements.

Given the number of Public Sector customers who may have similar requirements, either nationally or locally, it may be feasible to pool requirements with other organisations in order to either meet a minimum order quantity, or to seek a better price.

This can be carried out through formal purchasing consortia such as the Universities Purchasing Consortia in England/Wales and Scotland, framework contracts such as those created by Buying Solutions, or less formal arrangements.

The Right Time (to buy and to deliver)

The right time to buy will be influenced by the following factors:
• Availability
• Market conditions
• Competition
• Procurement policies
• Customer Demand

In practice in many Public Sector organisations, it is also influenced by funding streams and budgets – as will be seen; this is sometimes not helpful in achieving the right outcomes.

The right time to deliver will be influenced by:
* Supply lead time , which includes the suppliers lead time
* Organisational requirements
* Customer demand

The Right Place

Buyers need to ensure that the products or services are bought from the right supplier. Once appropriate sources have been identified, the market conditions will need to be assessed and a formal supplier appraisal may be needed, depending on spend, volume and risk, before committing to a purchase.

The Public Sector has greater restrictions on the identification and selection of suppliers than the private sector, but these mostly have the effect of opening up the initial assessment of potential suppliers to a wider marketplace and so, although time consuming, may lead to good outcomes. It is also often the responsibility of the buyer to ensure that the services are delivered to the right location.

The Right Price

Information on prices should be gathered to allow full analysis of market prices. For example, raw material prices could be monitored as such prices may affect the cost of services that are being bought, for example, the fuel costs in third party transport logistics.

Total acquisition cost (TAC) is a concept that can be used to cover the Price Paid plus all of the other costs that are involved or result from the purchase, for example, with services:

• Quality	e.g. errors, defects, returns
• Deliver	e.g. transport modes, time scales
• Delivery Performance	e.g. non availability, unreliability
• Lead Time	e.g. cost of waiting
• New Supplier	e.g. start-ups, assessments
• Administration	e.g. order processing

The question that needs to be answered is: Exactly what are all these costs beyond the price paid? Are they measured and understood? The importance of TAC is that it goes beyond looking at the purchase price and emphasises that there is more involved than the lowest price.

Factors affecting the immediate cost of acquisition are as follows:

- Initial price
- Cost of financing
- Terms of payment
- Performance and technical guarantees
- Liquidated damages
- Conformance with programme
- After-sales service/support

The Five Rights and Supplier/Buyers

The Five Rights actually connect customer/internal users, buyers and suppliers. The following commonalities can be identified.

Quality

Clarity with suppliers will better enable the meeting of quality requirements. A good specification will generally lead to a better outcome. Buyers who are very clear on their requirements may also generate a response from their suppliers that gives them some alternative options, and purchasing processes should encourage the provision of variant or alternative options that may give better value.

Quality needs to be designed into services before they are supplied and those organisations working collaboratively with suppliers can more easily ensure that this is the case.

Quantity

It is the placing of an order that triggers the ongoing buyer/ supplier relationship. Order size differences between the parties will require agreement, and may be one of the issues that need consultation with potential suppliers before finalising the specification. It may be that allowing all potential suppliers access to demand information and forecasts, will enable them to better plan and enable them to better match the buyer's needs.

Time

In the total supply lead time, the supplier's lead time only starts, after the all of customer's internal processes has been completed. If buyers/ customers are reporting delays or variations in the supply lead times, then it may not be always the "fault" of the supplier. An examination of lead times will therefore indicate all the process involved in the lead time "chain." Supply lead time is a critical aspect of procurement and has been examined in *Excellence in Procurement* (and is discussed more fully, for products, in *Excellence in Inventory Management*). In the Public Sector, the requirement to conform to public procurement standards with long lead times for Pre Qualification Questionnaire (PQQs) and tenders can add considerably to the lead time. This increases the emphasis that must be placed on planning and understanding the supplier's lead times in order to commence the procurement process at a time that allows the supplier sufficient time to complete their obligations.

Place and delivery

It can also be appreciated that delivery has common Key Performance Indicators for both the supplier (on the outbound delivery) and the customer (on the inbound delivery) such as deliveries being, on time, in full.

If both parties are able to record these on a per transaction basis and then share such measurements openly and periodically, they will find that this enables better communications and understanding.

Cost/price

When total cost approaches are used, there is really little to stop the sharing of the results with suppliers. Again, this can mean that they may be able to better suggest alternatives and options. It will also show "fairness," openness and "transparency" which are key concepts in Public Sector procurement.

The following are some of the signs that can indicate potential cost savings:

- There are many suppliers in different locations for a nationally consistent service use of a single, non-competitive source, where there is a competitive supply market
- No written contracts
- Existing contracts are old and are automatically renewed
- Multiple contracts with the same supplier
- Paper intensive ordering/approval process
- No real ordering/approval process, e.g for low value purchases
- Price for similar products/services are varied and are not in line with market benchmarks
- Different departments paying different prices for the same goods or services
- Departments placing orders without consultation with procurement
- Orders broken into smaller lot sizes to avoid a procurement threshold value

Differences between the procurement of products and services

There are some important differences between products and services.

The procurement of services is viewed by some as being indirect procurement, whereas direct procurement covers products, goods and materials.

This leads some people to (wrongly) feel they can commission service delivery without following procurement processes. The following simple differences can be seen:

	Products	Services
Quality	Tangible so testing is possible	Intangible therefore difficult to access
Quantity	Large to low orders	Often low quantity
Time	Regular frequency	Irregular frequency
Place	Sourcing can have global origins	Locally dependency is normal
Cost	Low to high	Often high

Services have many unique attributes and so they require a different approach than a standard product procurement solution and these are covered fully in the book *Excellence in Services Procurement* (Crocker, Moore and Emmett). Meanwhile the following can be noted on services procurement:

- Service needs are often unique; processes and sourcing options will differ by service category, for example, it will seen that the eventual price charged will often depend upon the users own measures of fulfilment/satisfaction.
- Spending control on services is often decentralised; different functions and departments are usually buying different services. Centralised buying, as used with standardised product contracts, is not usually an automatic option for services, as standard workflows have to fit with specific local requirements. Local knowledge must also be available so that new users, categories and suppliers can be easily and readily served.
- Subjective factors come into play with services buying; buyers purchasing services will generally, have to give more emphasis on relatively subjective factors; such as skills, knowledge, experience, references and sometimes, the specific identification of individual people. There is a need when doing so to try to be as objective as possible, and thereby ensure that all suppliers are treated fairly.

- Services are also more complex and difficult to price than goods; marketing, for example, involves many intangible activities. How do you price the creativity involved in coming up with an excellent promotional slogan? Investment in consultancy may be extremely worthwhile, but how do you measure the value or the success? Do you get more value paying a higher daily rate for a "big name" consultancy, or a lower daily rate for a niche consultancy or sole trader?
- The total process must be tracked rather than just the order delivery management; unlike goods purchases, the value of services doesn't happen on receipt/usage, but often only at the end of the contract or even when the service people have delivered and left. It is much more difficult to manage a services contract than for product supply. The total process engagement must be tracked to ensure that the expected value was delivered, for example:
  - the temporary worker showed up each day as required
  - the supplier did the work that was expected
  - the consultant completed the project on time and in full (and the recommendations were valid and implementable)
  - the supplier met service level agreements (SLAs)
- Therefore buyers must track the whole performance of service providers, to make sure that the expected value was delivered; for example, supplier invoices must not be paid without confirmation of the applied rates or verification of the value delivered.
- Services procurement is more locally dependent; unlike goods and material procurement, which can be specified centrally, nearly every department in an organisation may be actively buying and receiving services. Moreover, language requirements and other special requirements, and supplier networks are often regionally dependent. For example there may be a need for suppliers with Welsh or Gaelic language capability in some areas.

Product characteristics

For more absolute differences between products and services, we can see that products are those things bought and owned, that will satisfy a want or need.

Product characteristics are as follows:
- Features; are those characteristics beyond the product's basic functioning
- Performance; is the designed output levels that may have been engineered into the product to give a specific level of reliability for given operating conditions.

- Conformance; this is how far the product's design and operating characteristics match the requirements.
- Durability; is the product's expected operating life.
- Reliability; the probability that a product will not malfunction or fail within a specified period of time.
- Reparability; the ease of fixing a product that malfunctions or fails.
- Style; how good the product looks and feels to the buyer

Services characteristics

Services are also bought to satisfy needs and are defined as:

"The performance or act from one to another that does not result in ownership."

Services are an intangible exchange that may or may not be connected to a physical product; they are perishable and cannot be stored. They constitute a significant proportion of all Public Sector procurement expenditure. Compared to products, the performance of services may be often highly variable and unreliable, as whilst products can be engineered and certified/ tested to give a standard and known reliable performance, services will nearly always rely on the performance of people.

With services, whilst there may associated products and goods, such as plant, equipment, or ICT hardware, that have a real part to play in the service performance, ultimately it is the people delivering the service that will give the value/satisfaction.

Services characteristics are as follows:
- Are intangible:
  - cannot really be seen, tested, touched, felt etc.
  - have to be experienced/bought
  - may be perceived differently by different customers
- Are produced and consumed at the same time
- May have a variable performance
- Are perishable and cannot be stored

Services can however, also be directly involved with products as follows:
- Installing; the work done to make a product or service operational in its planned location

- Training; ensuring the customer's employees can use products properly and efficiently
- Consulting; data, information systems and advising services that the seller offers
- Repairing; describes the quality of repair service available to buyers of the company's product.
- Delivering; how well the product and supportive service has been delivered/received/used

As mentioned above, the procurement of services is covered more fully in *Excellence in Services Procurement*.

Procurement by the strategic requirements

As we have shown procurement needs to occupy a strategic role within the organisation. It should also arrange procurement according to the strategic requirements of the organisation, or simply, by what is the most important for the organisation.

Once a need has been identified, the next step is to determine the importance which is applied to the product/service that is required.

ABC/Pareto analysis provides a basis to identify where spends are the greatest and where most effort should be directed to reduce costs.

Pareto analysis can also be most usefully run separately for product procurement spend and for service procurement spend where the 80/20 rule states that, in most cases, 80% of the procurement spends are concentrated with 20% of the suppliers used.

Additionally, risk and other factors are involved and tsupply risk factors can be ranged from high to low, against the following criteria:
- Experience with the product/service (high risk for a new, untried services to a lower risk for repeats)
- Supply/demand balance (short supply /excess capacity)
- Supply chain complexity (many parties involved to "direct" purchases)
- Financial aspects of supply disruption (high to negligible costs)
- Safety consequences of disruption (high to low hazards)
- Design maturity (new to established services)

- Product design/Service complexity (complex to simple)
- Public interest or benefit (low to high)

The other factors can also be rated from high to low against the following criteria:
- Market structure (many sources to a monopoly supplier)
- Value of spend (high to low spending)
- Supply/demand balance (spare to no capacity)
- Efficiency of buying process (identical for all, to tailored buying)

To account for both spend and risk from non-supply purchases can be broken down into four categories based on the work of Kraljic:

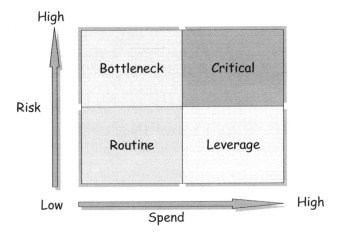

This indicates that different purchases have different strategic requirements for a business. It also can give a broad indication of how buying and the supplier relationships should be conducted and in general terms the following will be involved:

Leverage; Low supply risk, high spend items
- Leverage items are those where a high volume is purchased with a high number of suppliers leading to strong competition. Here, therefore, the lowest cost can easily be found. Buyers are able to leverage by maximising economies of scale and by offering large spends in return for low prices.

Routine; Low supply risk, low spend items
- Routine buying of standard services, needing efficiency of procurement process

above all else. Minimal effort is needed for sourcing these items due to the relatively little impact procurement can make to reducing purchase costs. Therefore acquisition costs are reduced by the use of procurement (credit or debit) cards, EDI, internet ordering and call offs with users directed to place orders direct with suppliers; who then report on the usage.

Critical; High supply risk, high spend items

- Critical items and services require closer supplier relationships to ensure they are always available, and that prices are reasonable. Additionally the service required maybe a specialised one and will involve longer term relationships and possibly partnering approaches with suppliers. These items can also be difficult to source due to low numbers of suppliers. Close supplier relations are needed with possible use of joint working and multi-functional teams.

Bottleneck; High supply risk, low spend items

- The need here is to ensure the supply and reduce the risk of non supply and disruption. Suppliers are often few in numbers. These items would not rate as important if analysing spend alone, but due to difficulties in sourcing there needs to be concentrated effort to secure supply of these items. The supplier often having a strong position as a single source.

Levels of risks

Risk is the impact of uncertainty and results from:

- an unexpected event, for example, unseasonal weather
- false assumptions, for example, on a supplier's performance
- human failure, for example, the misinterpretation of requirements

The sources of risk can be as follows:

- Poor planning
- Insufficient competent resources
- Unrealistic timescales
- Evolving technology
- Poor communication
- Insufficient task definition
- Financial restrictions
- Legislative requirements

The level of risk will depend on a variety of factors, such as those already covered above; the strategic requirements of the product, spend and the usage. The acceptable level of risk will vary from contract to contract.

Risk can rarely be eliminated, but, it can be managed or transferred to another party; the key principle is that risk should be allocated to whichever party can best manage it. However, risk must always be managed; merely "dumping" the risk on a supplier is likely to create an eventual failure, and the buyer's organisation will then be directly affected.

Commercial risks may be taken as the degree of risk in a transaction is often seen as being linked to the potential for commercial gain, with some "risky" deals leading to better prices (and others failing completely). Specifically for procurement, the following are examples of such commercial risks:
• Supplier liquidation
• Poor performance
• Supplier failure to meet environmental requirements
• Cost and/or price inflation
• Changes in law

Public Sector organisations are often reluctant to consider "risky" transactions because of the need to justify any failed purchases. By doing so they can miss out on opportunities to source products and services at low prices. What is required is a balanced assessment of the risks and potential benefits in a transaction.

Risk factors must be identified and then the probability of each risk occurring should be estimated. Risks can then be placed in rank order and the likely impacts of each risk on success factors are determined.

The risk assessment process therefore has the following four stages:
• Identify potential problems and causal factors
• Consider possibility of problems arising
• Weight factors and assess impact
• Devise strategies to control risk

The idea here is to categorise/segment to focus resources so that we can concentrate on the important few, not the trivial many, for example when using Kraljic, the following can apply:

Strategic items are:

- Critical, say 5 % of suppliers = Tier 1 Strategic suppliers.
- Bottleneck, say 10% of suppliers = T2 Key suppliers.

Tactical items are:

- Leverage, say 35% of suppliers = T3 Preferred suppliers.
- Routine say, 50 % of suppliers = T4 Other suppliers.

However, in many organisations resources are allocated on the basis of the number of transactions undertaken, rather than the risk and value associated with each transaction. This can lead to the undervaluing of procurement as mainly a tactical activity.

Procurement Strategy

As we have noted earlier, many organisations actually operate procurement sub-optimally. We also noted that the value, risk, cost, service etc are all involved in a complex series of trade offs and suggested that these must be examined with all relevant parties to optimise the "whole" organisation/supply chain. Therefore suppliers, customers and internal functions must be integrated in a meaningful way. Many organisations need aligning to their core drivers, such as serving customers "needs".

This in turn impacts on the core business competences and capacity. It will also require internal integration and the removal of functional or departmental silos, or to "win the home games first", (supply chain rule number one (of eight) that are fully described in *The Supply Chain in 90 minutes*, Emmett 2005).

Externally, this will mean developing a clear strategic view and fit of suppliers using the Kraljic procurement portfolio analysis described above, or one of the many variants developed by other academics.

The following ideal-typical view presents an **overview and outline strategy for procurement**. As with all ideal typical views, it is not "absolute" but is intended to demonstrate the alternative methods available and that "one size does not fit all." Each organisation needs to develop their own version appropriate to their needs and situation.

Aspect	Bottleneck Items	Critical Items	Routine Items	Leverage Items
Supplier numbers/ availability	Fewer specialist monopoly/ oligopoly suppliers	Few to More suppliers	Many suppliers	Many competing suppliers
Power	With supplier	Interdependent	Independence	With buyer
Alternatives	None to few	Few to none	Many	Many
Costs of disruption	High	High to medium	Low	Medium to low
Relationships	Long term. Supply agreements.	Long term "partnerships" and collaborate with selected trustworthy and reliable suppliers.	Short term and often "distant" and "arms length."	Short term "deals" with possible long term buying consortiums, alliances, groups to concentrate buying power.
Requirement	Need security and certainty of supply. Then find alternative sources.	Need security and continuity of supply.	Need to simplify product variety and the ordering/ supply process.	Need low cost supplies.
Service quality	Critical	Critical	Marginal	Marginal
Procurement Staffing	Hi level buyers with market knowledge and contingency plans.	Top level buyers in the start up, implementation and monitoring.	Low level buyers, procurement maybe actually contracted out.	Medium level buyers.

		Comprehensive questionnaires. Competitor analysis can be used. Agreements for shared risk and responsibility. Public sector: Restricted tender/ Competitive dialogue	RFI/RFQ with possible ITT/ competitive bidding. Public sector: Open or restricted tender or low value route	Elemental questionnaires with some RFI/RFQs. ITT and competitive bidding with reverse/e-auctions. Public sector: Open tender E auctions
Sourcing methods	RFI/RFQ Public sector: Restricted Tender or Single source Negotiation			
Orders	Quick responses.	Possible framework agreements with call offs and vendor managed inventory.	User direct call offs with agreements; otherwise spot buys/self managed with P-cards/web ordering.	Standard POs.

An important aspect to consider is how the different strategies line up and if they are really being consistently applied in the organisation. For example, an organisation may proclaim that "quality is number one", but then select suppliers based on the lowest price.

The point here of course, as with any strategy, is that it is the implementation and application that is critical; the design is the easiest part. Merely trying to implement by the planners and strategists "waving the wand" is damaging, wrong and can be fatal. It is a pity that more strategists in organisations (and in politics) do not recognise this simple eternal truth.

Finally to summarise for the public sector, the following Kraljic segmentation maybe applied (diagram overleaf):

Kraljic : Purchasing portfolio for Public sector

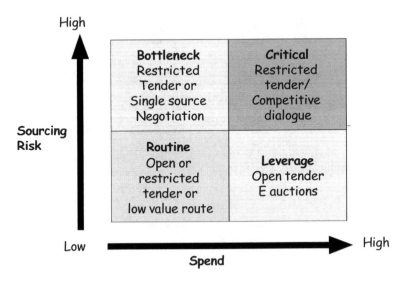

2: The procurement cycle stages

The standard procurement process follows the following procurement cycle:

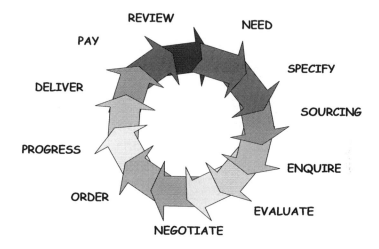

This procurement process cycle involves the pre-order, the order and the post order stages, as follows:

The Pre-Order stage:
This covers Need/Requirements – Specify – Sourcing – Enquiry – Evaluation –Negotiation/Selecting.

The time taken to complete this pre-order stage can be long, especially with contract approvals for new projects and the following example from a public sector company (in the Oil & Gas sector) illustrates their contract approval lead times.

Contract Approval Stage	Involves	Time
Receipt of the requisition.	Agreeing the specification/ scope of work (SOW)	8-12 weeks
The strategy approval of the scope of work/specification.	Internal approval	1 week
	Partner approval	6-8 weeks
	Government approval	12-16 weeks

Supplier/Market approach e.g. with ITT	Sending to receiving the ITT response.	Variable, but say 1-4 weeks
Receipt of the ITT to the award recommendation. e.g. use of Tender committees	Internal approval	1 week
	Partner approval	6-8 weeks
	Government approval	12-16 weeks
The contract award	Contract placed	1 week
Total Timescale		**48-67 weeks**

After the preorder stage, the following stages are involved:

The Order stage:
Ordering – Progressing/Expediting – Delivery/receipt
The Post order stage:
Payment/Invoice verification – Reviewing

We will explore each of these, and start with the pre order stage. Please note this discussion largely covers the principles behind such stages, we shall context these further with examples, where appropriate, of the public sector and will cover specific public sector directives in Part 3.

Needs/Specifying

Handling Orders and Requisitions

An initial requisition may be used to identify the user or customer needs by for example, simply defining the product coding required. Here the details on a requisition will include:

- Name and contact details of the customer/user. This ensures that costs are internally allocated correctly, the contact is also available should there be any queries.
- Item details. This needs to be provided in enough depth to enable sourcing from a competitive market. Too much detail can restrict the buyer's ability to identify potential sources.
- Delivery details. This will be required either direct to customer or into storage. It will include the time of delivery and instructions regarding changes and late arrivals.

- Signature of authority. Procurement will maintain a list of those with the authority to spend budgets and where applicable the spend limit.

With more complex items and for projects, contract plans will be used. In these cases a thorough analysis of need and supplier capabilities will be carried out prior to making the final Invitation to Tender (ITT) for products and materials.

Specifications and Standards

As explained earlier there are some important differences between products and services. Product/service specifications and standards will need to be identified, in liaison with the user or customer. Specifications are a description of what a customer/user wants and therefore communicate what is required to meet the needs. They are a statement of need from internal sources that is to be satisfied by the procurement of external resources. Specifications need to be clear; they may therefore take the form of industry used standards, or of coding/classifying products; they may also identify characteristics of potential sources to provide materials and products.

Standards differ from specifications. Whilst every standard is specification, not every specification is a standard. Standards are all about obtaining the expected performance or the expected output from the use of a product or service. Standards have been originated by organisations such as The British Standards Institution (BSI), The International Standards Organisation (ISO) as well more industry led bodies such as with drugs (e.g. BPC), insurance (e.g. Lloyds), and mechanical engineering (I.Mech.E).

Where such standards are found, it will usually imply that there are many supply sources; however the use of such a standard may preclude other suppliers, which in turn, may be against legislation on preventing competition.

Where standards are a part of specifications, it is useful to check that the current version is being used as standards are often regularly updated.

Product coding

An organisation may have a method of identifying products through the use of some form of coding system. The coding system maybe a unique one (for example, the former Materials and Equipment Standards and Codes (MESC) 10 numbers coding that was used worldwide within the Shell group, see below) or, it may be a coding system that conforms to industry standards (for example, the UK food industry bar code labelling of products).

Whatever coding method is used, the reasons for it are universal:
- Provides a unique identifier per product line/item
- Prevents duplication of stocks; for example by ensuring coding is used by suppliers and customers/users
- Provides standardisation; for example, coding a "new" product for the first time can identify that similar products already exist and therefore possible duplication is avoided.
- Simplifies product identification for all suppliers, customers and users
- Can help in determining stock locations; for example within a store holding engineering items where all those products in one main coding category are kept together.
- Assists in pricing and costing; for example with food supermarkets EPOS systems

Example: Shell Material Equipment Standards Code (MESC)

Materials were understood across +130 world wide companies in 94 countries covering over 125,000 items

To classify:
- Main group XX
- Sub group XX
- Sub-sub group XX

To identify:
- Item number XXX

To categorise e.g. who created, special conditions etc:
- Indicator X

Example for item 76.05/39.120.1
- 76 =fittings and flanges
- 05=screwed API steel
- 39=elbows 90 degrees
- 120= 2 inch. class 3000
- 1= item is centrally coded

Determine the specification types

Specifications should comply with the following criteria:
- Are the requirements stated clearly, unambiguously and with only the essential characteristics stated?
- Will it enable suppliers to decide how to cost their offer?
- Can the suppliers offer be evaluated against the specification?
- Does the specification create opportunity for all suppliers to make an offer?
- Does it include any legal requirements?

The development of specifications will usually require liaison between users, procurement and possibly potential suppliers. Trade associations and other users can also help, as can independant consultants who can check and verify the final draft specifications.

Specifications may take the form of the following:
- Technical specifications: such as a highly detailed description; e.g. engineering products.
- Sample specifications: such as to assess the suitability of chemicals or fabric.
- Brand specifications: such as a specific brand which may denote the customer's preference and identify a standard. As this will however limit the supplier options, then any such use will need to have been specially justified.
- Design specifications: such as to identify dimensions and outlines.
- Functional specifications: such as to ensure the product performs 'fit for purpose' or what it has to achieve
- Form specifications: such as shape and appearance.
- Performance specifications: such as the output range within which the item must function.

Role of procurement in specifications

Ultimately, procurement aims to procure products and services which are fit for purpose and the characteristics that give this, may be determined by the specification.
From the users' specifications (or using existing coding), procurement is then better able to:
- Provide information on available supply routes
- Provide a supplier appraisal

- Identify risks on suppliers and products
- Identify where the organisation is able to standardise

Once the product or service requirements have been established/specified, it is important to summarise the details with the user or customer to confirm that what is being sourced is to the specification they require. Additionally, lines of communication will need to be established to ensure there are minimum delays should problems occur and areas of responsibility, should be highlighted and confirmed.

Performance specifications/contracts

The nature of the product/service being procured may determine that a performance related specification is required, perhaps becoming part of the formal final contract. Performance being, the output(s) required from the product or service, therefore, the aim here is to provide a clear and objective view of the expected output.

The following questions can be asked. The answers will assist in determining the objective performance outcomes, such as the following:

- Clarity; what has to be done and who is accountable with clear levels of responsibility and authority.
- Competence; do the knowledge and skills exist in supplier and users?
- Consequences; why is it being done?
- Competition; what other tasks are there to do? Prioritising may be needed.
- Co-operation; who else is involved?
- Control; how will it be known that the desired and satisfactory end has been reached?
- Commitment; do suppliers they have the intention to do it willingly and well?
- Context; are the right surroundings and support available?

Performance contracts

In the UK public sector for example, the provision of services such as ambulance, police, hospitals and fire rescue, have used performance contracts widely in recent years. The aim being to ensure that government objectives can be met by the setting of targets to be achieved that deliver improved performance.

These expected conditions can however fail to materialise if, for example, managers with information and bargaining power but no strong incentive to "comply", manipulate targets to ensure performance is judged satisfactorily.

For performance specifications to work correctly, objectives must be explicitly stated with assigned weighting and priorities, and then translated into clear and agreed performance improvement targets, ideally with clear incentives and disincentives about compliance.

Performance contracts are an enforceable agreement between suppliers and buyers that link incentives and disincentives to the contracted performance outputs. The supplier is required to provide guarantees, for example, a timely completion of a project and for the achievement of performance specifications, for example on quality and cost.

Liquated damages, in English law, may be a part of such contracts; this is a pre-determined estimate of loss by the buyer and payable by the supplier in the event of failure to meet agreements. Liquated damages for delays are determined by a time scale (e.g. daily) and normally will equate to the buyers financial loss. Liquated damages for failure to meet performance are normally based on an amount for each percentage point the failure falls below the guaranteed performance level.

Differences between Technical and Performance Specification

The following shows the important differences between the two types of specifications:

	Technical specifications	**Performance specifications**
Supplier	Receives an exact and clear specification.	Responds to the outcomes required in the required operating conditions and environment
Buyer	Certainty of what is being bought. However these may not the "best", as other options that may satisfy the need are excluded	Must very clearly specify the requirements and outcomes needed
Technical risk	With the buyer	With the supplier

Supplier Innovation	Low/little	Higher/likely
Examples	Simple and branded products	Complex projects

It should be noted that the above technical specifications and the subsequent technical assessment in the evaluation process, are different. As we will see later, the technical assessment looks at compliance with the specification; (and this is either a technical or a performance specification) and also the performance parameters of the specification.

Sourcing

Supplier & Market Conditions

The number and location of potential suppliers will influence the price of the goods in the marketplace. There are often many other buyers for services and products and this will ensure a review by the supplier of how "attractive" each buying customer is.

Markets may be expanding or contracting, this will influence the number of suppliers. The power of each party also has a part to play as shown below:

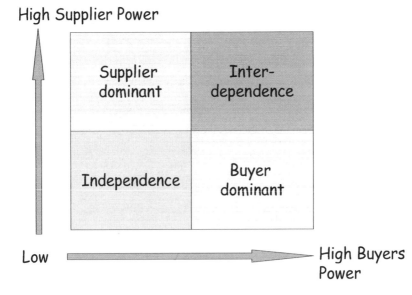

The following differences can be seen.

The buyer is dominant when there is:
- A small number of big buyers
- Buying of a large percentage of a sellers output
- Ease for buyer to switch
- Many sources of supply
- Low transaction costs
- A "take it or leave it" view from the buyer

The seller is dominant when there is:
- A small number of big sellers
- Supplying to many buyers
- Difficulty for buyers to switch
- Few sources of supply
- High transaction costs
- A "take it or leave it" view from the supplier

Supplier Availability

Procurement needs to be aware of any expansion or contraction of the markets from which they are sourcing.

There may be several reasons why the markets appear unattractive to suppliers including:
- The standards that need to be met
- The amount of competition
- The investment that needs to be made
- A low profit level

It should also never be assumed by buyers that every supplier is "desperate" to supply them with products or service. Suppliers also have a view of their market and therefore this will affect a supplier's view of buyers, for example (see diagram overleaf):

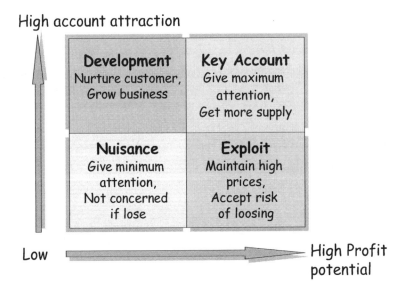

High account attraction

Development	Key Account
Nurture customer, Grow business	Give maximum attention, Get more supply
Nuisance	**Exploit**
Give minimum attention, Not concerned if lose	Maintain high prices, Accept risk of loosing

Low ➜ High Profit potential

PESTLE Analysis

Procurement need to consider factors that affect the sectors in which they are buying. PESTLE analysis maybe used here, this involves the following:

- Political considerations, such as government policies.
- Economic considerations, regarding the employment of finite resources and the effect on supply and demand.
- Socio-cultural considerations, for the people employed to produce and manufacture the materials and products along with the customer base.
- Technological advancements and the possibility of alternatives.
- Legal requirements and contractual documentation and processes.
- Environmental considerations and policies of the suppliers and the procurement organisation.

Many of these factors interrelate and once information has been gathered on the market conditions, it will be possible to compare this to the internal capabilities, as opportunities may exist to contract out non-core activities or services, such as a make or buy decision.

At the time of writing the UK Political situation is changing significantly and rapidly, and this may require regular PESTLE analyses to account for new developments. At other times it may only be necessary to carry this out on an annual basis.

Make or Buy?

Strategic make or buy decisions will involve the overall organisational strategy. Operational make or buy decisions will be based on the capacity and capability of the buying organisation, relative to, the analysis by the procurement department of the potential suppliers.

Sub-contracting may be appropriate where the internal resources are finite, the costs and risks will here clearly indicate that this option is the most viable. Alternatively, the sub-supplier may have greater experience. Buyers will need to ensure that performance measures have been clearly defined for sub-contracting and that all legal considerations have been covered in the contract. There is a potential for outsourcing to be considered as a politically lead activity rather than a pragmatic procurement lead activity, and so sensitivity to external perceptions and potential consequences must also be assessed and if necessary managed.

Procurement Options from Economic Sectors

Prices will overall be influenced by normal economic supply and demand elasticity.
In the primary sector that covers raw materials from farming/fishing (food, beverages, and forestry), quarrying/mining (minerals, coals, metals) or drilling (oil, gas, water) a dictated market price may be found. This in turn works through into the secondary sector in the conversion of these raw materials into products, therefore affecting the price make-up of components and finished products.

Purchases from the manufacturing sector require a good understanding of cost breakdowns, so that a realistic price is obtained; whereas, procurement from the service sector requires greater emphasis on performance definition and measurement.

Procurement Options of Existing or New Sources

Some of the advantages of using existing suppliers include that they can provide information on performance from the existing historical data. Additionally they will have knowledge of the normal practices policies and expectations. When changing to a new supplier, one has to bear the costs of changing, as well as an element of risk. However, new suppliers should not be "disadvantaged" and markets need to be monitored so that opportunities can be developed where spend, risk or usage mean a change is needed.

Procurement Options of Local or Global Solutions

Local suppliers have the advantage of offering reduced lead times and lower transport costs, against the risks and costs associated with global logistics.

Global suppliers, however, do offer opportunities in lower prices achieved from the use of cheaper resources, materials and components. Fluctuating exchange rates would need to be taken into account along with lead time and legal aspects (foreign business law can be complex).

It should be borne in mind here that whilst purchasing may believe they have a local supplier for products, in fact, commonly, these may actually be sourced by the local supplier from a global source.

Consideration of local sources can be involved in assessing the MEAT solution, but it must be emphasised that (in most situations) it is not permissible to select or exclude EU suppliers purely on the basis of geography.

Procurement Options of Single or Multiple Sources

Multiple sourcing encourages competition and innovation; it also protects against the risk of having "all ones eggs in one basket". Single sourcing should only be considered where:
- The market dictates there is only one supplier
- The value and usage defines the material or product as critical.
- A long-term relationship can be established.
- The overall competitiveness of the market is not damaged.

Procurement Options: conclusion

The available options for sourcing will be affected by the product or service being sourced, its availability, location, the number of suppliers and buyers, along with market growth.

New opportunities for sourcing must always be considered for services and products that are critical on a risk or spend basis to the organisation. As global markets are becoming the norm for larger organisations, this offers potential new suppliers and possibilities for negotiation around larger volumes. Additionally, the growing trend for smaller supplier bases with closer links requires a more intensive supplier management with longer-term relationships.

Enquiry & Evaluation

Enquiry by requesting for information

This may take the form of a pre-qualifying questionnaire (PQQ) that is used to invite suppliers to apply for potential business. It ensures that the supplier conforms to certain required criteria, before, further detailed information is provided to them. Pre qualification can use a standard request form that should make clear to all who receive it:

- The mandatory conditions to be fulfilled

- Which parts require a response

- The form and length of responses required

Questions can be asked that will require explanation answers, so that the ability of the supplier can be better judged against the following criteria:

- Financial position

- Previous experience

- References (if not to be considered as part of the tender evaluation process)

An outline example follows of a pre-qualification that covers the supplier capability for offering a service (for freight):

1. Companies outline of requirements
(This is to give the suppliers an indication of what is on offer and what is required from them)
2. Supplier details
(This is to get basic supplier details such as contacts, company structure, and professional qualification/affiliations)

3. Financial details

(This is to get details on financial support/backing, insurance covers/liability)

4. Equipment and Facilities

(This is to get details on the necessary equipment and facilities)

5. Management Skills

(Key Contacts and their skills/experience of the people who will be handling our business on a day to day basis, Training and development policy, technical questions may be asked here to "test" the management capability)

6. Referees/references

7. Customer Service/reliability

(Statement of how you would prefer to work with us, IS 9002 or other external accreditations, methods to improving service/performance?)

In making and dealing with enquiries to suppliers, approaches need to be seen as ethical and a "level playing field" must be maintained for all proposals.

A set procedure should be laid down to deal with the response proposals based on size and spend. Analysis of the proposals can include commodity value, delivery, quality, technical merit, after sales service, security of supply, health and safety and environmental policies. It must be noted that the same criteria cannot be evaluated twice in a procurement tender i.e. at both the Pre-Qualification Questionnaire (PQQ) stage and the Tender Proposal stage, and so care must be taken to ask questions at the appropriate stage of the process.

Pre-Qualification Questionnaire (PQQ) in the public sector

In the public sector, Buyers may also choose a Prequalification Process which will ensure that bidders are able to deliver on the tender requirements.

In practice, PQQs are sometimes wrongly requested at the same time as the final proposals, as some buyers wrongly assume that they can be considered simultaneously. In fact the PQQ must be considered before there is any review of a formal tender proposal. The fact that they share a submission deadline does not stop them from being quite separate processes; only those suppliers who meet the PQQ criteria can then have their tender proposals considered.

The aim of the PQQ therefore, is to gather information that is used to select those to be invited to submit a tender.

It is common that the PQQ will be received, and increasingly completed, online via an E-tendering portal. If such electronic PQQs are used, simple drop down tick boxes can be used for the selection criteria, with provision made for suppliers to provide further information on each of the criteria, either via text box or via attached documents. This allows suppliers to add additional information that cannot be easily given as a Yes/No answer; examples might include a company without 3 years prepared annual accounts who can explain why this is, or, that if selected, a level of insurance cover will be increased for the tender phase.

The PQQ can certainly be seen as a Pass/Fail stage, as the PQQ identifies those suppliers who will be invited to put forward bids. However, responses to the PQQ stage cannot form part of the process for selecting the best bid, even if this is carried out on the same day. There being a requirement to distinguish between the "selection" phase (i.e. PQQ) and the "award" (i.e. tender proposal) stages of any public procurement.

The OGC has published two templates for procurement PQQs and these are shown below:

Checklist: OGC PQQ Template - Business section

Full name, address and website of the Potential Provider:
- Company Name
- Address
- Town/City
- Postcode
- Country
- Website

Name, position, telephone number and e-mail address of main contact for this project.
- Name
- Position
- Telephone Number
- Fax Number
- E-mail

Current legal status of the Potential Provider

- Sole Trader
- Partnership
- Public Limited Company
- Private Limited Company
- Other (please state)

Date and place of formation. Please provide any changes of name, registered office and principal place of business.

- Date of formation
- Place of formation
- Date of registration
- Registration number
- Certificates enclosed (Y/N)

Brief Description of the Potential Provider's primary business and main products and services.

Brief history of the organisation, no more than 400 words, including details of any parent and associated companies and any changes of ownership over the last 5 years including details of significant pending developments, changes in financial structure or ownership, prospective take-over bids, buy-outs and closures etc. which are currently in the public domain.

Evidence of registration with appropriate professional/trade body

Is the Potential Provider a consortium joint venture or other arrangement?
If so, and if it is available, please provide details of the constitution and percentage shareholdings.

Checklist: OGC PQQ Template - Financial issues

Name and address of principal banker together with banker's reference.
- Bank Name
- Address
- Town/City
- Postcode
- Banker's reference enclosed (Y/N)

Accounts information; copy of the full report and audited accounts for the last [x] financial years. If the accounts submitted are for a year ended more than 10 months ago please enclose the latest set of management accounts.
- Profit and Loss Accounts
- Balance Sheet
- Full accompanying notes
- Director's/Managing Partner's Report
- Auditor's Report
- Overall turnover for last [x years]
- Turnover in relevant services
- Operating Profit
- Profit in relevant services
- Current Assets
- Current Liabilities
- Long Term Liabilities
- Net Assets
- Numbers of Staff working in relevant services

Insurance
- Employer's liability, public liability, professional indemnity insurance (if appropriate)
- Name of insurers, policy number, expiry dates, and limits

These OGC templates give a guide on the information to be included to cover the nature of the requirement and the details of the contracting body. They also provide an excellent framework for Public Sector Buyers, as they cover all the essential required information when selecting appropriate suppliers.

The OGC standard format is often modified by Buyers to meet their own organisation's requirements. While this ensures that the form is appropriate for the Buyer, this should not be undertaken lightly, as for example, a seemingly trivial change, even in the order of the questions asked, will impose a burden of work on a supplier for no real benefit. Suppliers often complain about the bureaucracy of public sector procurement and any difference in requirements on various PQQ forms can contribute to this.

Changes in the precise nature of the questions may require potential suppliers to research their own organisation, rather than just simply copy standard answers used for other PQQ processes. This does not generally add value to the process, but does add to the work required to complete a PQQ form. If additional questions are appropriate, they should really be added to the end of the PQQ (regardless of whether that has a negative effect on the "flow" of questions) and whenever possible the standard PQQ form should be used.

To make it easier for SMEs to win public sector contracts, a number of initiatives have been conducted with potential suppliers. Here suppliers had only to complete a single PQQ form to make them eligible for bids covering a range of contracts with a range of suppliers. The results of pilots undertaken by both St. Helen's and Haringey Councils were generally seen as successful and consequently, similar initiatives may help increase the competition and confidence in the procurement process, without, incurring additional costs.

Use of standard PQQ templates

In December 2010 the government mandated the use of a standard PQQ template by all central government departments from 1 January 2011 (Procurement Policy Action Note-mandated use of core pre-qualification questions in central government, Action Note 20/10 December 2010). The aim is to streamline, simplify and speed up the public sector procurement process and make it easier for SMEs to do business with the government. A PQQ will therefore include a core of standard questions, followed by project specific questions and/or sector specific questions if necessary. This will make it easier for SMEs to bid for business, and if the process is adopted more widely by public sector bodies it will be a big step forward in opening up the procurement process to competition.

Additional PQQ Criteria

Further information over and above the standard questions may be required in order to determine whether suppliers should be invited to tender for the contract.

It should be remembered that Buyers are not allowed to use the same criteria at both the PQQ and Tender evaluation stages of the process. This was established in Emm. G. Lianakis AE and Others vs. Dimos Alexandroupolis and Others (ECJ Case C-532/06), and is emphasised in OGC Action Notice dated April 2009. This ruling also stipulates that after the publication of the selection criteria (for either or both stages), new criteria cannot be introduced for the purpose of differentiating between suppliers. This therefore places great emphasis on the need to consider how Buyers are going to choose between suppliers. Clearly at an early stage of the process, it is is not possible to ask general questions and then try to pick a winner from the answers!

Additional information that maybe required in PQQs includes:
- Statement of technical facilities and capabilities
- Quality accreditations, standards and/or processes
- Professional, Educational and vocational qualifications of staff
- Asset register of tools, plants and equipment available for the contract
- Experience of comparable contracts within a given period
- Details of economic and financial standing
- Confirmation that the organisation, directors and senior staff have not been found guilty of offences that would mandate exclusion from the process

Such additional criteria must have a demonstrable link to the tender requirements. It would not, for example, be acceptable to insist that bidders for a waste management contract have a PhD in economics, but it may be appropriate to insist on appropriate NVQs for operators.

Communication with unsuccessful PQQ bidders

Potential suppliers benefit greatly from receiving feedback on their submissions, and this is both an obligation under the EU directive and best practice for lower level tenders. Some public sector bodies are however reluctant to provide detailed for feedback for a combination of factors, such as the effort involved in doing so, the potential for suppliers to attempt to engage in changing the decision, and the threat of legal challenge to the decision based on information given in the feedback.

These of course may be very real concerns, but without feedback, suppliers are unlikely to be able to be able to improve their performance and therefore they cannot add to competition for tenders.

As a minimum, suppliers should be told the main issues on which their PQQ was deemed to have failed to meet the requirements. (Where the failure is made on an issue where the supplier has proved a supporting comment recognising their inability to meet the requirement, then the feedback should recognise this and comment on it).

Enquiry by tender

Tendering is defined as:

"The procedure, by which potential suppliers are invited to make a firm unequivocal offer of the price and term which, on acceptance, shall be the basis of the subsequent contract."

If tendering is required, then an appropriate tendering method must be used. In the public sector this is subject to specific directives from UK and EU government and we will be covering such directives shortly. Competitive tendering is a formal process involving the following steps:

- Identification and selection of suppliers from whom to seek bids
- Issue of invitation to tender (ITT) documentation to the qualified suppliers
- Receipt and assessment of tenders
- Selection of a preferred tender

Competitive tendering aims to obtain compliant tenders from qualified tenderers in a single round of tendering.

The invitation to tender document may be only sent to those who have been pre-qualified (as discussed above); a procedure that will often save much time and effort for both parties.

To achieve this, the best available information must be prepared and issued under identical conditions to all those being invited to tender. The key principles for tender invitation and submission are as follows:

- Conditions for all tenderers should be the same
- Confidentiality should be respected by all parties
- Sufficient time should be allowed to prepare tenders
- Sufficient information should be provided for the preparation of tenders
- The terms and conditions of contract should be clearly specified

All the purchaser's requirements should be set out in the Invitation to Tender (ITT) document and is made up as follows:
- Instructions to tenderer
- Form of tender
- Contract award criteria
- Technical specification
- Drawings
- Health and safety plan
- Pricing schedules
- Free issue materials or resource (if applicable)
- Terms and conditions of contract

The formal procedure for the tender must be stated in the instructions provided to the suppliers with the same instructions provided to all tenderers, along with identical details regarding the buyer's requirements.

There are three general methods for tendering, and these are as follows:
- **Open tenders;** these invite everyone and are only really useful where a small number of suppliers are expected to respond.
- **Selective tenders;** these invite those few suppliers who can meet the selecting criteria and have been pre-qualified. Here the number of responses is controlled, saving the high costs of dealing with a large number of responses, as can be found with open tenders.
- **Single tenders;** only one tender bidder with whom the tender is then negotiated. This may be where the technical complexity of the product being bought restricts the marketplace, or where there is a monopoly.

The public sector tendering procedures use the following three methods and we will cover these more fully later:
- **Open tenders;** this process may be used where there are few suppliers or the buying organisation is attempting to develop new sources.
- **Restricted tenders;** this limits the number of suppliers to tender, but, according to EU regulations, there must be a sufficient number invited so that the tender is seen as competitive.
- **Negotiated tenders;** here the buying organisation may negotiate with selected suppliers. This would be used where no tenders had been received through the other methods available, or where a monopoly exists.

- **Competitive dialogue;** here the specification is developed in negotiation with a range of potential suppliers before a final restricted tender stage. This is suitable when the requirement is particularly complex and/or very high value.

Specific timescales will be set for the tender process and the suppliers informed. Registered post or recorded delivery should be used to return tenders; however email returns being now more widely accepted as are bids through electronic tender portals. Late bids must be rejected unless an extension is given to all applications. This ensures the process is seen to be fair and no supplier has an advantage over the others. The deadline for receipt of tenders should reflect both post deliveries and when the tenders are likely to be opened.

In the public sector, two individuals, who should not be involved in the evaluation, will be appointed to open the tenders/access the emails. Tenders should be registered and recorded, with complete details of the supplier. Next, the tenders are examined against the technical and commercial checklist and at this stage; any offers that do not meet the essential criteria are eliminated. Tenders should be treated as confidential with access to bids being restricted to the tender panel with documentation being maintained in its original condition in case needed for later review. Note that there may be requests for access to the tender documents under the Freedom of Information Act.

Tender review boards may be ad hoc for a particular project, or be standing tender boards that may be multiple in number with varied levels dependant varied dependant on the spend, as per the following example:

Example of tender procedures in a Government owned oil exploration and Production Company

Spends of over $50000 go via Tender Committees at three levels:
- Internal Tender Committee (ITC); Spend over $50000 to $2 Million. Sign offs are dependant on managerial grades with break points of up to $500K, up to 1 million and up to $2 million.
- Higher Tender Committee (HTC); $2 to 10 million. Sign off by committee made up of managing directors of government owned companies
- Central Tender Committee (CTC); over $10 million. Chaired by Government and signed off by the Oil Minister.

Where strict and "open" tender procedures are being used, for example as used in the public sector, then it should be noted that any anomalies in the above tender principles could require the tender to be revoked and the process be re-started. This obviously slows down the process and incurs additional costs, and so care must be taken when writing the initial tender specification and establishing the process to ensure that it is legally compliant, and covers all the organisation's requirements. Legal challenges can arise when organisations do not follow EU, national or the organisation's own procedures. We will now more fully examine public sector tendering.

Tendering in the public sector

Tendering is one of the main processes used for public sector procurement, and is required by EU directive for many purchases (See Part 3 for fuller details). The usage can be seen below:

Kraljic : Purchasing portfolio for Public sector

High

Bottleneck Restricted Tender or Single source Negotiation	**Critical** Restricted tender/ Competitive dialogue
Routine Open or restricted tender or low value route	**Leverage** Open tender E auctions

Sourcing Risk

Low → High

Spend

As will be seen, tendering can be used to achieve objectives in all quadrants with the best form of tender being considered and applied for each purchase, rather than adopting a one size fits all approach, for example:.

- For Routine purchases, open tenders are a way of engaging with a wide range of suppliers, however with a large number of responses for a relatively low value item, then there is a high cost of acquisition.

- For Leverage purchases, with higher spend, the improved prices achieved will often justify the high costs of evaluating tenders.

- For Bottleneck and Critical purchases, tendering really does little to mitigate supply risk, which is the major issue with such purchases. As a process it can be helpful in structuring the procurement, and categorising the supply risks, but it does not help to resolve them. Indeed for Bottleneck and Critical purchases one of the common problems found in the public sector, is that there are not often enough suppliers for an effective tender competition.

Whilst there is controversy about full use of the tendering route in public procurement (such as it being bureaucratic, potentially expensive to administer, does not guarantee good prices, and additionally restrictive because many suppliers will not respond to tenders) and we will open this up in the final part of this book, the answer to why it used is found in what Tendering *does* guarantee.

The prime focus of public sector procurement is not just to obtain high quality goods and services at the optimum price. It has other dimensions such as:
- Legal and regulatory compliance
- Public perceptions of ethical behaviour
- Public perceptions of fairness and openness
- Political considerations about the use of public money
- Political and economic considerations about the wider marketplace

These additional dimensions mean that it is not sufficient for a buyer to be able to point out that they have achieved a good price and good quality; they have also to be able to demonstrate that the process for doing so was fair, non-discriminatory, legally compliant and appropriate.

The recurring nightmare for a public sector procurement officer is seeing one of their procurement decisions as the headline in a local or national newspaper. To avoid this happening they have to make sure that whilst their decision is the right one, it is also defendable; this is where the Tender route is so valuable.

The aims of tendering are to run a procurement process that is:
- Transparent (i.e. well defined, and therefore open to suppliers),
- Traceable (i.e. well documented at all stages)
- Defendable (i.e. legally compliant, and ethical)

Issues with Tendering

Although tendering is a valuable tool for the public sector, there are still problems with its application.

One of the major problems is the time and resource required to run a tendering process properly. The preparation and evaluation of a tender require considerable time, and resources (often a three to five person team is required to evaluate the bid proposals, and a similar number may need to contribute to the development of the specification). In addition, the tender has to give suppliers/bidders sufficient time to prepare their proposals; the timescale for bids is specified in the OJEU legislation covered in Part 2.0. This means that it is difficult to run a formal tender process quickly, and tenders under the OJEU process will usually take one to two months from start to finish.

Additionally, the tendering approach does not provide protection for collusion between suppliers. If a cartel has been established, the bidders can establish between themselves just how to meet the tender requirements, and through payments or hidden contracting arrangements, they can then distort the procurement process which in turn, leads to higher prices (and sometimes to poorer quality). Although it is possible to try to prevent this by attracting new suppliers into tender competitions, there have been a number of cases in the UK public sector of cartels being unchecked over many years.

Case Study: UK Construction cartels 2009

In 2009 the Office of Fair Trading (OFT) fined 103 companies a total of £129.5m for illegal bid rigging, relating to 199 tenders between 2000 and 2006 with a combined value of over £200m. The OFT accused 112 companies of colluding over contracts worth over £3bn.

The main practice agreed between the firms was of "cover pricing" where the firms would agree who would win a contract, and other firms would then submit bids with higher prices in return for cash payments and/or preference on other contracts. The winning bidder would thus have little or no competition for the contract, but to the awarding authority there was the illusion of competition. The companies fined included some of the UK's leading construction companies such as Carillion and Balfour Beatty.

Additionally, the OFT imposed fines of £ 39.2m on six recruitment agencies specialising in the construction industry, after granting immunity to two other agencies for their role in uncovering the cartel. The agencies were found guilty of agreeing a joint anti-competitive approach to a new entrant to the recruitment market with a new business model, Parc UK. The guilty companies agreed to boycott Parc UK, and to fix fees that they would pay to Parc and other intermediaries.

A similar but actually quite separate problem to this "cover pricing" issue is that some suppliers may believe that in order to appear as a committed supplier then they have to submit bids for all tenders on offer, even if they do not have the resource capacity to deliver the contract.

They then submit a bid that is deliberately highly priced, so that they have the opportunity to make the case for their business, but they are not interested in winning this particular contract. In unusual cases, the only bidders for a tender may be suppliers (acting independently) who are following this approach, thereby leaving the buyer with a choice between inappropriately submitted high bids.

A further problem is that in order to run an effective tender process, there has to be a clearly defined specification against which suppliers can bid. There are of course, some situations where it is just not possible to define the best solution at the outset of the procurement process, or where the suppliers may have innovative ideas or concepts that could be applied. In these cases, the tender approach may not give the best results, and a negotiated or competitive dialogue approach may be more appropriate.

The running of the tender process is another problem area, with the most common issue being that suppliers having a different levels of information about the tender either through formal communications or access to informal routes. Occasionally the formal tender rules are not followed, leaving the buyer open to a legal challenge from bidders.

Official Journal of the European Union (OJEU) Tenders

There are two tender routes available for OJEU tenders, Open and Restricted. The processes used are also appropriate with lower value tenders that are below the threshold value, although here the process is often not as strictly followed as with OJEU tenders.

The current "direction of travel" in European Union Public Procurement is towards the use of the formal tender routes for contracts below the OJEU thresholds in order to ensure contracts are awarded in an open manner – unless they are of "very modest value" (see the case Germany v European Commission, T-258/06 in the Court of justice of the European Union 2010).

The Generic Tender Process to be followed is shown below:
- Stage 1: Notification of requirements
- Stage 2: Pre Qualification
- Stage 3: Tender
- Stage 4 : Interview/Presentation
- Stage 5 : Decision/Award of contract
- Stage 6: Notification

The precise form of the tender process for OJEU tenders is clearly defined, and will be covered in detail in Part 3.

Notification of requirements

In order to ensure adequate competition for tenders, it is vitally important to advertise and promote the existence of the tender to potentially interested suppliers. It is also important to ensure that the principles of open competition and fairness are applied.

In the case of OJEU tenders, the tender notice will be published through the Official Journal of the European Union. Although this demonstrates that the tender is available, it may well not be accessed by some potential suppliers particularly SMEs. Further steps can therefore be taken, and these may be the only steps taken for tender processes below the OJEU thresholds:
- Publication on own website
- Publication on www.businesslink.gov.uk and/or other aggregated websites
- Adverts in trade journals and/or newspapers
- Direct contact with potential suppliers.

Known suppliers can be made aware of a publicly advertised tender opportunity, as long as the opportunity is also being genuinely widely publicised. Consequently, buyers may wish to ensure that well qualified suppliers do not miss out on.

Care must be taken though to ensure that are opportunities are made available to a wide range of potential bidders. Advertising only in niche or specialist publications may not be sufficient. Buyers in ethnically diverse communities may also wish to ensure that tender opportunities are readily available to all communities by issuing notices in a range of languages, and advertising in newspapers or websites that service those particular communities. These communities can also be made aware of public sector opportunities; in general, by using targeted "Meet the Buyer" sessions, and using "How to Win Business with the Public Sector" leaflets, ensuring these are in a range of languages.

For some low value purchases, in order to make a rapid and efficient procurement, buyers may choose to run a restricted informal tender process by inviting a small number (3 or more) of suppliers to submit proposals against a specification. In such cases, the Buyer should take sure to ensure that:

•   There exists adequate competition between the suppliers selected,
•   Other suppliers are not being unfairly discriminated against,
•   Other suppliers are aware of processes where they may make a case to be included on such short lists

Again, "Meet the Buyer events" and "How to win Business" leaflets will help to ensure that suppliers are aware of how they can put themselves forward for consideration. In June 2006, The European Commission published an Interpretive Communication on the Community Law, effectively for low value tenders. This communication is applicable to contract awards which are not fully subject to the provisions of the Public Procurement Directives.

The document reconfirms the principles of equal treatment of bidders and non-discrimination, and therefore implies an obligation of transparency to ensure there is a degree of advertising that is sufficient to open the market up to competition (including suppliers in other EU Member states). Implicit here is ensuring that suppliers do have sufficient time between the notice and the PQQ and/or Tender deadline to develop an appropriate bid proposal.

The Invitation to Tender

After selecting a number of bidders capable of meeting the requirements of the contract, they will be invited to put forward proposals.

As well as the detailed specification of the requirement, it should contain the elements identified in below:

- Form of tender
- Conditions of contract
- Schedule of Prices
- Scope of work
- Administrative instructions
- Technical Specification
- Technical Drawings (if appropriate)
- Free issue materials and services (if appropriate)
- Details of the tender process
- Any Terms and Conditions of contract not covered above.

The Open Tender process

In the open tender process, any interested parties are invited to submit a proposal. As mentioned above there may be a PQQ requested to accompany the proposal, and only those proposals from suppliers who meet the requirements of the PQQ can move to the proposal evaluation stage. However, these processes will usually occur on the same day, and although the PQQ and tender evaluation processes are legally separate, they will appear to the suppliers to be part of the same tender evaluation process. The process is illustrated schematically below, followed by the relevant timescales:

EU Open Tender Procedure

Tender Notice in OJEU
↓
Suppliers respond
↓
Invitation to Tender to *all* interested parties
↓
Tender proposals received
↓
Tenders evaluated
↓
Stand still period
↓
Contract award
↓
Contract award notice in OJEU

Minimum Timescales – Open Procedure
-52 days (36 days following a full Preliminary Indicative Notice (PIN)/Buyer Profile notice)
-7 days for electronic publication of the notice
-5 days for provision of contract documents on internet
Minimum 40 days from dispatch of contract notice (net 24 days following a full PIN or Buyer Profile notice)

The process for open tenders below the EU threshold should follow the same format. The Tender evaluation processes being similar for both the Open and Restricted Tender routes, however, typically in the Restricted route, the technical evaluation is more complex.

The Open Tender route is suitable for Lowest Price tenders, and for Most Economically Attractive Tender (MEAT) routes. Lowest Price Tenders are more likely to be evaluated under the open route, as they are by definition covering the buying of commodity goods or services, and will have a wide range of suppliers may wish to bid for their provision.

Note that the process can be speeded up in a number of ways. Firstly the accelerated process can be used where there is an overwhelming case for the use of a faster process.

Secondly issuing all documents electronically on the internet (which is becoming standard practice), will allow a shorter period between placing the notice and the deadline for tender submissions.

Finally the issue of a Preliminary Indicative Notice (PIN) will allow the use of a shorter period between the notice and tender deadline.

Restricted Tender Process

The Restricted Tender route is similar to that for the Open tender route, and is shown schematically opposite:

EU Restricted Tender Procedure
↓
Tender Notice in OJEU
↓
Suppliers complete PQQ
↓
Invitation to Tender to *qualified* bidders
↓
Tender proposals received
↓
Tenders evaluated
↓
Stand still period
↓
Contract award
↓
Contract award notice in OJEU

Typically between 3 and 8 suppliers are sought to participate in the Restricted Tender route. For tenders below the OJEU threshold, the Buyer may choose to select a number of bidders to invite. In other cases, and for those procurements above the threshold, the Buyer will run a PQQ process to determine which suppliers should be invited to put forward a proposal. The requirement for any PQQ stage will add to the time required for this process. There can also be concerns when it is not possible to attract sufficient qualified bidders to justify running the subsequent tender phase, or where the PQQ phase either passes, or, eliminates too many bidders. Meanwhile the timescales for this route are illustrated below.

Restricted Tenders and Competitive Dialogue Process
Requests to Participate
37 days from dispatch of notice (15 days if accelerated)
-7 days for electronic notice (-5 days if accelerated)
Total 30 days from dispatch of notice (net 10 days if accelerated)

Tenders in restricted procedures
40 days from ITT (36 days following a PIN/Buyer Profile notice or 10 days if accelerated)
-5 days if contract documents published on internet
Total 35 days from ITT (31 days following a PIN/Buyer notice, or 10 days if accelerated)

The reason for selecting the Restricted route is often because of a highly complex or risky technical component to the procurement, and so the commercial terms are often of lesser importance than the technical evaluation.

Communication with potential bidders

It is essential to ensure that all potential bidders are treated equally. In order to do this it may be useful to ask potential bidders to register an Expression of Interest (EoI). This is not a selection activity, as with a PQQ, but the EoI assists with the fair treatment of bidders by ensuring they they all receive the same information.

Bidders may well seek a privileged position by requesting information from the contracting authority on a formal or informal basis, for example, by using their contacts to find out information unknown to other bidders. This has to be avoided, and it is common to stipulate that bidders using such approaches may find themselves excluded from the bidding process. In practice of course, it can be difficult to detect or prevent such approaches, and they may be tolerated, unless, there are some clearly unethical aspects.

Modern technology has made it easier to communicate with potential bidders on an equal basis. There are two main routes; e-mail and web based e-tendering/procurement portals. In both cases, suppliers are invited to submit questions to be answered by the buying organisation. The answers are then sent out (by e-mail, or by placing the answer along with the descriptive document on the portal), to all of those bidders who had expressed an interest at the same time.

In some cases, it may be appropriate to hold a supplier briefing. This is when potential suppliers/bidders will collectively meet with the buying team so that they can clarify their understanding of the tender requirements. Some buyers have a view that such meetings may facilitate the development of collusive bids, as the potential bidders are now all being introduced to each other, this making it easier for them to form a cartel. However, if such an outcome was feasible, then the supplier briefing may not be the cause, as most suppliers will tend to be already aware of their competitors and could therefore be already able to collude. The benefit of holding a single briefing for all suppliers are in the reduced time and effort required to ensure that all potential bidders receive the same information at the same time.

Finally here, it is vitally important to keep a record of all communications with potential bidders. Not only will such communications potentially form a part of the eventual contractual agreement, they may also be required as evidence if an appeal is lodged against the award decision.

Bid opening

A primary aim of the tender process is to ensure that all suppliers are treated equally. One of the areas where there is potential for this not to happen, is in the opening of tenders.

The submission deadline for receipt of tenders should be fixed at an appropriate time, for example, by considering the Royal Mail guarantee of deliveries before 0900 hours and before 1300 hours. The deadline should reflect such normal business practice, unless there is a particular reason for the deadline being at another time.

All bids received should be anonymous until opened, and therefore be submitted only in plain and non liveried envelopes. These may be provided by the buying authority to ensure that there are no marks identifying the bidder on the envelopes and also to ensure the use of the appropriate reference codes to identify the specific tender process to avoid confusion if multiple tender processes are being completed on the same day.

Two people, not included in the evaluation, should open the bids and the names of these people should be recorded.

Late bids should not be opened. This may be obvious, but when there is a significant gap between the submission deadline and the opening of the bids there can be a temptation to allow the admission of late bids. This should be resisted because it creates the opportunity, however unlikely, for a late bidder to have an advantage over a timely bidder though the gaining and application of knowledge of new information. In the relatively common case of a known problem causing difficulties for bidders to meet the deadline (such as postal strikes) then it may be appropriate to formally extend the deadline for submissions.

Late bids should be returned unopened with an accompanying explanation. No benefit can arise from opening late bids as by definition, they are not compliant and therefore cannot be eligible for winning the contract. Additionally, if the late proposal was in any case inferior to other bids then it actually adds nothing to the competitive element of the tender. If the proposal is superior to those bids that have complied with the time limit, then all it can do is to create buyer dissatisfaction with the compliant bids; this is neither productive nor fair to those compliant bidders.

To reduce the potential for late bids, the opening of bids should commence quickly after the tender deadline. An hour delay is ideal, so opening could commence at 14:00 hours after a 13:00 hours submission deadline. The opening of the proposals should be carried out by a team of at least two, who must record who has bid for the contract, whether it met the deadline, and whether it is compliant in the number and form of copies requested.

Evaluation of tenders

Whilst the assessment process depends on the scope and nature of the contracts, normally there will be a technical assessment and a commercial assessment. This should be conducted as a joint technical and commercial assessment exercise, but it may be appropriate to conduct the technical evaluation component first in order to only look at the commercial elements of proposals meeting the required technical standard.

The technical assessment looks at things such as:
- compliance with the specification; (either the technical or the performance specification)
- performance parameters
- quality
- maintenance over the operating life of facilities or equipment

The commercial assessment will look at things such as:
- price
- terms of payment
- programme risks
- any commercial qualifications

The objective of the tender assessment is for the purchaser to establish which is the best offer, based on the selection criteria identified in the ITT. If price is the only criteria, then the tenderer submitting the lowest price should be awarded the contract (i.e. a lowest price tender). It is of course not always sufficient to only look at price and the purchaser often needs to decide the most economically advantageous tender (MEAT) or the best value for money. This means that the tendered prices are only one criterion in the evaluation. The criteria used to establish MEAT should be identified (usually with weightings) in the ITT. The precise selection criteria and weightings to determine the MEAT will of course depend on the precise nature of each purchase, and so there can be no standard set of criteria and weightings.

To determine MEAT, it is often necessary to establish the total cost of ownership or whole-life cost (TCO or WLC).

Factors affecting the immediate cost of acquisition (total acquisition cost or TAC) include the following:
- initial price
- cost of financing
- terms of payment
- performance and technical guarantees
- liquidated damages
- conformance with programme

Medium-term TCO/WLC considerations:
- build costs
- running costs
- costs of spares
- operation and maintenance costs
- after-sales service/support

Long-term TCO/WLC considerations:
- component replacement life
- retro-fitting costs
- dismantling costs
- disposal costs

Disposal and environmental costs are increasingly important in the evaluation of TLC due to the increasing pressure to improve environmental performance. The result of the MEAT assessment is to rank tenders received in accordance with the assessment criteria specified in the invitation to tender documents. This establishes the best overall bid, which is then recommended for the award of contract. Note that the contract is not awarded until after the so-called Alcatel standstill period, during which all bidders must be notified of the decision.

Comparison of tenders is a relatively straightforward exercise but complications can arise when tenderers offer alternatives and options. Whether alternative proposals are acceptable or not should be indicated in the ITT, and alternate bids must be evaluated according to the same criteria given in the ITT.

The financial evaluation of options is carried out in accordance with the same basic principles as given above, but prior to this a decision must be made as to whether the alternative to be considered is appropriate. For example, a novel item of plant may be offered on the basis of improved performance and cost saving but this may involve extra costs in redesigning and fitting associated plant. In these instances a full use of total acquisition cost (TAC) and total cost of ownership (TCO) can be helpful. Then the analysis of acquisition costs, operating costs and disposal will all have been fully considered.

It may also be valuable to identify where cost and value are added through the supply chain processes, for example, in the production of the product where a key requirement will be having reliable and fixed/known lead times.

Post-tender negotiation (PTN)

This involves negotiations with tenderers. If undertaken, then it is important that it is carried out in a structured and controlled way to avoid second bidding opportunities at a 'Dutch auction'. Any post-tender negotiation must be carried out on the basis of a recorded plan and strategy, setting out the negotiation objectives and giving the same treatment to all tenderers. Indeed, some have a view that PTN is unethical (as negotiations will often only take place with a "selected few") and therefore, PTN is not allowed or practiced formally by the public sector. Members of a buying team with a background in the private sector may be familiar and comfortable with this approach, and may need to be advised that it is not appropriate in the Public sector.

Scoring of tenders

Scoring of tender submissions is a time consuming and surprisingly tiring process. In addition to legal obligations there are a number of practical issues to be considered to ensure that the correct decision is reached in a timely manner.

Legally, the evaluation of tenders has to be fair, non-discriminatory and transparent. To achieve these ends the tenders must be evaluated against the weighted criteria identified in the original Tender notice/ITT or the descriptive document. It is not permissible to introduce new selection criteria at this stage of the process (even if you have forgotten to give as selection criteria important factors, such as price). If the criteria need to be changed it may be necessary to withdraw the procurement, and restart the tender process. In the unusual event that new circumstances require a change in the requirement(s), the evaluation panel must decide whether the bids can still be appropriately reviewed on the basis of the published criteria, or whether the tender needs to be withdraw and the requirement re-published.

The evaluation panel has an obligation to review the bids on the basis of the information presented, rather than any additional information known to the panel members; to do otherwise would be to show bias to known suppliers over new suppliers.

Case Study: Example of Award Criteria

The example below of applying the award criteria is derived from the European Commission's Practical guide on EC-funded aid contracts for consultancy services:

Tender Evaluation Summary

Technical Evaluation	Bid X	Bid Y	Bid Z
Evaluator A	55	88	84
Evaluator B	60	84	82
Evaluator C	59	82	90
Total	174	254	256
Average Score	58.00	84.67	85.33
Technical Score	-	99.22	100.00
Financial Evaluation			
Total fees	-	£951.320	£1060.452
Financial Score	-	100.00	89.71
Composite Evaluation			
Technical Score x .80	-	79.38	80.00
Financial Score x .20	-	20.00	17.94
Overall Score	-	99.38	97.94
Final Ranking	**Eliminated**	**1st**	**2nd**

(http://ec.europa.eu/europeaid/work/procedures/implementation/practical_guide/index_en.htm)

The key points of this example are:
Evaluation of the bids are based on the criteria identified in the original tender and supporting document

The evaluation is split into a technical component (80% of the total score) and a commercial component (20% of the total score), as indicated in the original tender

Both technical and commercial components are evaluated out of 100 points, based on various criteria

Within the technical component there is a threshold score of 80 marks out of 100, and only suppliers exceeding this threshold pass through to the evaluation of the commercial component

The technical and commercial scores are converted to percentages, and then weighted as indicated in the original tender (80/20: Technical/Commercial) to determine the final score

In determining the technical score out of 100 points against the various criteria, it is useful to consider what would constitute top marks, and what would be a non-compliant bid.

The following scoring schema, developed by the UK Northwest Regional Development Agency, is an example of how the panel could allocate marks for each criterion, in this case out of 5, but similar schema could be developed for scoring out of 10.

Scoring	Choose and enter a score per criteria
5 points	Significantly exceeds expectations, in a way which is very beneficial to the project
4 points	Very high level of compliance with no reservations about the ability of the supplier to meet the requirement
3 points	High level of compliance, with possible minor reservations
2 points	Reasonable level of compliance, some reservations
1 point	Minimum level of compliance, significant reservations
0 points	Non-compliance

In evaluating tenders the panel should always ensure that the proposal will meet the ITT specification, meet the designated terms and conditions, and if possible add value to the purchase for no extra costs.

Technical evaluation should ensure that all of the technical requirements of the bid are met. Commercial evaluation should ensure not only the price is appropriate, but also that risk and legal issues are addressed.

It is useful to consider the scoring of bids when developing the ITT, and ensure that the criteria used will allow the panel to properly distinguish good bids from poor bids.

Practical issues of evaluating tenders

In the case of a restricted tender the number of submissions will usually be in the range 3 to 8, which can be managed in a reasonably short period of time. The number of eligible submissions in an open process can be many times that number, and treating all submissions equally and fairly can become a significant challenge.

The first essential is to ensure that the team evaluating the bids has sufficient expertise and knowledge to form an accurate impression of the bid. Where the bid has a technical element, it is common practice to separate the technical and commercial elements of the bid. In this case the evaluation team may be split and the full team only meet after the technical team has completed its evaluations.

The greater the number of participants involved in the evaluation process, the longer it is likely to take. This is however, to be balanced against the likely reality that stakeholders in the contract may actually want to have a representative present as they see this will better guarantee their "buy-in" to the final decision. Ideally the team should be between 3 and 5 individuals, and comprise of those who were involved in developing the tender requirement, the scoring criteria and will have some subsequent involvement in the implementation of the contract. This continuity may be difficult to arrange but leads to the greatest likelihood of identifying the best bidder, and successful delivery of the contract.

Before evaluation of the bids commences, the team should clearly declare any relevant interests or involvements with any of the bidding parties, such as personal relationship or previous business relationships. In unusual cases, it may then be necessary for a panel member to withdraw from the evaluation.

The team should have a clearly appointed chairperson, who may be independent. This is to ensure that procurement rules are followed, appropriate discussions are conducted, and in particular, the tenders are being evaluated on the basis of the information provided, rather than personal knowledge by the team members.

Where ever possible, the team should operate in a room that is secure (to ensure confidentiality of discussions and documentation), separate from the normal office environment (to reduce distractions), well lit and ventilated (to facilitate concentration), and sound proof (to avoid leakage of information).

The team should take regular breaks to ensure concentration levels remain high and that the team do not become jaded. If the evaluation is likely to take many days or weeks (as might be the case if there are 100 bids to evaluate), then it is sensible to break the evaluation process every 2 or 3 days so that the team can attend to other issues and not be too weary of evaluating. Clearly, to be fair to all bidders, the team should not allow themselves to become too tired; the last bid should be dealt with as "freshly" as was the first one.

When the number of proposals is however not too large, it is sensible for the entire evaluation panel to read all of the proposals before commencing the scoring process. If though there are a very large number of bids, then it may however be more practical to ensure that each bid is read by one or more team members before starting the scoring process.

In scoring the bids the team should be looking for consensus on a bid, but not total unanimity. If one team member scores a proposal at 0, and another at 5, then an average of 3 is not a fair scoring of the bid. The team members should seek to understand the reasons for any large discrepancies in scoring, and must resolve any such bids so that there is a common understanding of the proposal. They must also be aware of the natural tendency of people to seek agreement, and then be prepared to put forward their dissenting views when appropriate.

When a large number of bids are evaluated there is often an unconscious drift in the scoring criteria. It is therefore good practice to regularly go back and quickly rescore a proposal evaluated earlier in the process to maintain a consistent approach to marking.

Award of contract

Post tender evaluation finishes when there is a decision on the award of contract; it being not permissible to negotiate with bidders. It may however be reasonable to communicate with the selected bidder in order to clarify, confirm or fine-tune elements of winning bid. These elements should be minor and must not change the nature or scope of the bid to such an extent that it is unfair to other bidders.

The successful/preferred bidder and unsuccessful bidders can then be informed of the intention to award the contract. It is useful to note here that should the successful bidder choose to actually commence preparatory work ahead of the contract award, then they do so at their own risk and cost, as until the contract award is completed, there is no obligation on the buyer.

Meanwhile, the contract itself cannot be physically and finally awarded until the end of the 10 day Standstill or Alcatel period (this is to allow other bidders may launch a challenge to the decision). If a challenge is lodged then legal advice must be sought. When no challenge is lodged within that period the contract may now be awarded. It should be noted that there may still be a legal challenge from unsuccessful bidders after the standstill period, but this should not usually stop delivery of the contract.

Communication with unsuccessful bidders

Unsuccessful bidders are usually keen to be informed of the reasons that they were not successful so that they may be able to improve their offer for future contracts. Whilst many Buyers want to improve the competitive position of potential suppliers, they are often reluctant to give any detailed feedback for a number of reasons:

- the effort involved in doing so
- the potential for suppliers to attempt to re-engage in the process in an effort to change the decision
- the threat of legal challenge to the decision based on information in the feedback

Suppliers often find that Buyers are more willing to be open with information in a telephone call or personal meeting rather than in writing (either in a letter or by e-mail). Buyers should be wary of this, as the information they divulge will carry the same weight, regardless of the method of communication.

The OJEU procedure states that the contracting authority should as quickly as possible but within 15 days of a written request inform candidates of the:

- reasons for the rejection of the bid, including any decisions that the bid was not compliant, or the non-equivalence of the works, goods or services that were offered
- characteristics and relative advantages of the winning tender, as well as the successful tenderer or parties to a framework agreement

In practice, this is usually done by giving the top winning score in the evaluation process, along with, the score of the unsuccessful bidder.

Particular details of the unsuccessful bid may also be raised to assist those suppliers to improve any future offer, rather than to encourage a revised bid. Whilst many Buyers will often give the total scores rather than the scores for individual criteria, it is good practice to allow suppliers to fully understand the details of how their bid could be improved.

Buyers should in any case be aware that under the Freedom of Information Act, they may be required to provide details of both the bids submitted and the evaluation process that lead to the decision to award to a specific bidder.

With this in mind, contracting authorities should reject suppliers' confidentiality clauses wherever possible, although this will not stop suppliers claiming them. Under the Freedom of Information Act, public authorities cannot agree to hold any information "in confidence" which is not actually confidential in nature. If they attempt to do so, they may find that a court will rule that the information should be released. However, an exemption may be applicable if disclosure of the information to the public would constitute an actionable breach of confidence.

Buyers should therefore be aware that the details of all bids and their evaluation may eventually be made public, emphasising again, the need to ensure that all aspects of the decision making process are fair, accurate and well documented.

Finally, contracting authorities will be expected to contact bidders directly to inform them of the decision, and of their rights to appeal the decision during the so-called Alcatel Standstill period. The contract award should also be listed in the OJEU (if the opportunity was advertised there), and any other portals and journals that carried the original tender notice.

Terms and conditions of contract

Compliance with the general terms and conditions of contract is usually a condition of bidding for the contract. If bidders seek any amendment to the terms and conditions, this should be resisted if possible, and if it cannot be, then it should be referred for legal advice.

Terms and conditions will usually cover the following:
- Contract prices and payment terms
- Payment schedule
- VAT (recoverable or non-recoverable) (note that in the UK public sector this issue can often be confusing, and therefore needs a clear statement)
- Process for price variations
- Nominated contact points
- Definition of contract requirements and service levels
- Applicable legal system, i.e. law of England & Wales, or Scotland, or Northern Ireland
- Dispute procedures
- Change procedures
- Force Majeure clauses
- Termination of contract clauses
- Completion/End of contract clauses; the contract itself may be terminated for a number of reasons, which are usually articulated in the contract;
  - Insolvency
  - Change of ownership or control of the supplier
  - Default or non-performance
  - Force Majeure
  - Non-performance of elements of the essence of the contract

RFQ/Tender Checklist

1. Tender Overview
Overview and background information for tender

2. Administrative Requirements
Fee for tender documentation
Where and When to submit proposal
Form of submission (paper copies, CD etc.)
Identification of bids
Process for rejecting late bids/ identified bids/incomplete bids etc.
Bid opening process
How proposals will be evaluated
Process for gaining additional information/clarification
Tender contact names, addresses, e-mail details
Duration of proposal validity
Publication of award
Process for feedback
Commencement date
Commissioning meeting

3. Technical Requirements
Critical Success Factors
Functional Specifications
Hardware/Software requirements
Communications requirements
Free issue materials
Allowed alternatives/substitutions
Disposal/return of products

4. Management Requirements
Staff and personnel requirements
Project plan and deadlines
Delivery and installation schedule and plan
Training requirements
Documentation required

5. Supplier References and Qualifications
Supplier's relevant experience Financial information required (Financial Records) Qualifications of nominated staff List of similar customers/projects Names of references including contact details
6. Supplier's proposal
Supporting information
7. Pricing
Product/Service prices Day rates for nominated staff or staff levels Rate for additional supply Delivery charges Training and documentation charges Taxes, Duties and Insurance Spare part prices
8. Contracts & Licenses
Law, Terms and Conditions Currency Payment Terms Performance Bond Non-Disclosure Agreements Arrangements for Collaborative bids Non-collusion agreement Sub-contracting conditions Intellectual Property rights and ownership Dispute procedures Warranty and Guarantee periods and procedures Ongoing license arrangements Unforeseen circumstances (force majeure) Subsequent negotiation process

9. Appendices – supporting information
Relevant diagrams, spreadsheets, flowcharts
List of provided equipment/material
Outline project plan
Company standards and procedures
Standard Terms and conditions

Checklist: Hints and Tips on running a Tender Evaluation Process

- Think about how you will score bids when you write the ITT; it will save time and help to ensure that you get information in comparable format
- Leave sufficient time to evaluate the submissions; it can take a long time to do justice to a submission, maybe an average of an hour per submission. Make sure that bidders are aware that the process will take time
- Only mark what is in the proposal; tempting as it is when an existing supplier does not do themselves justice the only fair thing to do is mark them on what they write – other bidders might also be underselling themselves
- Specify how you want the pricing information; day rate or hourly rate, and what levels or job titles – these can vary a lot between suppliers, so is better that they work out how their fits your requirements than you spend ages trying to work out whether an Executive is senior or junior to an account manager
- Be clear about what you actually want and what is important – how you will distinguish between bids
- Score the bids the way you said you would; which requires thinking about it first, so that you don't give equal marks to a company with good policies, but no quality of work, and a brilliant supplier who forgot to include their environmental policy
- Be clear about the financial criteria; do SMEs and new starts really stand a chance?
- The people who write the ITT should be the people who mark the bids (or at least part of the team)
- Remember that you can get jaded evaluating bids; leave a day a week for other work, consider taking an hourly break on a 48/12 minute cycle

- Your idea of a good bid can change as you read more bids; consider going back and rescoring the first couple of submissions again to ensure that scoring is consistent; don't always start with the same bid when evaluating multiple submissions- move through the alphabet, or order of receipt
- If something is not included in the submission or not clear you can ask for further information, as long as all bidders get the same opportunity

Checklist: Points about Biding for tenders

1. Look and Feel of proposal gives feeling of quality; this may not give you any points but may give you the benefit of the doubt

2. Answer the questions
- Make sure you address all the points identified in the tender
- Show the client respect by doing it their way
- Be clear about how what you write answers the question
- Don't be afraid of saying "yes we can do this"

3. Don't rely on assumed knowledge
- If it is not on the paper it will be overlooked
- Do tell the client what you do and why you are the best candidate
- Do state your vision, mission and values – but don't over elaborate

4. Fulfil all the obligations for legal work etc.
- Even if not relevant for you or this proposal
- If they ask if you have a policy attach it as well

5. Be clear about the pricing
- Don't give ranges
- Indicate how it is constructed if necessary
- Give it the way they ask e.g. including VAT, excluding expenses

6. Make sure the structure of the bid is clearly laid out
- Match the structure of the tender so sections are easy to find
- Clarity and Brevity are essential – it saves work for the clients

7. Provide the right number of copies, and the right number of bound/unbound

8. Explicitly state how you meet the requirements
- Don't just say we specialise in this topic, say we can do this piece of work

9. Don't bid for anything and everything; if there are a number of lots, only go for those you really want and can do

10. Tailor your bid to meet the particular tender
If bidding for multiple lots make sure there is something that says what you are offering for each lot
Don't just stick in a standard approach, tailor it to the job and keep it short

11. Submit it on time

12. Make it clear that you want to win, that are very keen to win, and if necessary why you want to do this particular piece of work (and not just the money)

13. If you have alternative proposals also make a proposal the way they asked; don't just put down your ideas and ignore what they have asked for.

14. Use references and referees relevant to this tender
- Don't just use your best or standard references
- Need to be within past two or three years
- No more than 3 or 4 are necessary unless there are special reasons (e.g. one for each aspect of a large tender).

Comments and options on Assessment

There are many aspects that can be assessed on a supplier's ability, attitude, organisation, finance, structure, products and production methods. We will look now at all of these:

1) Assessment of Supplier Ability
Suppliers may be assessed for their capabilities to supply, for example:
- Capacity (ability to deliver required volumes)
- Capability (ability to deliver to required standard)

- The number and quality of their workforce
- The number, age and quality of equipment
- The size, layout and location of premises
- Quality policies
- Environmental policies
- Lead time reliability records

2) Assessment of Supplier Attitude

Suppliers may be assessed for their interpretation of the market and especially in long-term relationships. Their attitude will depend on:

- Shared goals
- Organisational strategy
- Client management
- Future prospects

3) Assessment of Supplier Organisation

Suppliers may be evaluated on the type of organisation, for example:

- Organisational culture
- Lines of communication
- Levels of trust and delegation
- Levels of integration
- Internal and external relationships
- Management style
- Sub-contracting arrangements
- Level of local employment (as long as not anti-competitive)

4) Assessment of Suppliers Financial Data

From information given by the supplier or collated from other sources, the financial information needs to be evaluated to determine:

- Profitability. This measures the performance of the supplier to exceed costs and make a profit.
- Gearing. This looks at the long-term loans that the company uses for funding where high gearing suggests the company is open to financial instability.
- Liquidity. This identifies the cash flow position of the supplier.
- Stock Turn. This identifies how expedient the company is at rotating goods through the company. It is based on financial turnover divided by the value of the stock on hand; it is not a measure of the actual physical goods stock turn.

5) Assessment of Suppliers' Organisational Structure

From the information gathered, it will be possible to identify the strengths and weaknesses in the suppliers' structure and culture, for example:

- Hierarchical structures may be cumbersome, bureaucratic and may restrict communication and extend lead times due to their inherent "silo" functional process structure.

- Flatter stuctures offer quicker response times for decision making and communication, for example where supply chain management is adopted as a philosophy and will result in a cross functional management structure

6) Assessment of Supplier Product Data

By research into the price structure, the required specifications and the quality standards, it will be possible to identify those suppliers can produce the product to the needed requirements at appropriate prices and margins.

Related products on offer from the supplier may create opportunities for the purchaser to multi source and reduce the cost of purchasing, and achieve better pricing.

7) Assessment of Supplier Production Process

When applicable, with information on capacities and production facilities, it should be possible for the purchaser to identify the strengths and weaknesses in the supplier's ability to provide the product. The internal supply chain of the potential supplier can be usefully analysed to identify possible cost savings. Production equipment and procedures can also be analysed to ensure they are up to date and appropriate to the standard required.

8) Assessment by Weighting; method one

With so much information available from the appraisal system it will be necessary to identify the criteria which are most important in identifying the preferred source. Weighting can therefore be applied to the attributes related to the critically and can be determined by the procurement department and the user/customer. This is essential for OJEU tenders, and advisable for other tender processes (unless there are exceptional circumstances which prevent the identification of appropriate weighting, in which case the order of importance should be given).

For example with long-term relationships, organisational strategy would be allocated a high weighting to reflect its importance – perhaps 30% of marks, or top priority.

The following is an example of an elemental questionnaire/weighting where from questions asked of the supplier, an initial identification is made of the ability to meet the requirements of quality, quantity, time, place and price can be established. Next, the purchaser can nominate a grade for each area, scoring from one, as unacceptable to five, as meeting all requirements and providing added value (as with the scheme shown above from NWDA).

Area:	1	2	3	4	5	Comments:
Quality: Procedures Manual Audits Testing Policy						
Quantity: Capacity Flexibility Bulk Individual Discount						
Time: Admin Production Collation Despatch Priority						
Place: Group Address Individual Optional Referral Notification						

Price: Bulk Discount Cost Breakdown Warranties Flexibility Improvement		

9) Assessment by Weighting; method two

Another example of applying a weighting factor follows:

Area	Max Points	Score
Quality	40	
Quantity	30	
Time	10	
Place	10	
Price	10	

The above example emphasises that a high importance has been given to the quality of the product delivered, along with ensuring the right quantity is delivered. This suggests that the item is essential to production and that the price paid is not as important. A lower rating is applied to price, place and time as these factors are seen as not having as great an impact on the operations as the others.

Clearly the purchaser will compile the details of each area with justification for the scoring being given.

Who is responsible for the pre-order stage?

This stage covers Need/Requirements – Specify – Sourcing – Enquiry – Evaluation – Tendering/Negotiation/Selecting that all work towards the implementing of a contract and order placing. The level of a procurement department's involvement in managing contracts and order fulfilment must be established. This will require clarity with the commissioning department as to, for example, who has responsibility for:

- Support and advice; for example the decision on which source to use may be with the budget holder/end user or, if the product has not been sourced before, then there may be an opportunity to develop a supplier.

- Contract negotiation; here it could be the direct responsibility of the buyer to negotiate terms and conditions on behalf of the user or internal customer.

- Contract management; who should have the responsibility to manage the total procurement process from identifying the need, agreeing specifications, identifying potential suppliers, supplier appraisal, contract negotiations and contract implementation, including the performance measurement.

- Collaborative partnerships; these would need to be based on trust and cooperation, shared information and shared goals, and without these, then the partnership merely becomes a long-term contract.

It is important that organisations determine who owns the relationship with suppliers, and whilst we have explored this topic more fully in our book ***Excellence in Supplier Management (2009)***, the standard answer is that as the need is determined by the user, then the user has the responsibility.

In textbook terms and theoretically then this seems entirely logical. However, in organisations where the responsibility is ill defined or, where office politics have a part to play, then it can happen that most users choose to believe that it is the procurement department that has the responsibility for the relationship with suppliers. They also often believe this to be true without making any formal delegation; therefore they have a viewpoint of "after all we passed it on to you, so get on with it."

Whilst one can fully appreciate that the procurement department is involved in sourcing and finalising the deal, it should not be the case that procurement are systematically left to do this in a vacuum and in total isolation from the rest of the organisation. Unfortunately however, the authors know of too many examples where this actually happens.

Order placing and Contracts

It is essential when placing orders/implementing contracts, that all parties involved are aware of their roles and responsibilities. The supplier must be conscious of their responsibilities regarding the delivery of the products or services in line with their contractual obligations. The purchaser must ensure that the contract is managed in accordance with policy, and ensure that the customer is kept aware of any developments. The user/customer must keep procurement informed of any changes to the process or design that may affect the supplier contract. If it is likely that the demand will vary (e.g. demand for road salt depends on the prevailing weather conditions) then the customer must try to establish precise forecast information.

Orders, contracts and supply agreements

The contractual arrangements must be structured to match the particular requirement. Requirements vary and this section will look at these variations; it therefore represents an overview of the procurement order and contract practices.

Examples of different types of arrangements are as follows:
- Spot orders are placed as and when required
- One-off purchase orders (no repeat purchases)
- Framework agreement is for a fixed term for a specified supply, but with no initial commitment to buy
- Call-off agreement, for example, fixed price contracts for a specified supply, therefore there is an agreement to buy
- Contract with varied rates, dependant on certain criteria, for example, on volume quantity order, on early payment etc.

These may have been set up through a bidding process, by competitive tendering or by negotiation. Public sector bodies may also access framework contracts established by third parties, such as Buying Solutions Ltd.

Procurement is responsible for ensuring that the best-fit commercial conditions are applied to the particular purchase. In applying these, procurement must take account of any relevant legislative requirements. For example, chemicals are subject to the COSHH (Care of Substances Hazardous to Health) regulations, the waste electrical and electronic equipment (WEEE) Directive, while the Health and Safety at Work Act (HASAWA) applies to the majority of purchases.

Low-value purchases can be satisfied by the invitation of bids from a small number of suppliers, without the formalities and costs of tendering as long as this process does not distort the market or unfairly exclude potential bidders. The bids must be provided in a form allowing comparison, so that the best can be selected. These types of requirements are normally covered by a simple purchase order with standard terms of contract printed on the back.

Managing supplier agreements, orders and contracts

The type of agreement made and used, will in part be dependant on the process and procedures followed by the organisation, and set processes will ensure that suppliers are being dealt with fairly. Having the right type of agreement ensures the organisation is trading on a sound legal basis. The type and form of contract can be standardised, but can also be adapted to suit varying situations.

A contract plan may also be used to identify the work to be completed and the resources required. If this is being used, it will require a concerted effort by the buyer and user/ customer prior to the sourcing.

The size of the contract will need to be established, both financially and in terms of resources required. Internally, this involves estimating the staff hours and systems resources involved, and if a product is involved, then an analysis of production costs will be useful.

Confirmation of budget availability or 'phasing' will need to be established where applicable, with cost centres. These will effectively form the authoritative level by which the contract will be based. Phasing may also be influenced by the budgeting and funding processes, whereby some funds may only be available before a deadline or only become available after a certain date. Although this is common, care should be taken to ensure that internal budget timescales do not result in inappropriate commercial methodology (e.g. paying before delivery, or withholding required stage payments).

Procurement should be involved early to ensure the procurement process and decision meets the needs of the user/customer. Long-term agreements will need to be closely managed, as the basis for these agreements is often cost reduction and value-add to the benefit of both parties. Due to the time and resources invested in such relationships, it is in the buyer's interest to commit an adequate amount of time to managing these contracts.

Contract award

Following the previously discussed tendering or negotiation process, the contract will have been formally awarded and publicised. The contract' that has resulted from the tendering or negotiation process, will comprise of the following:

- the original enquiry document or ITT (including subsequent clarifications and communications)
- the terms and conditions included in the ITT
- the selected tender proposal
- any subsequent relevant correspondence between the tenderer and the purchaser, particularly that arising from the tender assessment (e.g. questionnaires) and post-tender negotiations
- the letter of contract award
- any further changes to the scope or timescale of the contract that are agreed by the buyer and seller (ideally written in a letter or minutes of meetings)

It is only necessary for the purchaser to confirm acceptance of the supplier's bid to form a binding contract. For simple contracts, the contract generally only comprises a contract letter that refers to the enquiry, tender and questionnaire, relevant terms and conditions and any other relevant correspondence or minutes. For some very large contracts, contracts staff might produce an agreed contract document, comprising a comprehensive consolidated version of all the agreed provisions of the enquiry, bid and questionnaire. This represents the total and final agreement between the parties.

If any post-tender discussions have led to changes to the original bid submitted, the supplier might be asked to submit a revised tender document incorporating all agreed changes. If these changes are significant it may be necessary to re-run the procurement process rather than adapt the proposal. The letter of contract award must set out clearly the basis of the contract and stipulate any conditions precedent to the award (i.e. any conditions with which the tenderer must comply before the contract is regarded as firm).

It is the responsibility of procurement to ensure that:

- the appropriate terms and conditions are specified
- any modifications to standard terms and conditions are minimised, and recorded
- there is a definition of when offer and acceptance takes place

- there is an approved digital signature or equivalent
- all legal principles have been followed

English law

These notes are based on the requirements of English law. Scottish law differs from English law in both principle and practice, and legal advice should be taken if dealing regularly with trade between the two countries. The law that relates to England and Wales derives from four main sources:

- Common law
- Equity
- Statute law
- European Community law

The common law is the very centre of English law. It is the body of law and precedents built up over many years based on judges' and the courts' decisions on cases heard and the customs of the various courts of the land.

Equity is another form of law derived from the results of cases decided by the courts. Both common law and equity differ from statute law in that the latter is laid down by parliament in the form of published Acts of Parliament, maybe following EC law.

It is common law that provides us with the following definition of a contract:

"A contract is an agreement between two or more parties which is intended to be enforceable by the law."

There are various statutes directly relevant to contracting – the main ones are the Sale of Goods Act 1979 (SOGA), amended by the Supply of Goods and Services Act 1994 (SGSA) and the Unfair Contract Terms Act.

To make an enforceable contract, three essential elements must be present and correct:

- capacity (the power or authority) to act
- intention to create legal relations
- agreement (follows from offer-acceptance)

We will look at each of this overleaf:

Capacity

This means that both parties must have the legal authority and ability to enter into a contract. In simple terms, the parties should usually be 18 or over and of sound mind. If one or other of the persons entering into a contract does not have the necessary power, the contract may be void (unenforceable) or voidable (the innocent party has the option to set the contract aside, i.e. the contract may operate as a valid contract until one of the parties takes steps to avoid it).

There are certain groups who do not have 'capacity' and so cannot enter into contracts:

- minors (though exceptions exist)
- those with a mental disorder
- those under the influence of alcohol
- corporations (which require agents to form contracts on their behalf)

Companies are usually registered under the Companies Acts and their power to act depends on their constitution and the nature of their business. A company's constitution consists of two major documents: the Memorandum of Association and the Articles of Association. The importance here is that if a company enters a contract to do something that it has no contractual power to do, then the other party to the contract may not be able to enforce it. In other words, the company may escape its liabilities under the contract.

Because it is impossible to state exactly all the powers necessary to do everything a company may need to do; there are also implied powers. This means that the courts will take it for granted, even if it is not specifically stated in the company's constitution, that a company's powers include taking normal steps incidental to running a business (e.g. employing staff, buying materials) and powers appropriate to the particular type of business. Usually anything which is a natural or reasonable extension of permitted activity will provide adequate capacity and, therefore, a valid contract.

Intention to create legal relations

Both parties must intend that their relationship will have a legal effect. This is taken for granted in commercial or business transactions but not in social or domestic arrangements. However, even a social or domestic arrangement may be contractually binding if both parties have made it clear, expressly or by conduct, that such was their intention.

Offer – Acceptance – Agreement

An agreement arises when an offer is made, followed by, an acceptance of the offer. The **offer** may be express or implied:

- Very often a contract is formed after an express offer. For example, John offers to sell his second-hand car to Jenny for £1,000.
- Implied offers are also common. For example, a customer at a petrol station, serving himself with petrol, is making an implied offer to buy the petrol.

An offer may be made to a definite person, as in the case of John and Jenny above; this is the normal situation. However, an offer may also be made to the world at large; for example, this can happen where a person offers a reward to anyone who may help to find a stolen valuable item.

An offer does not take effect unless and until it is communicated to the offeree. An offer, once made, does not remain open forever. It may be terminated in various ways, it may therefore:

- Be withdrawn by the offeror, unless it has already been accepted (however, withdrawal is not effective until it is communicated to the offeree)
- Be rejected by the offeree
- Lapse if the offeree fails to accept it within a reasonable time
- In addition, the death of either offeror or offeree terminates the offer

Meanwhile, **acceptance** is defined as: "An unconditional assent to all the terms of an offer." It must be absolute and unqualified. A qualified acceptance is not acceptance and is instead a counter offer (or cross-offer). For example, if Jenny says to John 'Yes, I'll take your car, but only for £900", then this is not an acceptance. In fact it ranks as a new offer (a counter-offer): Jenny is offering to buy John's car for £900. This offer may or may not be accepted by John. Unless and until John accepts, there is no contract.

Acceptance must be communicated to the person making the offer (either directly or through a reliable third party). Acceptance is only effective when it is received by the offeror (and not when despatched by the offeree). The contract only exists from this time.

The 'battle of the forms' occurs in a situation of 'offer' and 'counter-offer'. It describes the common situation when a seller and a buyer are each trying to deal on their own standard contractual terms and conditions. Where there is a discrepancy between the conditions offered and those accepted, it may not be clear whether the buyer's or the seller's terms and conditions apply.

It is worth noting that a contract may be formed without the exchange of documents through verbal "offer-acceptance-agreement". In other cases acceptance may be implied when a contractor is allowed to start work even though there is ongoing discussion about the terms of the contract.

Electronic contracts

The increasing use of e-business means that contracts are now being formed by electronic communication, so there are now various pieces of legislation to govern e-business transactions; these include the Electronic Communications Act 2000. The European Union's E-commerce Directive 2000/31/EC set out to remove barriers to the availability of information society services within the EU. The Directive states that provision must be made for the drawing up and conclusion of contracts electronically. The UK Electronic Communications Act 2000 therefore ensures the legal validity of e-contracts and The International Chamber of Commerce's uniform rules on e-trade settlement state that an electronic offer and/or acceptance becomes effective when it enters the information system of the recipient in a form that the system can process.

Legal principles of consideration

Consideration is the bargain or exchange aspect of the agreement; it is a promise on one part for an act on the other or can be a promise for a promise, i.e. quid pro quo. Without consideration there is usually no contract (though there are limited exceptions to this rule).

There are certain rules applying to consideration:
* Consideration must be valuable, but, need not be adequate. This means that what is offered by one party to the contract must have a monetary value, but that value need not be equal to what is offered by the other party. In such a case, one party will have got a bad bargain, but the courts do not concern themselves with that: provided the consideration has some monetary value, however small, it is sufficient to make the contract valid (this is why you hear of companies being sold for £1).
* Consideration must not be past. In other words, you cannot force someone to do something for you on the strength of something you did for them in the past.
* Consideration must be given by both parties.

- In commercial contracts, consideration is normally money, but it need not be. For example, some contracts are on the basis of barter or exchange.
- A framework agreement with no specific commitment is not a 'contract' because there is no consideration, so consideration is sometimes injected by making a nominal payment (e.g. £5).

Contractual terms and conditions

It is the responsibility of the buyer to ensure that the company is protected legally. "Caveat Emptor" – let the buyer beware, being the rule here.

Procurement must consider and decide which are the right commercial terms and conditions to apply. These could be bespoke to the organisation or might be based on available international or national standard forms. Examples of these are as follows:

- IMechE/IEE (Institutes of Mechanical Engineers and Electrical Engineers respectively), Model Form General Conditions of Contract; MF/2 for Supply of Electrical, Electronic or Mechanical Plant; and MF/3 for Supply of Electrical and Mechanical Goods
- CIPS (Chartered Institute of Purchasing and Supply) Model Form of Conditions of Contract, available to members on www.cips.org.uk

Many public sector bodies publicise their standard terms and conditions on the internet, and these can be studied and adapted for use by other bodies. Model forms of contract will allow for basic terms and conditions to form the main frame of all company contracts and with specific clauses being added according to the nature of the product or service being purchased.

Unless made explicit through specific (express) terms in the agreement, terms will be implied, according to the local legislation that has been developed to deal with commercial disputes in the business environment.

Conditions and warranties will form the basis of the terms, accentuating the importance attached to each of the obligations, which form the agreement. Clauses can be used to secure against risk, but also as a bargaining tool. The buyer can agree the inclusion or deletion of clauses for small concessions. The terms and conditions of sale or of contract do set out the obligations and liabilities of the parties; they are a statement of risks. The key risk areas to be dealt with are as follows:

- price

- payment
- defects
- completion and delays
- standard of care and workmanship liabilities and indemnities

Essentials of a valid contract

The essential ingredients of a contract are as follows:

- Agreement. This is formed when one party has accepted the offer of another (ideally but not essentially in writing)
- Consideration. Without consideration there is usually no contract (though there are limited exceptions to this rule). Consideration was more fully covered above, but is simply, where each side has promised to do or to give something to the other
- Intention. The parties must intend their agreement to have legal consequences
- Form. In some cases, certain formalities (in writing) need to be observed
- Capacity. The parties must be legally capable of entering into a contract
- Genuineness. The agreement has to be entered into freely and involve a "meeting of minds"
- Legality. The purpose of the agreement must not be illegal or contrary to public policy

Where a contact has all these requirements, then it is said to be valid. If one party does not live up to the promises then the other party may sue for a breach of contract. Meanwhile, if essential elements are missing, then the contract will be void, voidable or unenforceable:

- Void means the whole contact is null and that at no time has a contract existed (despite what either or both party may believe)
- Voidable covers contracts founded on misrepresentation and some agreements made by minors. The contract may operate as a valid contract unless and until one of the parties takes steps to void it.
- Unenforceable means it is a valid contract but it cannot be enforced in the courts as one party refuses to carry out its terms.

The conditions of the contract will form the main body of a contract and breaching these terms and conditions, allows the claimant, the right to disown the contact or assert their right to damages.

Warranties are terms but carry less influence, as whilst a breach of warranty allows the claimant rights to claim damages, they cannot disown the contract. Usually, express terms are formulated to limit responsibility, the amount of damages that may be incurred and any changes in price.

Specific Clauses

There are many specific clauses that may form part of a contract and these can include:
- Addresses: communications must be sent to the address stated.
- Arbitration: how disputes will be settled.
- Assignment: controlling who the work is contracted to.
- Default: non- delivery.
- Entirety: what is not in the contract does not exist.
- Force Majeure: mitigating events out of your control.
- Law: deciding which countries law is used in foreign contracts.
- Liability and Indemnity: protecting against the risk of consequential or indirect loss.
- Notices: what means of communication will be used to pass information.
- Payment: when and how payment is made.
- Sub-contracting: restrictions on sub- contracting.
- Unenforceable: Protecting the whole contract from individual terms, which cannot be enforced.
- Variations: how variations to the contract are approved.

The terms on which a contract is concluded may include more than just the terms expressly laid out in the contract. For example, additional terms can be implied:
- by fact (an implication that is obvious to both parties),
- by statute (legislation),
- by the courts (with precedent set in cases)
- or by custom (for example, the trade acceptance that one case of a product contains one dozen items e.g. bottles of wine)

Privity of contract

The doctrine of privity means that a contract cannot, as a general rule, confer rights or impose obligations arising under it on any person, except the parties to it. Common law has reasoned that only a promisee may enforce the promise, meaning that if the third party is not a promisee, then they are not privy to the contract; therefore only a person who is a party to a contract can sue on it.

However, if the doctrine of privity was inflexibly applied it would cause considerable injustice and inconvenience; accordingly many exceptions to it have been developed, the main ones being as follows:

- Collateral contracts: A contract between two parties may be accompanied by a collateral contract between one of them and a third person relating to the same subject-matter. There must, however, be an intention to create a collateral contract before that contract can be formed.

- Agency :The concept of agency is an exception to the doctrine of privity in that an agent may contract, on behalf of his principal, with a third party and form a binding contract between the principal and third party.

- Statutes: Certain exceptions to the doctrine of privity have been created by statute, including price maintenance agreements; and certain contracts of insurance enforceable in favour of third parties. For example, under the Road Traffic Act 1972, an injured party may recover compensation from an insurance company once he has obtained judgment against the insured person.

Meanwhile, The Contracts (Rights of Third Parties) Act 1999 reformed the common law rule of privity of contract. Section 1 provides that a third party may in their own right enforce a term of a contract if:

(a) The contract expressly provides that they may do so

(b) The term purports to confer a benefit on them (except where on a proper construction of the contract it appears that the parties did not intend the term to be enforceable by the third party).

The relationship between a buyer, a supplier and the supplier's supplier can have critical impacts; consider the following case study:

Case Study: Upstream Suppliers in the Supply Chain: Alpha Co.

Alpha Co. is an assembler of high volume branded electronic consumer goods. Alpha Co. integrates technologies, defines products, designs finished goods, prototypes and assembles the core product. All accessories, packaging materials and component production are outsourced.

Plastic Parts Ltd.

PPL is a first tier supplier of mouldings and uses three sub-suppliers to supply components — Gloss Paint Ltd, Special Coatings Ltd and Liquid Gaskets Ltd. Originally it had been anticipated that materials would be pulled through the supply chain based on monthly demand forecasts and weekly delivery requirements. In theory, PPL would sell moulded parts to Gloss Paint Ltd who painted the parts and scrapped a percentage due to their process yield. The painter sold on the remainder either back to PPL or on to Special Paints for metallic coating. Special Paints would add their value then sell the parts onto Liquid Gaskets. It was expected that the suppliers would order, from the next lower tier supplier, the volumes required by the next Company in the chain plus their anticipated or actual yield rate loss.

Start up

Difficulties became apparent as none of the companies had anticipated Forrester effects or quality, defect liability issues. A lack of production synchronisation resulted in Alpha Co. purchasing involvement on a daily basis to expedite parts between moulding and the factory. This was done on an ad-hoc basis by telephone and weekly visits. Other key issues identified were a lack of co-ordination between the independant companies, low process yields and missing batches of parts. Feedback on quality began to be received from the distribution centre that products had too many imperfections. When checking it was found that Gloss Paint Ltd had a lack of employees that were skilled to the required level; additionally the managing director of Gloss Paint insisted on working shifts in the hand-finishing booth to achieve the yield and volumes required.

An intermediate solution

This relied on Plastic Parts inspecting the components after each supplier had added its value. Plastic Parts had to act as guarantor for the receiving supplier that the inbound components were of the appropriate quality. Any defects then created would be, at least in theory, the responsibility of the receiving supplier as a result of damage during its value adding operations. The main supplier returned damaged or otherwise rejected parts to the previous supplier for credit note purposes. Plastic Parts was then in a position to determine the amount of money owed to each company. This solution allowed the inbound logistics chain to supply the assembly plant with at least some of the part sets required.

Gross volumes of the product were planned to be in excess of three hundred thousand units. During the production run, less than ninety-one thousand units were produced due to inadequate supply, damaged parts, and late delivery. To avoid this occurring on higher volume product runs for other regions, generic design changes were implemented, based on the use of alternative technology solutions that allowed for a simplified supply chain to be developed.

The delayed ramp-up and the inability to deliver sufficient volume of acceptable component sets reduced the total number of products produced by more than 69.8%. This created a net financial loss for both production and the product creation programme. The relationship with the principle customer of Alpha Co. was also negatively affected as a result of failing to deliver almost stay batches on time.

Statute

The terms implied by statute are particularly relevant in contracts for the sale of goods. A contract for the sale of goods is an agreement where the seller transfers or agrees to transfer the property in goods to the buyer for a money consideration (the price). The Sale of Goods Act 1979, amended by the Sale and Supply of Goods Act 1994, implies certain terms into contracts for the sale of goods, for example:

- Goods must be as described, of satisfactory quality, and fit for any purpose that the consumer makes known to the seller.
- Goods are of satisfactory quality if they reach the standard that a reasonable person would regard as satisfactory, taking into account the price and any description.
- Aspects of quality include fitness for purpose, freedom from minor defects, appearance and finish, durability and safety.
- It is the seller, not the manufacturer, who is responsible under the Act.

If goods are not of satisfactory quality the buyer is entitled, if they act within a reasonable time to reject the goods and get their money back. The Supply of Goods and Services Act 1982 extend the provisions of the Sale of Goods Act to contracts which are not just purely for goods. This Act implies into contracts for the supply of a service the terms that:

- the service will be carried out with reasonable care and skill,
- within a reasonable time, and
- where no price has been agreed, for a reasonable charge

These terms apply unless they have been excluded and there are strict limits on the circumstances in which an exclusion or variation will be effective. Any material used must be of satisfactory quality. The law treats the failure to meet these obligations as a breach of contract and the consumer is entitled to seek redress.

The use and application of exclusion clauses is subject to the provisions of the Unfair Contract Terms Act 1977. This Act regulates the use of exclusion clauses and severely limits the concept of freedom of contract. In non-consumer sales (where a business is selling to another business) any exclusion clause can only be valid if it passes the test of 'reasonableness'.

The Act lists a number of guidelines to determine whether a term is reasonable. Of these, the strength of the bargaining positions of the parties is the most relevant. In commercial relationships, the courts will deem most businesses to have equal strength and, therefore, most exclusion clauses will be regarded as valid. Therefore, the implied terms of the Sale of Goods and Supply of Goods and Services Acts can be excluded.

Intellectual Property Rights (IPR)

When products and services are purchased, the supplier has certain rights under law on the creativity and innovation in the same way as if they owned physical property. The owner of the IPR can therefore control and be rewarded for the use so that this will encourage further innovation and creativity for the benefit of all.

In some cases IPR give rise to protection for ideas but in other areas there will need to be more elaboration of ideas before protection can arise. It will often be not possible to gain IPR unless they have been granted, however some IPR, like copyright, arises automatically without any registration.

The main types of IPR are as follows:
- Patents cover inventions, those new and improved products and processes that are capable of an industrial application

- Trade marks for brand identity of goods and services, this is to allow for differentiation between different traders
- Designs for product appearance that cover the whole or part of product resulting from the features like lines, contours, colours, shapes, texture or materials of the product itself
- Copyright for material such as literary, artistic, music, films, sound recording and broadcasts, including software and multimedia

However, IPR also covers broader aspects like trade secrets and plant varieties; additionally more than one type of IP may apply to the same creation IP; for example a glass "Coca-Cola" bottle is covered by both trade marks on the names "Coca-Cola" and "Coke" and also on the design (shape) of the bottle.

Legislation on copyright is covered by the Copyright, Designs and Patents Act 1988, and full details of this (and all the other legislation covered in this section), can be found on:www.legislation.hmso.gov.uk/legislation/uk.htm.

From a procurement aspect it may be useful to agree with the supplier on the IPR, so as to be able to use or acquire for example, tooling, designs and materials to manufacture items in the case if any supplier defaults. From a supplier point of view, IPR is one of the major sources of competitive advantage and marketplace differentiation. Accordingly when this applies, buyers will need to ensure that IPR are part of their normal evaluation and assessment process. In the case of ICT software, it may be essential for the buyer to have some IPR over both the source code and the look and feel of the presentation of the software, to protect against the supplier stopping trading, or to allow future updates to be sourced competitively.

EU Influences on contracts

Consider the following: A businessman is negotiating a contract with a company in another State of the European Union, but neither party wishes to apply the law of the other country. A lawyer is advising parties to a contract involving parties in different States. An arbitrator has to decide a dispute under a contract "to be governed by internationally accepted principles of law".

All these need to know the principles of contract law shared by the legal systems of the Member States and to have a concise, comprehensive and workable statement of them.

The Principles of European Contract Law Parts I, II and III provide this and have been drawn up by an independant body of experts from each Member State of the European Union under a project supported by the European Commission and many other organisations.

The principles are stated in the form of articles with a detailed commentary explaining the purpose and operation of each article. In the comments there are illustrations, ultra short cases which show how the rules are to operate in practice. Each article also has comparative notes surveying the national laws and other international provisions on the topic.

The Principles of European Contract Law Parts I and II cover the core rules of contract, formation, authority of agents, validity, interpretation, contents, performance, non-performance (breach) and remedies.

Part III covers plurality of parties, assignment of claims, substitution of new debt, transfer of contract, set-off, prescription, illegality, conditions and capitalisation of interest.

The Commission on European Contract Law

A common law does not (yet) exist in the European Union. The above Principles have therefore been established by a more radical process and no single legal system is used as their basis. The rules of the legal systems outside of the Communities have also been considered and the existing conventions, such as The United Nations Convention on Contracts for the International Sales of Goods, 1980 (CISG). In short, the Commission tries to establish those principles which it believes to be best under the existing economic and social conditions in Europe.

The Commission has made an effort to deal with those issues in contract which face business life of today and which may advance trade, especially international trade. However, the Principles do not intend to apply exclusively to international transactions.

The European Parliament has proposed the enactment of a binding European Contract Law as the ultimate goal after careful studies and preparations. It remains to be seen what happens in the political arena involved, especially when many consider that the different member states contract laws present no real barriers and that there are more important barriers to trade such as fiscal taxation and the lack of coordination on EU directives. Meanwhile the Consolidated Procurement Directive 2004 for the Public Sector and the New Directive for the Utility Sector has been agreed and changes the way that these regulated sectors have to contract for goods, services and works.

This emphasizes the changing nature of legislation and demonstrates the requirement for Procurement professionals to maintain "a watching brief." Such legislation knowledge would also be required for the "normal" health and safety legislation, environmental legislation and the waste electrical and electronic equipment (WEEE) Directive. Many lawyers and technical experts keep track of such issues, and communicate significant developments through blogs and newsletters – it may be useful to register interest with a number of these specialists.

Checklist: Contracts with Customers and Suppliers

Although in law a simple telephone call can constitute a contract, and therefore would be binding, if would be foolish to rely on unrecorded and unsigned agreements, even to vary the terms of a standard contract.

A written contract not only enables you to record what is done for a customer, it also gives the opportunity to state how important matters, will be handled. But a contract can be a millstone if it contravenes one of the many laws on 'unfair' contract terms.

Professional advice should therefore always be sought.

Meanwhile the following questions may help either party:
- Do you have a contract or written terms of business?
- Do you confirm in writing all telephone agreements or changes over the phone to written terms?
- Are you relying on a copy of somebody else's terms? (These may be defective, inappropriate or illegal)
- Do you know who you are really making the agreement with? (are they able to enter into that agreement with you?)
- Do you record the registered company number of the customer or supplier on your agreements?

- Does your contract exclude liabilities for negligence?
- Do you know that you have rights concerning the acceptance and rejection of bought goods?
- Do you always read your suppliers terms of business, including the small, hard to read grey print on the back of their invoices?
- Do you always check out business references?
- Do your terms of business make it unambiguous what you will do, when it will be done, how you will be paid, and what will happen if there is a dispute
- If you are buying overseas, have you settled which countries legal system will apply?

Handling Contracts and Partnerships

A contract register can be used to monitor progress and spend. This will also identify those suppliers who are being used and when. This also allows the buyer to identify opportunities to extend short-term relationships and review long-term relationships. Levels of authority will be set to control spend, such as with basic requisitions and orders. It is assumed that with longer term, high-risk and high spend contracts, that the authority levels will be authorised by senior management.

The level of buyer involvement in managing contracts must be established and this may take the form of any or all of the following:

- Support and advice; for example the decision on which source to use may be with the budget holder/end user or, if the product has not been sourced before, then there may be an opportunity to develop a supplier.
- Contract formation; here it will be the direct responsibility of the buyer to negotiate terms and conditions on behalf of the user/customer.
- Contract management; here it is the buyers' responsibility to manage the total procurement process from identifying the need, agreeing specifications, identifying potential suppliers, supplier appraisal, contract negotiations and contract implementation including performance measurement.

Collaborative partnerships may be established for strategic items of high value and critical materials and products. These will aim to reduce costs and improve performance for both the buyer's organisation and the supplier. To be a collaborative partnership, it will need to be based on trust and cooperation and without this, plus shared information and shared goals, then the partnership merely become a long-term contract. We examine further such collaborative arrangements later.

Different types of Contracts

All parties involved must be aware of their roles and responsibilities and the contractual arrangements must be structured to match the particular requirement. As already mentioned, requirements can of course vary and examples of different types of arrangements are found as follows:

- Spot orders are placed as and when required
- Framework agreements for a fixed term for a specified supply, but with no initial commitment to buy, and when eventually buying, the use of call offs. There is then an agreement to buy
- Contracts with varied rates, dependent on certain criteria, for example, on volume quantity order, on early payment etc.

Procurement departments are usually responsible for ensuring that the best fit commercial conditions are applied to the particular purchase and must also take account of any relevant legislative requirements. As explained above, all contracts will involve the legal aspects as follows:

- Offer
- Acceptance
- Consideration
- Legality
- Capacity

However beyond the "mandatory" legal aspects, there is a range and continuum of variations and choices to be made. What follows therefore is an ideal typical view to indicate this range.

Whilst for some, this idealised view will be entirely practical and realistic; for others, the following division will not be fixed and definite. There can be a mixing across this continuum and it is not therefore a "tablets of stone" view, but, is designed to show the key aspects that have to be considered before the buyer makes a choice; a choice of course that should usually be undertaken in conjunction with other internal departments in the organisation.

Contracts types

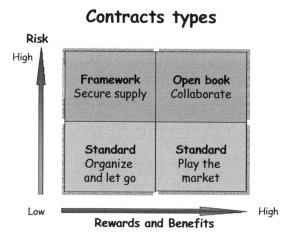

The buyer's views of risks are: any thing that may stop the operations of the business or prevent it from achieving its objectives.

For example, poor health and safety, unreliable supplier lead times, low product quality with high levels of defects, using new untried technology, working in political environments with constant changes to regulations, supplier closure, exchange rate variations.

The buyer's view of rewards and benefits are: reduces costs, improves service, quality, time to market, innovations etc.

The key aspects involved in the different contract formats are as follows:

Aspects	Standard Contract	Framework Agreement	Open book
Other names used	Closed Fixed price	Call-offs	Cost plus
Typical Kraljic items	Leverage and routine	Leverage, routine and bottleneck	Bottleneck and critical

Contract description	Standard fixed terms and conditions covering Quality, Quantity Time, Price and Delivery, plus many others, for example: -Assignment & Sub-Contracting -Arbitration -Bankruptcy -Equipment -Terms of Payment -Damages/ injury -Designs/ drawings -Liability -Passing of property —Inspection/ testing -Information -Copyright/ Patent Rights -Statutory Regulations -Termination	There is no initial commitment to buy as the agreement just anticipates doing business. It "prepares the groundwork" and details the standard contract terms and conditions. When orders are placed by issuing a PO (known as a call off in a framework agreement), upon the order acceptance by the supplier (without the supplier varying the terms), then there is a contract.	All costs are visible to the buyer, as the "books are open." All costs are therefore reimbursable to the supplier or maybe are paid direct by buyers. This is the "cost" aspect and the "plus" aspect can be: -a fixed management fee, or -a percentage of costs, or -agreed fees that maybe dependent on order volumes. As well as having fixed terms and conditions, there may also be some "moral" expectations/ agreements covering the preferred relational aspects.

Risk for buyer	Usually risks are well known and are often contractually passed to the supplier. (Although of course, any subsequent supplier failure will likely impact the buyer).	May be shared or maybe with the supplier.	Maybe not fully known in advance and may be accepted by the buyer.
Rewards/benefits for the buyer	Perceived as being "fully protected". Penalties for supplier non conformances. Likely to be able to easily withdraw.	As for standard contract but with no initial commitment to buy. "Ready to go" immediately when wish to place orders.	Full visibility of costs and therefore all of the processes involved. Collaborative working.

Disadvantages for buyer	Hides supplier's profit. Supplier may include too much "contingency" cost in the price and may cut corners to improve profits. Suppliers may only do what the contract says and do not innovate or suggest improvements.	Supplier may become "disappointed", for example, they have to wait for orders which can then fall below their expectations.	Buyer needs cost knowledge. High administration. Could be little incentive for the supplier to reduce costs and improve service; however, the supplier may also do whatever is needed to make improvements, as mutual gains and goals "rule."
Rewards/benefits and disadvantages for the supplier	Supplier from the buyer- "you have the business, for now;" the supplier is therefore uncertain of the future. Supplier does not have to suggest any improvements.	As for standard contract but on bottleneck items, some form of incentives are available as the buyer needs to secure supply.	Supplier incentives/ performance bonus. Incentives can follow from: -Cost reductions -Performance improvements -Delivery on time
Term	Short	Medium	Long
Performance expected	Standard	Satisfactory	Successful and can go beyond expectations

Trust	Low and is boundary trust that is determined by the contract.	Some trust beyond what the contract covers, and should become established by the reliable performances of both parties.	High and is goodwill trust. This has been built up during the working together experiences.
Relationships	Transactional, adversarial, contractual.	Cooperative	Collaborative, strategic alliance, mutuality, commitment.
Contract price	Known/ fixed by price agreements	Fixed by the PO/ contract, but may not have been initially fixed in the agreement.	Cost plus. The total cost price may be estimated in advance and therefore may become a variable if the estimating was wrong.
Buyer controls after orders have been placed	Low efforts needed as measures by non-compliance and can easily change suppliers if needed.	Low to medium effort needed	High effort needed and both parties may measure and jointly agree remedial actions
Control of costs	With supplier	With supplier	With buyer

It can be noted here that Open Book has been criticised as not being sufficiently transparent, and that it should be more open by being two way process rather than one way. Suffice to note here as well that the above Open Book description does actually cover cost transparency and collaboration and is therefore two ways working; we will however return to this debate later.

Specifically on **Framework agreements** in the public sector, these are used to minimise the need to run repeated procurement processes for goods and services required on a regular or semi-regular basis, it is therefore possible to establish a framework agreement with a number of suppliers.

As explained this is an umbrella agreement that sets out the terms on which the parties will enter into call off contracts in the future. In order to establish the framework, a standard open or restricted tender process is undertaken, the competitive dialogue process being unlikely to be appropriate for establishing framework deals.

Some frameworks have been established on behalf of the public sector by some of the 40 Professional Buying Organisations covering the public sector. The largest of these is Buying Solutions which is the national procurement partner for all UK public services and is part of the Efficiency and Reform Group within the Cabinet Office, set up in 2001 as a result of the Gershon report and covering some 500,000 product and service lines with 1,500 suppliers. Public sector bodies are able to use these frameworks or to develop their own.

There are restrictions on the use of frameworks, which aim to balance the ease of use and efficiency for buyers (and to some extent suppliers), with, the danger of distorting the supply marketplace by excluding new entrants.
- Frameworks must generally not exceed 4 years, usually a 3 year duration with a potential 1 year extension
- Substantial changes to the terms of the framework agreement cannot be made during the period of the framework
- The contracting authority or authorities (in the case of a consortium bid) must be identified at the outset of the framework, and cannot be amended during the period of the framework. Therefore it is not possible to add new authorities to an existing agreement.

The way that a supplier is "called off" to supply against an agreement should be indicated in the invitation to tender. Generally there are two standard processes:
- A mini-competition between some or all of the suppliers on the framework

- Call-off according to a fixed schedule described in the framework (e.g. alphabetical order, or allocation of all of one type of requirement to Supplier A, and another type to Supplier B).

In order to maintain fairness, some authorities allocate business in strict rotation according to alphabetical order, the so called "taxi rank" principle, where the company at the top of the list is invited to perform the contract, after which they go to the back of the list.

In some cases firms will be sent to the bottom of the list after an invitation has been issued regardless of whether they accept the contract or not. In other cases, firms are allowed a (limited) right of refusal. Some authorities follow a similar procedure with mini competitions and invite the top 3 firms on the list to compete, and select the winning bidder from those 3. The other 2 firms may then either remain at the top of the list or go to the bottom depending on the precise nature of the framework.

The taxi rank principle has the virtue of ensuring all firms are treated equally; however it does run the risk that the firm best suited to deliver a contract is not invited to do so, because, it is not their "turn".

Frameworks may act as an unintentional barrier to the participation of some business in the public sector. A frequent requirement in PQQs is the requirement to have three years' trading accounts. A firm just failing to meet this requirement for a framework having the maximum period of 4 years, could potentially then be excluded from supplying into the public sector for nearly 7 years. In such ways framework agreements can inadvertently act to exclude new start businesses. Their use therefore needs to be considered in light of government aims to create broader opportunities for firms to engage with the public sector.

Finally in this section on Contracts, a good contractual legal agreement may therefore provide the following:
- the overall groundwork and framework for the future supply
- a perception that we have minimised risk and have a "safety umbrella"
- a formal "place of last resort" to resolve any ensuing problems

However legal agreements will not prevent problems, nor will they provide protection on a daily working basis. Legal agreements will only provide a formal structured framework for handling problems that have already occurred – they do not absolutely ensure that we will get what we want. Dealing with problems can, of course, be handled without recourse to any formal legal involvement/judgements, as legal costs can be high/prohibitive and involve long time scales/delays. It should also be noted that legal cases can be unpredictable – a court may decide that the actual contractual agreement was not that believed by either side but in fact a third form. Legal action based on the contract should not be a first step in resolving problems, but only when it is the best option for achieving the best possible result.

As covered in **Excellence in Supplier Management**, some may question why the initial time and cost, in agreeing legal agreements, is entered into in the first place. In this book it is suggested that for the more complex purchases, most of the value obtained from the supplier is actually going to be driven by the post contract management, rather than from the up front negotiated contractual terms.

Suffice to note here that the different types of contracts have connections to Kraljic and therefore to procurement strategy and the relationships aspects. Therefore *"A successful relationship is mainly made, not on legal contracts, but on aspects like trust, fairness, respect, promises and mutual benefits that will occur daily between all of the players involved. It is how these are handled that will determine successful supplier management; success is often unlikely to be because of the rigour of the legal contract"* (From **Excellence in Supplier Management**).

Handling orders

General purchase orders for low risk/low spend items can be handled at local or administrative levels. These orders need to be checked for details before being dealt with. Alternatively, in some cases, procurement cards can be used where the customer will buy direct and their spending budget will simply be charged accordingly.

Blanket orders may have been established for items that have a recurrent usage as this will result in reducing the order costs. Another advantage here is that a variety of items can be controlled and distributed via a contractor who is left to self manage stock levels; perhaps using a Kanban system for items such as stationery, electrical components or small engineering fittings.

Replenishment

For materials that are held in stock then the replenishment decision is one of deciding when and how much to order (the time and the quantity). This is largely concerned with inventory policy; this being given a full consideration in the book, *Excellence in Inventory Management; how to minimise costs and maximise service* by Emmett and Granville.

Suffice to note there that holding stock literally costs, for example a major oil and gas company calculated its holding and carrying costs between 17% to 30% per annum of the value of stock being held.

Key Performance Indicators

The determining and handing over of Key Performance Indicators (KPIs) to be used in monitoring the delivery/service performance delivery, follows on from the order stage. The order stage therefore "scene sets" how the subsequent contract and orders should be handled. Accordingly, time spent determining and agreeing KPIs with all the relevant players, is time well spent to prevent subsequent confusion and disputes.

Supplier performance must be monitored in a positive manner to motivate better results. Long-term relationships for example, will only succeed where both parties are committed to continuous improvement. KPIs can therefore be used to ensure control of all procurement activity and highlight any deviation from the standards expected.

The actual KPIs used will depend on the product or service being purchased and they can then be monitored to ensure supplier interest is maintained in the contract and also to build historical data for reference; wwill discuss KPIs in more detail shortly when we cover the reviewing stage.

Progressing and Delivery

If all appropriate agreements have been made, including firm and agreed supplier lead times, then providing the buyer/customer has fulfilled their part of the bargain, then it should not be necessary to spend time progressing and expediting orders. Indeed with collaborative supply chain thinking coupled with appropriate supplier monitoring and performance reviews, then expediting can be seen as being an admission of defeat.

Expediting is also largely superfluous with Factory Gate pricing or with Incoterms Ex Works buying; an option available for example, when global sourcing where track/trace visibility is then proactively a part of the process.

However, for one-off purchases where there is no history or record of supplier performance, then some progressing and checking maybe required to ensure suppliers meet their contractual agreements. It can also be used for critical items required for example for scheduled maintenance, and also for where there are no proper arrangements or collaborative supply thinking.

When expediting it is necessary to determine:
- which orders to expedite
- the date(s) to check
- the checking actions needed, for example, writing/e-mail, personnel contacting,
- telephone contact (on B items), supplier visit (on A items)
- the system for record keeping

After delivery, on receipt into warehousing/stores, then the following activities are involved:
- Establish which unloading area is to be used; ensuring it is safe and suitable for the operation.
- Record the arrival of the vehicle and note the transport security locking systems, for example, container seal(s)number(s)
- Break the security locking system with the driver present
- Check the order documentation and record each item against the consignment note
- Ensure the vehicle is safe before unloading
- Unload the vehicle
- Assemble the goods in the goods receipt area
- Check the goods for quantity (use blind checking?),condition and possible damage
- Carry out any required quality checks
- Report any discrepancies and condition/quality at once
- Record/notify the system of receipt
- Move the goods out of goods receipt area as soon as possible to the appropriate destination:
  - location in the warehouse where goods are to be stored

- the staging/holding area they are to be held in (such as quarantine)
- direct to the user

Clearly the time taken to do this will impact of the overall supply lead time and this receiving lead time up to the time available to issue, may need careful management, especially in those operations where procedures require inspection by internal end users before goods are accepted.

It has been known to take some weeks for this process to be undertaken and the goods, meanwhile, are not yet entered into the stock management system. Where replenishment is being done remotely and away from the stores environment, we also have known new orders being placed, because of this "system gap" in the practical visibility. Meanwhile, more on stores and warehouse operations in available in *Excellence in Warehouse Management* by Stuart Emmett.

Payment and Reviewing

Payment

Clearly before reviewing each order on an individual order basis, the payment to suppliers needs to be completed. This will be in accordance with the schedule agreed in the contract terms and conditions. Payment terms are often a major aspect of the supplier appraising and evaluation steps.

Late payments are often the major source of friction between suppliers/customers. They can also be a breach of contract terms. The handling of any payment complaints from suppliers must also involve the procurement department; it is really not acceptable for procurement people to blindly direct such supplier queries to finance department. Supplier performance is important, and not being paid on time in accordance with agreements will be a major source of discontent and can ultimately lead to changes in suppliers' performance. Indeed we have come across many instances where a supplier blocks future orders or even refuses to do any more business solely due the "hassles" of getting paid on the agreed due date.

Procurement departments therefore must be aware of all payment problems and issues with suppliers. It is too late to get involved after a new order has been placed but then refused by the supplier.

UK Government guidelines are for payment in 14 to 30 days.

Reviewing

It will be recalled that all public sector organisations interact with a range of markets, in order to deliver a range of services. The procurement priorities for each organisation will vary, but will include elements of value for money, quality and legal compliance as well as other elements such as stimulating economic activity. These will in turn provide the basis for the procurement strategy. The sources and processes to be used are then identified by procurement in order to meet these strategic decisions.

The amount of reviewing, monitoring and control allocated to an agreement will depend upon the importance of the product or service being procured, in relation to the organisation's strategy.

Reviewing price

The cost of the material or product can be measured from two angles:

- Cost of acquisition

- Cost of the product

Traditionally, purchase price was the only measure used; however modern procurement methods recognise the long-term benefits of managing the total cost of ownership (TCO), and other contributions to economic impact.

Product material costs are made up of different cost elements including acquisition costs, cost of operation and cost of disposal. The costs involved in procurement of materials or products, will include the direct material and labour costs of production including expenses, production, overheads, administration, sales and distribution.

A cost model, if available, will identify the total costs including the profit made by the supplier.

The type of pricing agreement used for the contract will contribute to the make up of the cost elements. Fixed price agreements will be simple to calculate. Longer-term contracts will need to take into account fluctuations in raw material prices and other cost factors.

Reviewing Procurement Costs

Procurement costs must be monitored to ensure the buying process is cost effective.

The buyer should be aware of the costs involved in raising an order and this will involve all the direct and indirect costs, including salaries, expenses, departmental suppliers, heating, lighting, communications etc.

Ratios can be used to identify costs and indicate trends. These can include:

Department costs x 100 = % Procurement efficiency by total spend

Total value of orders

Department costs x 100 = % Average cost of orders
No of orders placed

Reviewing Total Organisation Spend

Total spend of any organisation can be defined as the suppliers agreed price, plus, the procurement costs. Information regarding spend should be readily available from the finance department, or from any procurement systems.

An ABC analysis of all agreements will identify the high priority contracts, which require closer control and monitoring. ABC analysis should be reviewed regularly to account for changes in market conditions.

Reviewing costs and risk factors

Procurement has a direct responsibility, both externally and internally, to check and see that all risk factors are accounted for. External risk factors will include the number of suppliers, length of lead-time and other considerations affecting price and security of supply. Where there are several suppliers, risk associated with security of supply may be low, however, continuity of supply may still carry risk where the quality offered by the available suppliers is of a low standard.

Internal risk factors will include project delay which may result in cost overruns and overtime, and failure to achieve target outputs.

Poor procurement performance will be reflected in the extras costs of:
- Re-ordering
- Re-handling and re-storing the replaced items
- Returning the non required items
- Loss of revenue or, delayed revenue creation
- Effects on reputation and goodwill
- Re-evaluation of performance and subsequent improvement/re-alignment costs

Key Performance Indicators

As already noted, supplier performance must be monitored in a positive manner to stimulate better results. Long-term relationships will only succeed where both parties are committed to continuous improvement.

KPIs can be used to ensure control of all procurement activity and highlight any deviation from the standards expected.

The actual KPIs used will depend on the product or service being purchased and they can then be monitored to ensure supplier interest is maintained in the contract and also to build historical data for reference.

Defining key performance indicators

In general terms, the KPIs will cover at least the 5 rights of quality, quantity, price, place and time, related to the goods/services being purchased and also to the relationship with the supplier. Examples follow:

Quality includes:
- Re-work
- Rejects
- Warranties
- Procedures
- Complaints
- Control

Quantity includes:
- Full or Part order receipts
- Discounts
- Minimum order levels

Price includes:
- Consumables
- Tooling
- Overtime
- Re-work

- Materials
- Labour
- Downtime
- Absenteeism

Place includes:
- Accuracy of delivery to location
- Tracking availability whilst in transit

Time includes:
- Lead times
- Emergency response
- Set-up

Relationship issues include:
- Service levels
- Skill levels
- Response times to requests

KPIs are measurable and therefore are objective criteria.

Subjective criteria can also be involved based on the buyer's perception of the supplier and their conduct of the contract, for example to commitment, attitudes and mannerisms including:
- Motivation toward individual contract commitments, future business etc.
- Response to constructive criticism, problem solving etc.
- Input into problem solving, innovation etc.

Additionally surveys can be used to collate subjective opinions; for example the supplier survey mentioned below.

Procurement KPI benchmarks

The following indicators can be useful to make such comparison's to enable learning and improvement.
- Total procurement expenditure as a percentage of revenue
- Procurement operating expenses as a percentage of total procurement spend
- Number of procurement staff as a percentage of the organisation's total staff

- Total procurement spend per procurement employee
- Number of active suppliers per procurement employee
- Procurement spend per active supplier
- Cost of operating the procurement function per active supplier
- Percentage of active suppliers for 50%, 75% and 90% of procurement spend
- Percentage change in number of active suppliers in a reporting period
- Percentage of total spend with any "deemed" sensitive suppliers e.g. local suppliers, small companies, BME owned etc
- Percentage of total organisational spend managed by the procurement department

Supply chain KPIs

The entire supply chain performance can also be measured and the following KPIs can be used.

Description	Measurement tool	Definition	Units
Customer orders fulfilment	On time/in Full rate (OTIF)	% orders OTIF	%
	Lead time	Receipt of order to despatched/delivered	Hours/Days
Customer satisfaction	Customer Survey	A sampling survey to ask for customers experiences, for example: -Support available -Product availability -Flexibility -Reliability -Consistency -Comparison to the competition	% satisfied
Supply management	On time/in full (OTIF).	As above	%
	Supplier Survey.	A sampling survey to ask for suppliers experiences, for example: as in the above customer survey	% satisfied
	Effectiveness.	Year over year improvements	%

	Lead Time	Time placed order- time available for use	Hours/Days
Inventory (measure for each holding place of raw materials, work in progress and finished goods)	Forecast accuracy.	Actual/Forecast sales per SKU.	%
	Availability.	Ordered / Delivered Per SKU.	%
	On hand.	Value on hand/daily delivered value.	Days
Cash flow	Cash to cash.	Time from paying suppliers, to time paid by customers	Days
Quality	Quality.	Non conformances, as appropriate	Per 100 or 1000 or million
Operations	Utilisations.	Used/Available.	} Units
	Productivity.	Actual/Standard.	} Hours
	Costs.	Actual/Standard.	} Costs
	Lead times.	Time start/time completed per operation.	Hours or Days
People Relationships	Internal.	Absence rates	%
	External.	Sampling Survey, as customers / suppliers above.	% satisfied
Costs	Total supply chain or per operation cost.	Cost per time period/ Units.	£ per unit

Applying key performance indicators

The process for applying KPIs and the gathering of data must be agreed with all stakeholders, along with the format in which the results will be produced. This could be a basic spreadsheet or a more visual group of data using graphs or gauges.

The levels of acceptance need to be set and the procedure for remedial action agreed by the establishing the reporting structure and the levels of authority, along with direct contacts and substitutes.

The level to which the KPIs are "drilled down" will need to be established, for example with Quality KPIs:

Quality KPIs

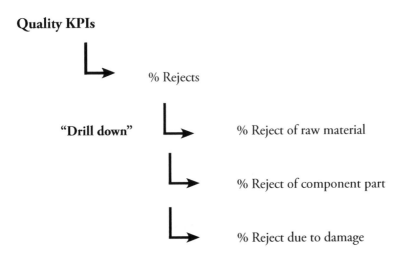

Using Weightings

A weighting system, like used in evaluation, can also be applied to prioritise the most important criteria. For example:

Quality   30

Delivery   25

Quantity   20

Price   15

Communication 10

This system can be simplistic (as shown here). But for complex and expensive projects, it can be highly comprehensive.

KPIs: Reporting structures

The reporting structure should ensure that deviations from the KPIs are clearly and easily communicated both in a cost efficient manner and as acceptable time frame. The reporting structure should link the supplier, buyer and customer in a horizontal visible frame. Meanwhile, the operational, tactical and strategic levels should be linked in the vertical hierarchy. Software can meet this need whilst a simple visual system can give adequate information in an appropriate format. For example, the 'Traffic High Light System' uses colour codes to report performance:

Green = Acceptable

Amber = Cautionary

Red = Unacceptable

This simple system can be implemented quickly and easily as a basis for more comprehensive performance measurement:

Supplier "A"

	Jan	**Feb**	**March**	**April**	**May**	**June**
Quality	Green	Green	Amber	Green	Green	Green
Delivery	Red	Amber	Red	Green	Green	Green
Quantity	Green	Green	Green	Green	Amber	Green
Price	Green	Amber	Green	Green	Green	Green
Communication	Green	Amber	Red	Green	Amber	Green

KPIs and Suppliers

Once key performance indicators (KPIs) have been established and a system created, the relevant parties will need to adhere to the process. If a significant change is involved, this should include a timed plan for the introduction and induction of individuals with identified responsibilities within the process. Responsibility levels, lines of communication and reporting should also be included. The supplier will need to commit to the programme and to recognise its advantages, for example, the performance measurements should also be of benefit to them.

The customer/user and any other interested parties must provide the required information expediently and recognise the benefits they will gain in terms of improved performance, reduced costs and greater co-operation. Without the co-operation of the customer and the other links in the supply chain, it can be impossible to collect the necessary data. Supplier rating schemes, also rely on the participation of the supplier and the buyer's internal activities, which both include goods-in and despatch, along with the customer.

KPIs: Effects on Suppliers

Suppliers must be given a thorough introduction to the supplier rating programme and understand their role. They must be encouraged to ask questions and be given thorough answers, so that, they can implement the process with little or no delays/errors. The buyer in turn will need to understand the supplier's strategies and objectives in order to apply the performance measurements and improvements effectively; of course, this information may have already been learnt when sourcing the supplier.

The supplier must be able to trust the buyer where the cost of commitment is substantial. For small to medium enterprises, the amount of effort and resources required for monitoring and maintaining performance measurement might be overwhelming; buyers should take this into account. Obviously, if the data is not accurate (either too optimistic or pessimistic) the system will not be successful in driving improvements and may create more conflict with suppliers than it resolves.

KPIs: Effects on Customers

Customers/users must also understand the value of performance measurement and recognise their role. Customers and other activities must interact with procurement as part of the responsibilities of an internally integrative supply chain.

Customers will need to be shown the benefits and cost savings and added value should be demonstrated. Equally the customer should be made aware that poor supplier performance that is not reported; would result in continued poor service. The buyer can then prioritise the customer's needs in order to maximise the benefits for them. Therefore in addition to understanding the suppliers' viewpoint, buyers have to understand the user/customer.

Monitoring Supplier Performance

Supplier performance should be measured over a period that is sufficient to capture any trends or fluctuations, such as seasonality. This however may not be necessary for projects to be completed within a specific time frame.

Performance monitoring must be a set objective, for which individual buyers must take responsibility. Each buyer can be given the responsibility of monitoring individual agreements or suppliers. Alternatively, the responsibility for monitoring, as an activity, may be given to an individual or specialist team.

Information must be gathered, stored and distributed in an acceptable format. It should be available to management and suppliers on a regular basis. Quantitative information on time and costs must be distributed to both suppliers and customers. This information should also take into account the quality expected from the supplier in terms of commitment and attitude.

Measurement should be made against historical data and projected improvements. The supplier should be driven toward continuous improvement to remain competitive; they should not be driven towards bankruptcy by making increasing and unrealistic price reduction demands. The value of improvements such as improved On Time in Full Deliver (OTIF) should be measured against the cost to the supplier – pushing for an improvement that adds little value but adds significant costs will usually result in future problems.

Comparisons can be made against similar suppliers to create a league table of performance. It would be appropriate to report supplier's performance against the best in class and their rank to encourage improvements in delivery – however the best in class may use this as a justification for higher prices in future.

Downgrading Supplier Ratings

Suppliers, who fail to keep within the set tolerances, must be notified within an agreed timescale. They should be given details of the non-compliance including dates and times. The supplier must also be informed of their reviewed grade and the records updated. This can be used to trigger a closer analysis of the supplier's performance to ensure the situation does not deteriorate.

The supplier needs to be given the opportunity to explain why they have failed to perform and where the deviation is severe, a meeting should be arranged to resolve the problem. The buyer should give the supplier guidance on how to achieve the required standard; this could include advice, co-operation, and the sharing of knowledge.

Where the supplier has to improve then a time scale should be set; additionally regular meetings may be necessary until the problem has been corrected, and the supplier can assure adherence to the expected performance requirements. Contingency plans may need to be drawn up in case of any recurrence, and in extreme cases it may be necessary to reassign the contract to another supplier (if this is permitted under the contract).

Upgrading Supplier Ratings

Suppliers who have maintained or improved their performance should always be informed and thanked, for example:

'A' class suppliers should be commended.

'B' class suppliers should be upgraded.

'C' class suppliers should be upgraded.

Good suppliers can be encouraged to sustain their efforts and similar suppliers gauged against the improvements attained by others. This information can be discussed with these improved suppliers to try to identify improvement opportunities.

Increased performance should be rewarded and rewards used as an incentive for suppliers to maintain and exceed the performance expected. Acknowledging suppliers' efforts is important in building relationships.

The rewards may be intrinsic in value such as, a certificate of achievement or other publicity. Buyers may create promotional opportunities, such as articles in newsletters and Press releases to highlight the importance of performance improvement.

Longer term contracts and repeat business reflects the aims of modern procurement practices such a, reducing the supplier base for critical items and forging closer working relationships where both the supplier and buyer are committed to continuous improvement. However these must always be framed in a context that is legally compliant and stimulates rather than hinders competition between suppliers.

Reviewing Supplier Performance

Supplier performance measurement methods should be regularly reviewed, to ensure they are still in line with the organisation's strategy and policies. Review meetings should be agreed with suppliers and customers/users and these should form part of the contract. For critical items regular reviews will be necessary.

The performance information collated will create a "performance profile" which will be invaluable to the buyer when analysing potential and existing buyers and for determining standards.

The suppliers' opinion of their own performance, as well as that of the buyers' organisation, should be taken into account. Where suppliers are undertaking identical measurement themselves, then the comparisons should present no surprises, thus removing any conflicts of the "you did/I did not" nature.

This can assist the buyer in making improvements to their internal supply chain, so also demonstrating a good working relationship with suppliers and assisting in the promotion of their organisation to other suppliers, as a quality client.

Having clear and agreed KPIs can help to prevent problems, consider how this might has assisted to prevent at least some, of the following "kaleidoscope" of problems:

Case Study: Jones Limited

Jones Limited produces a range of fast moving consumer products that are sold to retailers. They have traditionally enjoyed a strong position in this marketplace for many years. However, the market has recently become increasingly competitive with two companies who previously were producing for the wholesale sector. They are now able to produce on a marginal cost basis to the retail sector and therefore these new entrants have very low costs, and are also highly efficient.

Jones Limited now needs to become a leaner and lower cost producer and therefore the business needs to concentrate on:
- Making their standard products cheaper
- Keeping lower levels of raw material inventory
- Having customer demand driven production

There was widespread discussion and disagreement about the best way forward. Some of the board members were interested in the raw materials supplies side of the organisation and the contribution that it may make to increased efficiency and profitability. However, the Production Director (that the buying department reported to), said that in his opinion, most of the suppliers were a law unto themselves.

The Sales Director observed that Jones Limited was themselves suppliers to their retail customers and that Jones Limited had to worked closely with them; indeed the Sales Director was sure that they would be able to obtain demand information from the retailers so the Production could be more demand driven and that in turn, would perhaps mean having more responsive suppliers.

After much discussion, the Managing Director decided a new procurement manager was to be employed to move forward the buying department. This was made a Procurement Director designate position and would therefore report direct to the Managing Director.

As the newly recruited Procurement manager, you are well aware of the challenges of sourcing and managing suppliers. However you are concerned that there is a general lack of awareness of these problems within Jones Limited and you appreciate that you have an interesting few months ahead. You have undertaken an initial survey of the procurement function and this has revealed the following:

- Suppliers were being selected on the basis of a technical specification
- All purchases seem to be all treated in the same manner regardless of value or type
- Suppliers are generally selected on a lowest price basis
- There are two suppliers for the most of the products purchased; you were told that this was so that Jones Limited could play one supplier off against the other in price negotiations; indeed you heard the expression "squeezing suppliers" many times.
- No effective supplier KPIs exist

As if these general problems were not enough, you also learnt that specifically, two major suppliers of important raw materials were causing immediate problems: Packright Limited was demanding a 12.3 % price increase to cover for increase in fuel/energy prices due to the last escalations in the world oil market prices.

They have said that as they have now been talking to Jones Limited for over 7 weeks but have got no satisfactory answer, consequently if this increase was not forthcoming, then Packright have said that all deliveries would be suspended. Enzyme PLC were becoming unreliable by increasingly showing poor delivery/ late arrival performance, coupled with product damage as a result of poor packing or, in transit damage.

It was also clear to you, that relationships with suppliers tended to be short term and adversarial. You have observed some heated discussions taking place with Enzyme PLC over a late delivery. You were however unable to determine what the performance levels were supposed to be, as you were told that there were no supplier performance criteria available.

You are aware that you will need to engage with suppliers and therefore see that supplier management and relationships will need to be improved and whilst, you will be unable to develop and maintain deep relationships with every one of the suppliers, you are confident that something must be done.

You decided to have a discussion with some of your staff about the reality of working differently with suppliers so that they could see that the old methods were not always the best. Some of the comments you had heard were as follows:

- "I do not believe that suppliers can be a positive partner as they also deal with our competitors. They cannot therefore be trusted and we therefore have to be secretive with them on many things."
- "We do not have the time to work together. This will take up too much time; and we only have time have to focus on what is likely to be happening next week."
- "We are low cost driven, so anything else is secondary. It is them and us. They are our opponents!"
- "My job is to focus on crunching numbers, creating purchase orders and chasing up suppliers; it is not my job to be nice with suppliers".

Clearly in the real world of personalities and professional relationships that exist at Jones Limited, there are some obstacles to be climbed.

Loss and Disputes

Where there has been a poor supplier performance or it has been determined that there has been some loss and a dispute ensures, then legal considerations are needed. As stated earlier, legal disputes are potentially expensive, time consuming and uncertain – they should not be the first recourse in resolving problems. As buyers we need to remember that we are not the only party that can take legal action – suppliers can do so if they feel that the contract was breached by the buyer

Direct loss

In law, there is no clear definition of direct loss. This is due to the fact that when the courts consider damages, they will consider each case upon its own facts. What the parties have agreed in the contract and the circumstances of breach will be consider if a court decides to award damages. Where, for example, likely losses are loss of business, loss of profit and the increased cost of finding a replacement service, it can be argued that such would be direct losses.

Examples of what constituted direct loss are losses that flowed directly and actually, in the ordinary course of events, from breach of contract; particularly loss of profit, expenses thrown away and money spent as a result of the breaches, might all be recoverable as damages. Direct loss has been defined as that which flows naturally from the breach without other intervening causes, and that which is independent of special circumstances.

Indirect loss

This is the opposite of direct loss and it has been held that the words "indirect or consequential," did not exclude liability for damages which are the direct and natural result of the breach.

In a recent case on what constitutes direct and indirect loss, the judge defined "consequential" as *"such loss as the claimants may prove over and above that which arose as a direct result of such breaches the claimants may prove, in accordance with the rules laid down in the first limb of the rule in Hadley -v- Baxendale"*.

Where consequential or indirect loss is excluded in the contract, this does not necessarily mean that economic loss or loss of profits cannot be recovered. The increased cost for a claimant of, for example, finding a replacement service is likely to be considered as direct loss. However, damages for loss of business and therefore loss of profit will only be recoverable if they are closely related to any breach by the defendant.

Disputes and resolution

Clearly when disputes cannot be settled by the parties to the contract, then courts of law become involved. This can be expensive and is also public, which can lead to a loss of reputation on either or both sides, and will usually absorb a lot of management time as well as the costs of legal representation.

Alternative Dispute Resolution (ADR) is an alternative to litigation. Arbitration provides an opportunity even when direct negotiations have failed for parties to control the outcome of their dispute.

Alternative Dispute Resolution (ADR) is the collective term for the ways that parties can settle civil disputes, with the help of an independant third party and without the need for a formal court hearing. The term originated in America in a drive to find alternatives to the traditional legal system which was felt to be adversarial, costly, unpredictable, rigid, too professionalized, damaging to relationships and limited to narrow rights based remedies compared to creative problem solving.

The acceptance of ADR grew as the preferred term in business and civil litigation worlds as its popularity is based on the following facts:

- Quicker than litigation
- Relatively cheaper
- Can help to resolve disputes without damaging commercial relations

Methods of ADR

There are some very different characteristics and some of the methods of ADR are well known: the use of Ombudsmen such as the Parliamentary Ombudsman, and the various Regulators like the Energy Regulator, OFGEN and the Rail Regulator.

Mediation is also used successfully to resolve a wide range of disputes, whether or not they involve money, including cases involving problems with child residence and contact; neighbour and land disputes, clinical negligence and personal injury cases as well as in business and commercial areas. Mediation gives the party or parties in dispute, the opportunity to reach a settlement without a court hearing and with the help of an independant third party, a mediator.

The mediator's job is not to make a decision; instead they will help the parties to explore the strengths and weaknesses of their cases and to identify possible solutions helping them to reach a solution between themselves. Agreeing to use mediation does not prevent the parties from being able to eventually continue with court proceedings, if they cannot come to an agreement.

Mediation is a flexible process and an experienced Mediator can exploit that flexibility to achieve agreements between the parties that would otherwise be impossible. Mediation is a voluntary, non-binding, private dispute resolution process in which a neutral person helps the parties tries to reach a negotiated settlement.

Essentially, the following framework provides safe foundations on which to build.

Mediation procedures

1) Preliminary contact between the Parties and the Mediator to:
- Agree to mediation
- Agree terms of mediation including date/s, duration, location, representation, legal framework, costs and documentation.

2) Limited, brief written summaries of the case are submitted by Parties in advance to:
- Inform the Mediator
- Focus Parties on the real issues.

3) Initial joint meeting at which:
- The Mediator clarifies the position and establishes ground rules
- The Parties present a summary of their case to each other
- Issues are clarified.

4) Private, confidential meetings between the Mediator and each Party separately to:
- Examine the important issues and needs of each Party
- Encourage openness about weaknesses as well as strengths
- Discuss options for settlement.

5) Joint meetings as appropriate throughout the mediation at which Parties may:
- Negotiate directly
- Discuss differences, particularly in understanding of fact or expert opinion or likely legal outcome
- Set the settlement down in writing or agree further action.

The Mediator brings negotiating, problem-solving and communication skills to the process, deployed from a position of independence and neutrality, making progress possible where direct negotiations may have stalled.

During the mediation process the mediator fulfils several important roles:
- A manager of the process, providing firm but sensitive control conveying confidence that it is all worthwhile and giving momentum and a sense of purpose and progress
- A facilitator helping the parties to overcome deadlock and to find a way of working co-operatively towards a settlement that is mutually acceptable
- An information gatherer absorbing and organising data and identifying common ground shared goals and zones of agreement.
- A reality tester helping parties take a private realistic view of the dispute rather than public posturing and muscle flexing.

- A problem solver bringing a clear head and creative mind to help the parties construct an outcome that best meets their needs when compared with the alternatives of non agreement or an imposed decision by an arbitrator judge or jury.
- A sponge, which soaks up the parties' feelings and frustrations and helps them to channel their energies into positive approaches to the issues.
- A scribe who writes or assists in the writing of the agreement checking that all issues are covered and that all terms of the agreement are clear.
- A settlement supervisor, checking that settlement agreements are working and being available if problems occur this is occasionally requested.
- A settlement prompter, who if no agreement is reached at the mediation will help parties to keep the momentum towards settlement.

The essence of mediation and the reason for its success is that it introduces a powerful structure and dynamic into any negotiation or dispute discussion. The mediator acts as a catalyst being an independant neutral who is committed to helping the parties to settle, but who does not have a stake in the dispute either as a party or as an advocate or representative. In this way they can help challenge entrenched positions, and consider what happened and what is possible in future without preconceptions or personal history.

Less well known ADR methods include the following:
- Neutral Evaluation where a neutral third party provides a non-binding assessment of the merits of the case
- Conciliation which is similar to mediation but the third party (conciliator) takes a more interventionist role
- Expert Determination where an independent expert is used to decide the issue
- Neutral Fact Finding is used in cases involving complex technical issues where a neutral expert investigates the facts of the case and produces a non-binding evaluation of the merits.
- Med/Arb (a mixture of mediation and arbitration) is where parties agree to mediate but refer the dispute to arbitration if the mediation is unsuccessful.

The relationship between ADR and the Courts

For some time it has been Government policy that disputes should be resolved at a proportionate level, and that the courts should be the dispute resolution method of last resort. Although ADR is independant of the court system, a judge can recommend that parties involved in litigation enter into it. The court may also impose cost sanctions if it decides that one or more of the parties has been unreasonable in refusing to attempt ADR.

The courts will also take into account behaviour during the pre-litigation period including whether or not an attempt has been made to use ADR.

For some types of dispute, specific pre-action Protocols exist to set out the steps parties are expected to take before issuing court proceeding. For all other types of disputes parties are expected to follow the Practice Direction for Protocols. These details are available at:

www.dca.gov.uk/civil/procrules_fin/contents/practice_directions/pd_protocol.htm
(please be aware that web addresses soon become redundant, a search is often better)

Balancing Commercial and Social Objectives

So far in this section, we have looked at procurement generally and made some specific references, for example with tendering, to some differences between private and public sectors.

An appreciation of these differences is, we believe, very important simply because in Procurement most suppliers are found in the private sector which has very different standard practices. Additionally, suppliers can benefit from knowing more about the procedures in the public sector. Through mutual understanding it should be possible to have benefits for both parties.

To illustrate such differences further, the following summary was reported:

Feature	Public sector	Private sector
Main driver	Maintain the current due to resource constraints.	Growth.
	Political imperatives.	Commercial imperatives and customer satisfaction.
	"Survival" decisions are up to politicians, the managers "advise".	"Survival" decisions are made by managers.
	Image and politics.	Brands.
	Balance the books.	Make a profit.
Structure	Centralised and bureaucratic "by the book".	Any type of structure can be found.
Culture	Traditionally was a Job for life/security.	Job insecurity.
	Trade Union involvement.	Continual change.
	Little incentive to change.	Performance incentives often found.
	No performance linked pay.	
Ultimate responsibility	Politicians and elected bodies.	Shareholders or "self."
	Cannot go out of business.	Frequent close downs.
"Buying"	Tendering and long decision making.	Quicker decision making and price discussions.
	Price sensitive.	Less price sensitivity and more emphasis on "value."
	Fixed goalposts.	Goalposts change during negotiations

"Marketing"	Customer already exists and is disgruntled. Users have little choice or no choice, about using the service.	Customers have to be "sold". Competition exists and the aim is to get repeat business and retain the customer who can easily go else where.

Private and public sector differences
Source: UKHRD 3/2000 and Independant on Sunday 11/4-93

We will now concentrate more fully on the specific requirements and obligations of the Public Sector.

3: Public Sector Procurement Frameworks

Introduction and overview

Public sector procurement in the UK aims to achieve best value for the taxpayer, and at the same time to provide an opportunity for free and fair competition from suppliers across the UK and European Union. These aims are not always exactly compatible, and there can be times when the need for free and fair competition acts against best value by making it difficult for buyers to act quickly to take advantage of commercial opportunities.

Additionally, the requirements of EU procurement guidelines can add both time and cost to procurement processes. Sometimes, this may not seem commensurate with the procurement being undertaken, for example with relatively low value purchases.

The process is seen by many suppliers, and also by buyers, as bureaucratic and inflexible, especially when the benefits are spread or extended but the costs of procurement is immediate. Once understood however, the procedures are not as complex as they initially seen but their initial appearance does have a negative effect on some suppliers; particular SME suppliers who may be then reluctant to bid for contracts, or alternatively, to hire a tender writing specialist (which are employed by some large firms).

An additional hindrance is that it is not possible to modify the tender notice to reflect changed circumstances. This means that a tender may have to be withdrawn and resubmitted, causing delays and cost to both the contracting authority and the supplier.

Most UK public sector bodies therefore issue guidance to staff. These highlight obligations under the EU legislation, and also for lower value purchases. As all UK national law is secondary to the EU directive, the national laws and local council guidelines must be derived from the EU directive.

As already mentioned, there are three main routes for public sector procurement in the UK:

- open tenders
- restricted tenders
- competitive dialogue

In practice, there are also, many informal tenders, for small value purchases and we shall explore all of these routes shortly.

The process for deciding the appropriate route is often set by local authority internal guidelines/EU legislation and these often focus on the value of the contract, to the exclusion of the supply risk involved. It will be recalled from our discussion in Part 1.0 of this book that in the Kraljic model, both spend and risk need analysis is required. A form of the Kraljic model may be used to determine the most appropriate route and this is shown below.

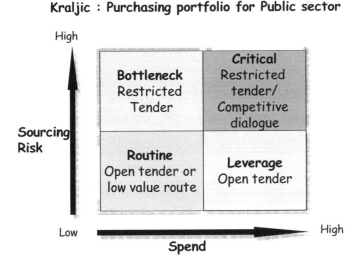

Kraljic : Purchasing portfolio for Public sector

The Regulatory Framework

Public procurement law in the UK regulates the purchasing of goods, works and services by a wide range of public sector bodies. The European Commission's Consolidated Directive on public procurement (2004/18/EC) was adopted in March 2004 and this forms the basis of the UK regulations. These are implemented in two separate pieces of legislation:
*   The Public Contracts (Scotland) Regulations 2006, and
*   The Public Contracts Regulations 2006 which apply in England, Wales and Northern Ireland

The two sets of regulations are similar, being based on the same overriding directive, and the minor differences between the two are outlined in the Appendix.

The aim of the European directive is to open up European public sector procurement to competition and also to promote the free movement of goods and services. This means public procurement, above a threshold value, must be open to all suppliers in all EU countries, and must also give all suppliers, a fair chance to win the business. It is not therefore possible to adopt for example, "buy local" policies that exclude suppliers in other regions or nations. Additionally suppliers must have an opportunity to both know there is a contract to bid for, and also then have a reasonable time to respond to the contract notice. They will then be eligible for feedback on their submissions, and able to challenge the award. The directive should also inform purchasing processes below the procurement threshold, and it may be necessary or appropriate to use the EU procedures for purchases below the threshold.

Bodies covered by the regulations

The regulations cover a wide range of organisations and with different thresholds. Bodies listed in Schedule 1 of the directive include central government, and have a lower threshold for notification in the Official Journal of the European Union (OJEU); this reflects the pre-eminent role of national governments in procurement.

Local authorities, and consortia formed by one or more contracting authorities will be covered by the threshold covering "other public sector contracting bodies". Exclusions from the regulations are possible, and may be sought in the light of national security issues for defence procurement.

Types of service covered

The regulations cover all public sector procurement processes, and for the purpose of the directive are separated into three categories:
- Supplies covers the purchase, rental, hire and/or leasing of products
- Services are further segmented into two, priority and residual and will exclude construction and design services, these are covered under "works"
- Works are contracts covering the provision of building, design and/or construction services or "works"

129

Public Supply Contracts have the aim to purchase, lease, rental or hire purchase (with or without an option to buy) of products. These will therefore commonly apply to the general procurement of products bought by the public sector, such as stationery supplies, ICT, office furniture and similar goods. Where the supply of products also includes as an incidental aspect the installation of the goods, it can however be considered a Supply contract rather than a "works" contract; an example being the installation of a new wall display screen, where the major element of the purchase is the screen rather than the installation.

Public Service Contracts have as their object the provision of services and are further segmented into Type A and Type B services.

- Type A services are "priority" services, and are fully covered by the regulations.
- Type B services are "residual" services, and are considered by the EU to largely of interest only to local (national) bidders and consequently are subject to less stringent regulation. These services therefore, do not require prior advertising of the contract notice, or open competitive tendering, but they must still follow the general requirement of being transparent, non-discriminatory, and offering equal opportunity to bidders. An example might be cutting grass.

Examples of public service contracts

Type A services include:
- Accounting services
- ICT related services
- Architectural consultancy services not covered under "works"

Type B services include:
- Education services
- Health services
- Recreational, cultural and sporting services

If products are supplied along with the service, but are of a lesser value than the service element, the contract can be considered as a Service contract.

Public Works contracts are those related to the design and/or execution of "works", meaning building or civil engineering works.

Concessions

A Public works concession is a contract of the same type as a standard public works contract, apart from the fact that the consideration for the works is the right to exploit the work (with or without further payment). An example might be the construction of a toll bridge, where the constructing body would also have the right to levy tolls for a period.

A Service concession is similar except that the consideration for the performance of a service is the right to exploit that service (with or without further payment).

Public sector thresholds

The OJEU procurement thresholds are revised every two years. The value is then set, based on the prevailing exchange rate, and do not vary, regardless of actual exchange rates, until the next review.

As an example, the OJEU limits applicable from 1 Jan 2010 are shown in the table below.

OJEU Limits from 1 January 2010			
	Supplies	**Services**	**Works**
Entities listed in Schedule 1	£101,323	£101,323	£3,927,260
	(£125,000)	(£125,000)	(£4,845,000)
Other public sector	£156,442	£156,442	£3,927,260
contracting authorities	(£193,000)	(£193,000)	(£4,845,000)
Indicative Notices	£607,935	£607,935	£3,927,260
	(£750,000)	(£750,000)	(£4,845,000)
Small lots	£64,846		
	(£80,000)		

The limits apply to the totality of the foreseeable procurement. This means that it is not acceptable to split a single requirement into smaller lots to avoid the OJEU threshold, for example, by requesting bids for only the first year of an anticipated three year project, or by splitting a single requirement into three smaller lots.

Where the value of spend is expected to be below the threshold, but is near to the limit, then the OJEU process have to be followed. In practice, this often means that public bodies set a further limit someway below the actual threshold, say 75% of the limit, and follow the OJEU process for all purchases above that value.

The trend is for the OJEU process to be seen as appropriate for purchases below the threshold, down to relatively low levels – potentially £20,000 (see *European Commission vs. Germany*, 2010).

Common Elements of the OJEU Public Procurement Process

Regardless of the procurement route undertaken, there are some common elements in all OJEU Public Procurement processes. The first is that the contract must be advertised by way of a notice in the Official Journal of the European Union using the mandated standard form; this is available on the EU's SIMAP web site (http://simap.europa.eu/index_en.htm).

Common Procurement Vocabulary

The Common Procurement Vocabulary (CPV) is an 8-digit numeric code used by the EC to assist buyers to classify their contract notices, and the enable suppliers to find relevant contract notices.

The CPV code can be confusing, as they are limited in number, revised rarely and so do not take account of some new ICT developments, and often do not provide a good match to the description of the contract. However they do provide basis for international suppliers to identify notices that might be relevant.

There is a hierarchy of codes, with the higher level or root codes mainly consisting of zeros, being progressively broken down into sub-sections. As an example:
- 72000000: IT services, consulting, software development, internet and support
- 72500000: Computer-related services
- 72510000: computer-related management services

For many public sector buyers only a limited number of CPVs are required, and it is common to keep a separate short list of commonly used codes for easy reference.

Choice of Procurement route

We have already covered the optimum procurement route by considering the following Kraljic model:

Kraljic : Purchasing portfolio for Public sector

For contracts over the threshold value, the procurement process must follow the appropriate OJEU process and the simplest way to determine this is to utilise the above Kraljic model..

Open tenders are most likely to be appropriate for low risk purchases, such as commodity materials and services. If the expected value of the contract is below the OJEU threshold, then the use of simple procurement processes may be appropriate.

For contacts with a higher degree of complexity and/or risk, either the restricted tender or competitive dialogue route may be appropriate. The competitive dialogue negotiated route may also be applicable in these cases where there is a lack of potential suppliers.

Lowest Price or Most Economically Advantageous Tender (MEAT)

The contracting authority must award the contract on the basis of either:
•   The lowest price, or
•   The Most Economically Advantageous Tender (MEAT).

The lowest price criterion is self-evident, but it is worth emphasising that in this case, no other elements of the tender may be taken into account (with the exception of the mandatory exclusions).

The Most Economically Advantageous Tender (MEAT) is the most commonly used criteria, not least because it seems to provide buyers with a little "wriggle room" in selecting the best bid. Factors other than price can be used either in addition to, or instead of, price, to determine the best bid. Typically these criteria will include quality, delivery, technical merit, life cycle costs, and added value.

The MEAT criteria are not as flexible as sometimes is assumed by buyers. The contract award evaluation criteria, and any other sub-criteria, must be set out in either, the OJEU notice, or, the tender documents (and ideally both). Once this has been done, then no other criteria can be used in determining the MEAT.

The exact weighting of each criterion and sub-criterion must also be given. This can be either as an exact number or, in cases where this cannot be provided in decreasing order of importance (for example, quality with the highest weighting, then innovation, then added value etc.). In evaluating bids it is not possible to deviate from these criteria and weightings. Consequently, significant consideration should be given during the preparation of the tender to ensure the criteria and the weightings, will allow for a proper differentiation of bids and the identification of the best offer.

Mandatory exclusions

Public Procurement processes in the European Union have on occasion been found to be criminally corrupted, and so the OJEU process insists on a mandatory exclusion from bidding of those supplier organisations that have been found guilty of:

- Organised crime activities
- Corruption
- Fraud to the detriment of the EC
- Money laundering

Organisations guilty of such activities are of course not likely to advertise this, and so the onus is on the public sector awarding body to review bidders to ensure that they are not guilty of any of the above, and are eligible for involvement in the process.

Organisations may also be excluded for a range of other issues:
- Not fulfilling obligations to pay taxes
- Not fulfilling obligations to pay social security contributions
- Being guilty of grave professional misconduct
- Financial irregularities such as bankruptcy, administration, winding up, sequestration of assets
- Being unlicensed to provide public services (where applicable)
- Being unregistered on professional or trade registers (where applicable)
- Not being authorised to pursue a trade or professional activity
- Serious misrepresentation of information

Timescales for procurement

The advantages of the OJEU process for procurement can be seen as:
- Opening up the supply market to potential bidders
- Ensuring that all suppliers are treated fairly and equally
- Giving suppliers recourse, if they are not treated in accordance with the guidelines

However, a drawback of the process is the length of time that is required to complete the procurement process. A long period of time is required to ensure that the notice is visible to potential bidders, and to allow them time to prepare appropriate responses. Short notice periods are vulnerable to giving advantage to those existing or other suppliers who have prior notice, as they know that the notice is coming, and have a longer time to prepare their response.

A reduction in the minimum time required is enabled by the use of electronic communication at all stages of the procedure, including, the transmission of notice to the Journal and the receipt of tenders. The standard minimum period for receipt of expressions of interest from bidders is reduced by 7 days to 30 days if the notice has been sent electronically to the Official Journal. This is still longer than may be seen with most private sector contracts, but still allows the required elements of fair and open competition. A Preliminary Indicative Notice (PIN) may also be issued ahead of the actual ITT to alert potential bidders to the forthcoming opportunity, and allow them to start preparations for bidding.

An accelerated procedure can be used in situations where there is a pressing need for urgent procurement. This should be an unforeseen situation or requirement, e.g. response to a natural disaster, rather than a lack of planning on the part of the commissioning body.

Timescale for EU procurement processes

Procedure	Process	Minimum Timescale
Open	Tender	52 days (36 if PIN)
Restricted	Expression of interest Tender	37 days 40 days (36 days if PIN)
Restricted Accelerated	Expression of interest Tender	15 days 10 days
Negotiated	Expression of interest	37 days
Negotiated	Expression of interest	15 days
Competitive dialogue	Expression of interest	37 days

Standstill (or Alcatel) period

This period is sometimes known as the Alcatel period, as a result of a European court of Justice ruling (C91/98) which led to the adoption of this process.

This period allows unsuccessful bidders to exercise their right to challenge the award of a contract. Contracting authorities have to notify all bidders of the contract award decision in writing.

Following this, there is a so called "stand still" period of 10 or 15 calendar days before the contract can be signed with the winning bidder, during which time; the unsuccessful bidders can request additional information and/or initiate a legal challenge to the decision.

The notification should also include or refer to the timetable of activities that can be undertaken before the final award, shown in the following table.

Day	Requirement
Day 0	Notification of award decision, containing all relevant information, to be e-mailed or faxed to all unsuccessful tenderers.
Day 1	Day after transmission (e-mail) - No action
Day 2	Deadline for unsuccessful tenderers to request additional de-briefing (midnight end of Day 2). This request must be in writing. (e-Mail or Fax)
Days 3-7	Responses to debriefing requests to be made within this period and by the end of Day 7 at the latest to ensure at least 3 working days between the last de-brief and the end of the standstill period. (If however there is a delay whatsoever in providing the requested de-briefing, then the standstill period must be extended accordingly).
Days 8-10	No action
Day 10	End of standstill period
Day 11	Conclusion – Final Award of contract if no legal challenge received.

Unsuccessful bidders can launch a challenge at a later time, but this should be within a reasonable time of them becoming aware (or should be aware of) the issue causing them to launch a challenge. This is typically 3 months, but may be determined in court, and such a challenge may not stop the award or delivery of the contract.

Open Tender Route

This procedure is used for the procurement of commodity products (or occasionally services) which does not require a complex tender process and would correspond to the bottom two boxes on the Kraljic matrix that have a relatively low supply risk.

A minimum of 3 supplier proposals must be evaluated and no negotiation with the tenderers is permitted.

Any interested supplier can submit a tender in response to the OJEU notice, and then when expressing interest, they have to be sent a copy of the contract documents. A Pre Qualification Question (PQQ) stage is often not required as a separate stage in this process, and respondents may actually be asked to submit the PQQ at the same time as their tender.

The authority then has the opportunity to review all of the submitted tenders, or only those meeting the selection criteria outlined for the PQQ. If the authority decides to review only those passing the PQQ stage, particular focus should be given to ensuring that elements included in the PQQ are not considered again in the tender stage.

Restricted tender route

This procedure should be used for the procurement of products or services with a higher degree of supply risk or complexity and therefore equates to the top two boxes on the Kraljic matrix. In this process, a PQQ stage should precede the invitation to submit tenders. Only those bidders who pass the PQQ selection stage should then be invited to submit full bids.

A minimum of 5 suppliers should be invited to tender. No negotiation is permitted with tenders after they have submitted their tenders, although a small amount of clarification and confirmation may be appropriate. Feedback must be provided to unsuccessful bidders at all stages, along with the reasons for rejecting their proposal.

Meanwhile, the definition of the final solution should be clearly defined in the ITT specification. If it cannot be clearly defined, the Competitive Dialogue process may be more appropriate.

Competitive Dialogue

This procedure should only be used for procurements in the top right box of the Kraljic matrix; those combining a high degree of complexity and supply risk with a high cost. This is a relatively new procedure from 2006 and allows the input of suppliers into the tender process. In practice it can be difficult to find a sufficient number of suppliers willing and able to bid for the contract.

It is intended to most replace the Negotiated route, which was previously used for such purchases, but this can still be used in very limited circumstances. In common with the Restricted tender route, it is normal to have a PQQ stage and then only to invite to bid those suppliers who meet the criteria.

Under this procedure, tenderers are invited to negotiate the terms of the advertised contract with the contracting authority. The aim of this is to utilise the experience, knowledge and ability to innovate of suppliers, in order to best meet the needs of the contracting authority.

A wide range of approaches and solutions may then be proposed. This can cause difficulties in evaluating the bids, especially as the selection criteria have to be identified in the initial notice, which of course, is before the potential solutions have been put forward.

The OEJU regulations do not set out any rules to govern the process of the negotiations, but as with all OJEU procedures, these should be fair, open and transparent. In practice this will mean treating all bidders equally and managing timescales so that all bidders have access to the same information at the same time.

A minimum of 3 suppliers should be engaged in the process and engage in the competitive dialogue. In some situations this may prove to be difficult because of the high costs to suppliers of participating in a competitive dialogue process.

Background to competitive dialogue

The competitive dialogue process is appropriate for high value procurements with a high risk of complexity and or risk. An example is the UK Building Schools for the Future (BSF) programme, where private suppliers were invited to be involved in the design, construction and funding of building schools.

Any supplier may request to participate, and the contracting authority will probably run a PQQ process to identify the suppliers best placed to take part in the actual dialogue process. The aim here being to develop one or more solutions to the sourcing requirement, and when that has been achieved the suppliers are invited to submit a formal, final tender on the basis of which the successful bidder is chosen.

Principles

The competitive dialogue process expressly recognises that suppliers may have more knowledge and experience in a given activity than the contracting authority. It also seeks innovative solutions to complex problems as these are difficult to achieve under the normal and standard tendering process. Therefore typically the dialogue is used for procurement processes for contracts of "many millions", rather than smaller projects.

A number of difficulties may arise with this procedure.

*   Firstly, identifying three or more candidates for the dialogue with the appropriate experience, skills and inclination to take part.
*   Secondly, the participating companies may seek recompense for taking part in the dialogue so they can offset some of their costs.
*   Suppliers may drop out of the dialogue, leaving a choice between a small number of potential solutions, or just one.
*   The time taken for a competitive dialogue can be long, typically a year, but at least months.
*   Finally, there can be difficulties in selecting the most appropriate bid if the solutions are very different in nature and approach, as the criteria for making the decision have been established at the beginning of the process, well before any solutions had been suggested.

Use

The process for a competitive dialogue is shown below
1) Issue OJEU notice
2) Return of expression of interest / PQQ
3) Evaluation of PQQ and selection of long list
4) Invitation To Participate in the Dialogue (ITPD), see below
5) The dialogue phase, see below
6) Call for final tenders , see below
7) Submission and Evaluation of Final Tenders, see below
8) Appointment of Preferred Bidder
9) Lessons learnt

A minimum of 3 candidate suppliers should be invited to take part in the dialogue, and in view of the nature of process a larger number is advisable. However, given the substantial costs likely to be incurred by both bidders and the contracting authority in running the process, then care should be taken not to invite many suppliers who have little chance; accordingly 6 suppliers should be the upper limit.

If fewer than 3 suppliers are assessed at the PQQ stage as being suitable to progress to the dialogue phase, it is still possible to proceed with this number, but it is not permissible to add in at this stage to ask or any new bidders who did not respond to the original notice.

The OJEU notice should set out the "needs and requirements" of the notice, and may also detail the award criteria that will be used at the end of the process to select the winning bid. At this stage the definition of the criteria are probably ill defined, and so it is acceptable (and preferable) to list the criteria in descending order of importance rather to give weightings.

The needs and requirements can be further defined in a descriptive document sent to bidders expressing and interest. This document should also define the selection criteria, and will be refined and developed through the process.

Invitation To Participate in Dialogue (ITPD)

The first revision of the descriptive document is likely to be the Invitation to Participate in Dialogue (ITPD), which should be sent to all bidders who successfully pass the Expression of Interest or PQQ stage. The ITPD should contain:
- A reference to the OJEU notice (publication reference number and date)
- Any supporting documents
- Administrative elements (language to be used for the dialogue, contact address and details etc.)
- Criteria for award of the contract (descending order of importance, or weightings)
- Supplier requirements (e.g. proof of information on financial stability or technical capability submitted at PQQ stage)

The Dialogue Phase

This phase starts when the ITPD has been sent to bidders. No formal process is stated by the OJEU regulations; therefore contracting authorities are free to develop their own process for conducting the dialogue.

It is important to recognise that at this stage, the aim of the dialogue is to *"identify and define the means best suited to satisfying the contracting authority's needs"*. This will require open sharing of problems, concepts and ideas, and the exploring of options that may not in the end form part of the solution proposed by the bidder. Bidders should not be constrained to include any potential solution in their final proposal, but be free to select whichever solution they think is most likely to meet the needs of the project.

All discussions should remain confidential, and information and concepts provided by one bidder should not be shared with other bidders without their express written approval (which of course, is unlikely to be given).

The dialogue may contain elements of formal presentations, written submissions, and verbal discussions. All elements of the contract can and should be discussed, including financial structures and terms and conditions of contract, and not be limited to just technical solutions.

In order to minimise the effort required by both bidder and supplier, it is acceptable to reduce the number of participants in the dialogue in "successive stages". The intention to do so must be stated in the OJEU notice and/or the descriptive document, and the reduction must be carried out in line with the award criteria set out in the OJEU notice and/or descriptive document.

It is possible to reduce the number of solutions being discussed in this way either in one step, or progressively (i.e. removing one solution each time), this being so long as at the end of the dialogue stage, there are still sufficient bidders for a genuine competition of at least 2 and preferably more. The process for deciding may be carried out by requesting the submission and evaluation of an initial tender response to allow a documented and evidenced process for the successive reduction. Alternatively bidders may choose to withdraw from the process at any stage.

During the negotiation the contracting authority has the usual obligations to treat all bidders equally, and so must ensure that all bidders have access to the same information at the same time, with no bidder given an advantage over another.

Some bidders may seek payments for participating in the dialogue. This is possible, but the contracting authority is not obliged to do so. If payments are made they should be made to all participants and not just one. Payments may be necessary in order to induce a sufficient number of bidders to take part in the process, and should be seen as a partial contribution to their costs of bidding, rather than an opportunity to profit from participation.

The dialogue continues until the contracting authority is satisfied that it has identified its requirements and can now define them with sufficient clarity to enable bidders to submit a Final tender which will then be the basis for selecting the successful bid.

The contracting authority must next declare that the dialogue phase is complete, and inform all of the bidders (preferably in writing). The authority must also be sure that all bidders do now have sufficient information to enable them to submit final bids. This may be achieved by issuing a final revision of the descriptive document.

Up until this stage it has been possible to discuss any and all points of a potential bid. After this stage the negotiation is effectively over, and any future negotiation must be limited only to "confirmation, clarification and fine-tuning" of the information submitted in the final tender. If larger revisions of bids are required, it may be necessary to withdraw the tender and to re-start the procurement process again from the initial notice stage. This is naturally to be avoided if at all possible.

In order to minimise the risk to all parties that the final tender will not meet the needs of the contracting authority, it may be possible, as a last stage of the dialogue, to request the submission of "indicative tenders" outlining the solution to be put forward in the final tender. The aim of this is to look for any issues or problems that have not been identified earlier, and resolve them before the final tender stage. This is not to "approve" the tenders to be put forward or in any way judge their acceptability; bidders not being bound by them in submitting their final tender.

Call for Final Tenders

Once the contracting authority calls for Final tenders, the dialogue phase is effectively over, and the process proceeds as with normal tenders. A formal written "invitation of submit final tenders" should be issued, with an appropriate deadline for receipt of submissions and a reference to the initial OJEU notice. Variant bids are encouraged, and so there may be more proposals to evaluate than bidding entities. Each bidder may have put forward their own solution(s), and these should remain confidential.

The criteria for award of the contract must be those identified in the initial OJEU notice and/or the descriptive document. Of course, these criteria were developed with little idea of the final form of the submissions and therefore the submissions may differ greatly with proposed solutions. The reviewers may well find themselves in the situation of comparing "apples and oranges" or even apples and trees.

If the weightings of criteria have been published then they must be adhered to, otherwise, the descending order of criteria indicated in the notice must be used.

Given the nature of the competitive dialogue, the descending order of criteria is more commonly used than weighted criteria. These must then be formalised ahead of the receipt and opening of any bids, and if possible should have been included in the Invitation to submit Final Tenders. Note that this is a clarification of selection criteria, rather than a change of criteria.

Evaluation of Final Tenders

The final tenders should contain *"all the elements required and necessary for the performance of the project"*. If the submitted bids do not include this, it may be necessary to withdraw the tender and start all over again.

When the Final Tenders are submitted, the only modification possible, is *"clarification, confirmation and fine-tuning"* of the proposals; this provided it does not involve changes to the basic features of the tender and are not likely to distort competition or favour one bidder over others.

In essence, this means that minor matters of detail only can be changed and in practice, this usually does not include price (and certainly not major changes in price). The concept of fine tuning does however allow for some minor improvements to the Final Tender, especially in unforeseen circumstances.

Case Study: BBC

The BBC used the competitive dialogue process for the Digital Switchover Help Scheme.

The approximate cost of the scheme is £600m, and the Completive Dialogue process was split into two parts run simultaneously:
- a pilot scheme worth approximately £1.5m
- the full national rollout worth and estimated £500m

The process took more than a year with the OJEU notice being published in February 2007 (after a period of development), and the final award being placed in February 2008.

Procurement costs for the BBC were estimated at £1m, and the three bidders for the main contract are estimated to have incurred costs of between £1m and £1.5m. This was seen as an acceptable percentage of the total contract value. The high cost was incurred in part because of the large number of people involved on both sides; the BBC had a team of 5 working full time on the project supported by other people on a part time basis, including 8 technical staff, senior management and support staff. Each BBC employee was matched one for one by an equivalent on the teams of each supplier.

In order to treat each supplier equivalently, the BBC staged meetings with each supplier in turn Monday to Wednesday, leaving the remainder of the week for internal work. A draft final tender was requested a week ahead of the final Tender to ensure that no issues had been overlooked or misunderstood.

Four companies initially engaged in the dialogue, but one dropped out during the process. Interestingly, the winner of the pilot programme (the findings of which were shared with all other bidders) was not the winner of the overall contract.

Best Practices

A number of best practices have been identified for using the competitive dialogue process.

Engage and consult widely amongst potential bidders before issuing the OJEU notice. This will allow the contracting authority to determine whether there are sufficient interested parties to allow a competition, and may also have an influence on the shape and nature of the requirement:

- Leave as much room for flexibility as possible while still conforming to procurement process requirements. In practice this means using the descending order of criteria, rather than weighted criteria in the initial notice. The earlier the indicative criteria can be developed and shared, the better.

- A dedicated team should be assembled to manage the dialogue process, and they should have sufficient time and resources to manage the whole process for a considerable period of time, potentially a year or more, on a more or less full time basis.

- Meetings with suppliers should be scheduled as close to each other as possible, ideally on successive days, so that no bidder has an advantage because of a longer time to prepare or longer knowledge of some new aspect of the dialogue.

- Maintaining confidentiality can be difficult over a long period. One suggested method to help in this is to formally raise the issue of confidentiality at the beginning and end of each meeting with a supplier, and ask a supplier to confirm the elements of their bid which they wish to be kept confidential (often all of it), and which they are willing to share with other suppliers (usually, none of it).

- Finally, the preparation of interim of provisional bids ahead of the final tender may allow both parties to identify potential problems and errors ahead of the final tender, after which no substantial changes are possible.

Lower Value Procurements

Contracts of a value lower than the thresholds identified earlier, do not have to follow the OJEU thresholds.

However, there are general obligations to ensure that all public sector procurement processes are inspired by the Directive, and that the process follows the general principles of non-discrimination, equal treatment of bidders, transparency, proportionality and mutual recognition of different standards and qualifications.

Any process used by public sector bodies for low value procurement must therefore be able to demonstrate how these principles have been achieved, that there was a reasonable and appropriate advertising of the contract (which does not need to be a formal advert), and there was some form of fair completion run to determine the best bidder.

The precise nature of the contract will influence which suppliers are likely to be interested, and should therefore be made aware of the opportunity

Council low value procurement process

Local authorities usually have a standard process for low value procurement that works on a series of thresholds. An indicative example (from Darlington Council) is shown in the table below:

Example of Local authority low value process

Value	Requirement
Up to £5000	1 written quote
£5000 to £75,000	At least 3 written quotes
£75,000 to EU threshold	ITT advert
EU threshold and above	Full OJEU process

The details of the threshold limit vary between councils, as does the process used to select suppliers within each band. Some councils have higher threshold values than those chosen by Darlington Council, and some have lower ones. Each local authority has to balance the cost of the procurement process with the value of the goods or services procured. It should be noted that this financial based system takes no account of the supply risk involved in the purchase; accordingly, a variant of the Kraljic model may produce a more robust process.

As identified above, some councils have a stipulation that any contract that approaches the relevant OJEU threshold (within say 10%, 20% or even 40%) should be treated as if it exceeded the threshold. In this way the council can be sure that the correct process is followed if the value of the contract has been underestimated.

Where there is a requirement in the process for three (or more) written quotes, care must be taken to ensure that the process does generate genuine competition. It is not unknown for this step to be compromised by the desire for a quick and efficient resolution, and for some buyers to take short cuts such as requesting quotes from 3 interlinked companies, or from a preferred candidate and 2 companies with little interest in the contract.

It has even been known for buyers to request a quote from a potential bidder (or bidders) and at the same time to tell one bidder what price would be seen as acceptable, and instructing the other bidders to quote high (in return for which they will be in the privileged position at some time in future).

These sorts of approaches pay some attention to the letter of the process for reasons of efficiency, while regrettably entirely ignoring both the intent and the legality of the situation. It is also a very short step towards having an unacceptable relationship with suppliers.

Publicity for transactions above £500

In 2010 the new UK coalition government sought to improve transparency about public sector procurement by issuing guidance on the publication about local government expenditure. This sought, particularly to smaller suppliers, to make the public sector marketplace more open and transparent, by ensuring that companies would be more aware of contract opportunities, and also which suppliers won each contract. This being intended to both stimulate competition and to allow smaller suppliers to seek sub-contracting opportunities. Additionally public procurement will be open to much more extensive public scrutiny than in the past, with individuals and interested bodies being able to analyse what was spent (although with limited information about why, or whether the purchase constitutes value for money).

It should also reduce the incidence of contracts being given "on the nod" to suppliers who have well established relationships with the commissioning body.

The elements are:
*   New items of local government expenditure over £500 to be published by all councils from January 2011. The £500 threshold does not cover salaries, and applies regardless of the size of the authority.
*   New local government contracts and tenders to be published in full from January 2011

This guidance at the time of writing is not prescriptive, and councils have flexibility about how this is achieved. However, the government has made it clear this will be enshrined in legislation if councils do not adopt it within their procedures.

The process of applying this guidance will mean that councils must identify for themselves the best method of publicising the contract award and tender documentation on a regular basis without incurring significant costs. The most likely solution will be to publish this information electronically on the web. Discretion may be needed if there are payments to named individuals such as sole traders rather than companies, as these may be sensitive for the individual concerned.

Councils will also have to establish processes for dealing with any challenges to the award of these small value contracts, and for ensuring that the costs and any time delays incurred in the publication of the opportunities are minimised.

Early adopters of this approach have been the Greater London Authority (http://www. london.gov.uk/who-runs-london/greater-london-authority/expenditure) which has been reporting spends over £1000 since 2008.

Best Value

Within the context of procurement, the UK Government's definition of best value is the *"optimum combination of whole life costs and benefits to meet the customer's requirement"*. This approach allows sustainability and quality to be taken into account when considering service delivery options, rather than just price. For example, considering whole life costs rather than just initial purchase price allows selection criteria to include factors such as fuel efficiency and cost of maintenance as well as social factors such as benefits to local people, community safety, diversity and fairness). Successful procurement strategies are based on whole life cost consideration including future revenue implications, and not simply the lowest initial tender price.

SME Concordat

A long standing aim of governments, both national and European, has been to ensure broad business participation in the public sector procurement processes.

SME businesses constitute the majority of businesses in the UK, but have a low participation in public sector procurement. Most SMEs:
- never bid for public sector work,
- believe that there is a lack of publicity about public sector contracts,
- feel the public sector is a more difficult client than the private sector because of red tape, lack of responsiveness and unrealistic timescales

Consequently more than 50% of SMEs believe that public sector procurement takes more time and effort than they can afford.

In order to improve the opportunities for SMEs to supply the public sector the UK government in 2005 asked local authorities to sign up to the SME friendly Concordat (Small Business Friendly Concordat: Good Practice Guidance March 2005, and addendum October 2005) as a voluntary, non-statutory code of practice.

The aims of this concordat, which was not legally binding, was to create opportunities for SMEs, Black and Minority Ethnic (BAME) owned and women owned businesses, and third sector organisations.

The aims of the concordat, obviously, do not override the obligations to comply with the EU directive where appropriate.

The Concordat consists of a number of policy statements that local authorities can sign up to deliver, which should make it easier for small businesses to win business. These are not onerous, and many are best practice for public sector procurement in any case, for example publishing the procurement procedure and responding to all bid submissions.

The key points are as follows:

Checklist: Local Authority Commitments

A key element of the 2004 National Procurement Strategy was that every council should adopt a corporate procurement strategy, including the SME Business friendly Concordat. The following points were put for forward to councils to adopt:

We will publish a corporate procurement strategy. The strategy will include a commitment to;

- The role procurement plays in delivering the Council's objectives and its contribution to the Community Strategy, workforce issues, diversity and equality and sustainability
- How we will encourage a diverse and competitive supply market including small firms, social enterprises, ethnic minority business and voluntary and community sector suppliers.

- A commitment to ensure that our approach to individual contracts, including large contracts and framework agreements etc. is supported by a sound business case and options appraisal.
- A commitment that where we decide that the best value option is to aggregate supply or let a longer term contract or framework agreement, we will invite bidders to demonstrate their track record in achieving value for money through effective use of their supply chain.
- A commitment to consider the role of SME specialist suppliers in delivering elements of larger contracts and framework agreements.

The Concordat undertakings include;
- We will apply our own rules and policies fairly.
- At pre-tender stage and during the tender process we will ensure that all tenderers have equal access to relevant information.
- We will keep the tender process as simple as possible in order to help minimise costs to suppliers
- If a pre-qualification stage is used we will use a Council-wide pre-qualification questionnaire containing common core questions with limited bespoke additions for each contract. We will work with regional and national partners to ensure a consistent approach to pre-qualification.
- We will assess potential suppliers against published pre-qualification and tender evaluation criteria. These criteria will be proportionate to the risks of the individual contract process. In particular the criteria relating to financial standing will not be set out to unreasonably exclude newer businesses.

Contract Management

We will treat suppliers openly and fairly. Suppliers will:
- Be paid on time and no more than 30 days from receipt of an undisputed invoice.
- Receive honest and constructive feedback on the supplier's performance of the contract.
- Be given notice of any performance problems and an opportunity, if appropriate, to put matters right.
- All contracts will require our suppliers to pay their sub-contractors, throughout the supply chain, within 30 days from receipt of an undisputed invoice.

Additionally:

- We will work with prime contactors – both at tender stage and during the life of a contract – to establish the contribution that small firms, ethnic minority businesses, social enterprises and voluntary and community sector suppliers can play in our supply chain. We will provide details of our prime contractors on our website.
- We will give potential suppliers an opportunity to discuss the procurement in order to understand our requirements and assess their own suitability. Nothing will be done, however, which would give a particular business or provider an unfair advantage in competing for a specific contract.

Feedback and Complaints

- We will offer meaningful feedback to suppliers following the procurement process in order that suppliers can improve for future tenders.
- We will seek feedback from suppliers, and their respective trade organisations on our tender processes and address, where we can, any problems that are brought to our attention.
- We will publish a complaints procedure.

4: Procurement Best Practice and Contexts

Supplier pricing

Price is the value of a product or service measured by money. It is the consideration to be paid or given, for an article, goods, service or something that was desired, offered and purchased. It relates to cost with the total sum involved including the price, plus, all that is associated with owning or using a product or a service (including the cost of procurement itself). In procurement, comparing prices enables evaluation and appraisal of the relative values offered by different suppliers.

Economists view supply and demand as balanced by the influence of price, and the point where equilibrium is found, is the point where supply and demand are equal. Therefore slight changes in price may cause substantial changes in demand; here the demand is said to be elastic, and for example, suppliers will consider reducing prices as a lower price will result in enhanced revenue. An example here is the growth of cheap air line travel.

Where however substantial price changes have little effects to the demand, then the demand is said to be inelastic. This will happen where:
- There are few substitutes or competitors
- Buyers are slow to change habits and practices and do not search for alternatives
- Buyers do not challenge high prices

An example here is the price of oil.

The theory on elasticity of demand applies in times of "perfect" competition where the market sets the price. Perfect competition may also apply in commodity markets, for example cocoa beans for confectionery manufacture, however some buying has to operate in "imperfect" competition and here the most common forms are:

Type	Number of Suppliers	Supplier Market Entry conditions
Monopoly	One	None
Oligopoly	Few e.g. oil production	Limited
Pure Competition	Many	Competition between suppliers

Pricing strategy

Price is an important issue in procurement – but not the only issue. In terms of the supplier and the buyer, the following are considerations on pricing.

Suppliers will consider:
- The market position occupied ranging from a monopoly position with the seller setting the price (subject to legislative controls), to pure competition where the market sets the price
- The nature of demand; elastic or inelastic
- What the buyer will pay; effectively charging what the market will bear
- Competitor's prices
- Supplier's need for the business
- Perceived long term value for the supplier, for example, payments, continuity of orders, reputation; accordingly perceived "one off short term bids" may affect the suppliers response
- Supply of standard "commodity" products or specialised "bespoke" products
- Product life cycle stage, for example, declining products may be price discounted and new products carry a premium price
- Order volumes
- Pricing options, see below
- Pricing for market penetration purposes by pricing low to win a larger share
- Their perception of what their product *should* sell for (which is often optimistically high – the so called endowment effect)

In turn, purchasers can consider the following on pricing:
- The risk attached to the purchase and the method of pricing, from firm price to cost pricing
- The position in the market; for example, a monopoly supplier
- The number of suppliers in the market and the possibility to source from another supplier
- Prices paid by other buyers
- The relationship of price to value
- Payment terms
- Price analysis to determine what is "reasonable"
- Order volumes
- Their own perception of what the price *should* be (which is often optimistically low)

Price analysis

Price analysis is the breaking down of a quoted price into its constituent elements for the purpose of determining the reasonableness, or otherwise, of the proposed charge.

The cost knowledge and information the buyer needs will come from past experience, from internal costing estimates or, from the suppliers provided cost information. Additionally, other management accounting practices such as life cycle costing, target costing etc are helpful. No procurement manager can be effective without a good knowledge of costing.

Price variation

Prices can vary at different times due to many reasons, for example:
- Quality, for example, use of branded goods rather than non-brand goods (e.g. Dulux paint rather than another less prominent brand)
- Quantity, for example, incentives in placing larger orders
- Time, for example, when buying in quiet periods
- Cost, for example, early payment incentives
- Place, for example, changing to ex works terms

Price indexing

This involves reviewing price increases, with, market price increases and makes a comparison with published price indices, for example:
- UK's Consumer Prices Index allows comparison of the inflation rate in the UK against that in the rest of Europe.
- UK's Retail Price Index; this is an average measure of change in the prices of goods and services. Once published, it is never revised.
- UK's CIPS Price Indexes covering basic commodities and some services
- USA's Bureau of Labour Studies; Producer Price Index

The usage of such indices can be extended beyond simple comparisons, for example, your prices have risen last year by 4% but you expected a reduction of 3%. However the external indexing shows an increase of 7%, therefore in effect then your prices have remained static.

Price and value

Price and value are not the same, with value often being viewed as what comes over the whole life of a product or service. An alternative view is that value is often seen as being what the customer perceives it to be and is something they are prepared to pay for.

By conducting analysis on existing materials and products in liaison with other departments, cost savings can be made throughout the supply chain.

Value analysis is often carried out as a team project with input from the user, research and development, procurement, warehousing and finance. As part of a team, procurement will collate data on products and materials from the marketplace.

Existing and potential suppliers can be involved in making suggestions to reduce costs and add value as well as looking for opportunities to reduce costs in product components and materials, packaging, storage and distribution, with also opportunities to add value to existing product design. Procurement may for example, suggest alterations to existing products within the early or mature stage of their life cycle.

Price Options

All the above factors will influence the final decision and in practice, the agreements between sellers and buyers will be of two types, firm price agreements and cost price agreements.

Firm price agreements are often said to be more advantageous to buyers for the following reasons:
- Suppliers bear all the risk of input price changes, meanwhile the buyer knows what is to be paid
- Suppliers have the maximum incentive to produce efficiently and on time, as the supplier has to pay for all cost increases, but will keep all cost savings
- A minimum of administration is needed

With cost price agreements, the supplier adds a fixed percentage to costs or agrees a fixed management fee, for their profit, and the buyer pays for all costs. This can be seen as being disadvantageous for the buyer as:
- Buyers bear all the financial risks

- Sellers have no incentive to be more efficient or effective as their costs are being paid "anyway"
- Administration can be difficult as buyers need to have all the appropriate knowledge of the sellers processing practices and cost structures

Cost plus agreements are however very common in the supply of services. Here the purchaser, especially if they have recently outsourced the service, will have "in-house" knowledge of the cost structures. Of course this knowledge will need to be updated over time.

Cost plus is also becoming increasingly common in projects and contracting. During the construction of T5 London Heathrow Airport there was also cost sharing of any savings or overruns; other aspects of the T5 contract are as follows;

The T5 Contract

The T5 Agreement is central to everything that's good about Terminal 5.

It is BAA's response to a project whose sheer size and complexity defy traditional construction management techniques. Legally binding, in essence it's a contract in reverse. Instead of specifying what redress can be taken in the event of things going wrong, it aims to stop problems happening in the first place.

This is done by fostering constructive behaviour and a recrimination-free environment. Key features include:

Ownership of risk
In contrast to most so-called partnership deals, risk is not shared between client and suppliers. BAA carries it all, allowing suppliers to concentrate on delivering results. The focus is on managing out the cause of problems, not their effects if they do happen.

Complexity management
The task of building T5 is split into 16 main projects, plus 147 sub-projects of between £30 million and £150 million each. The agreement binds BAA and its 60 key first-tier' suppliers only, these suppliers are themselves responsible for the

appointment and management of second- and third-tier suppliers, who must also work within the spirit of the agreement.

Close supplier involvement
To avoid the traditional and potentially damaging demarcation between design and build, key suppliers were brought on board at a much earlier stage in the planning process than is usual. This enabled potential hitches to be spotted before designs were finalised and construction began.

Integrated teamwork
Both within and across teams, the concentration has been on proactive problem-solving rather than the avoidance of litigation.

Shared values
Common induction programmes and regular communication initiatives help to ensure that all of the 6,000 workers from 400 supplier companies who can be involved at any given time share the same values and objectives, which include being proud of working on T5 and delivering the project on time, on budget, to quality and safely.

Source: Human Resources November 2004.

Clearly T5 represents more than just cost plus, but continues into a whole different collaborative relationship with suppliers; a theme we examine next.

Relationship-based approaches

Simply, the following supplier relationships can be noted:

Relationship	Examples of Procurement methods used
Transactional	Competitive tendering and spot buying
Co-operative	Negotiation and preferred suppliers with framework agreements
Collaborative	Open book and joint working towards continuous improvements

The change from more arms-length transactional relationships to closer working collaborative relationships can also reflect a move towards more adaptive and effective supply chains. It will also involve different levels of trust, shown below as levels one to three.

Level one trust	Level two trust	Level three trust
Boundary trust	Reliable trust	Goodwill trust
Contractual	Competence	Commitment
Explicit promises	Known standards	Anything that is required to foster the relationship
Standard performance	Satisfactory performance	Success beyond expectation
Mistakes bring enforcement		Mistakes give shared learning for advantage
Exchange data for transactions	Cooperate on information for mutual access	Cognitive connections and joint decision making
Animal brain		Human brain
Symbonic	Share	Swap
Time bound (as far as the contract says)		Open-ended, ongoing and leaving a legacy

These levels of trust also make for an interesting comparison between transactional and collaborative relationships and an "ideal-typical" comparison follows.

Transactional relationships	Collaborative relationships
Price/Risk	
Price orientation	Total cost of ownership
Price dominates	Shared destiny dominates
One way	Two way exchanges
Customer demands sensitive data	Exchanges of sensitive data
Customer keeps all cost savings	Mutual efforts to reduce costs, times and waste
All risk with supplier, the buyer risks little	Shared risk and benefits
"What is in it for me"	"What is in it for us"
Short term	Long term

Transactional Relationships | Collaborative Relationships

Negotiations	
Strong use of ploys in negotiations	Mutual gains "rule" discussions
Power based	Equality based
Win/lose	Win/win
"One off" deals	"Forever" together
Walk in and out of, change is easy	Difficult to break, change is difficult
Easy to set up	Difficult to set up
Adversarial and maybe inefficient for one party	Challenging to implement and continue with
"Partnershaft"	Partnership

Inter Personal Relationships	
No personal relationships	Strong personal relationship
Separated/arms length	Close/alliance
Low contact/closed	Shared vision/open
Predatory power based	Proactive and more people based
Hierarchical/superior subordinate	Equality
Blame culture	Problem solving "gain" culture
Alienated employees	Motivated employees

Trust	
Trust is based on what the contract says (contractual trust)	Trust is based on goodwill, commitment and co-operation
Little ongoing trust	Continual trust plus risk/benefits sharing
Power based "spin"	Pragmatic "tough" trust

Controls	
Strong on tactical/departmental controls	Strong on marketing strategy and supply chain alignment
High formal controls	Self controlled
Rigid contracts	Flexible contracts
Technical performance and the specifications "rule"	Work beyond just "one" technical view
Resource and capacity capabilities	Mutual long term capabilities
Measure by non compliance	Both measure and agree remedial action

Changing from more transactional methods to collaborative approaches goes far beyond the technical issues, of say ICT connectivity, and fully embraces soft skills. The view from sponsors of collaborative approaches is that if all players would work well together that a lot more would get done more efficiently and more effectively. It is seen that the evidence is overwhelming. However many people will not subscribe to such a mutually sharing collaborative supply chain management approach; indeed, in the public sector, this is often seen as preventing fair competition. For others, especially in the private sector, a major reason is much of their buying is for leverage (Kraljic) items with buyer power.

Therefore two way collaboration sits here as an uneasy concept; we will look at power in procurement below. One other major reason however, is that soft skills are the hard skills for many people in business. Indeed, supply chain management collaboration between companies is unlikely to succeed, without appropriate recognition that soft skill development is required. Issues of trust and blame can also make people reluctant to engage in a partnership. If it is unsuccessful the buyer could be blamed for being naïve in trusting a supplier – the buyer may feel unlikely to be criticised for being sceptical about a supplier, even though it lost a beneficial partnership opportunity.

Power

Relationships in procurement between buyers and sellers will vary; power is not always equally distributed. For example buyers have power when:

- They have a high spend
- They are a large organisation with a good reputation that sellers desire to be associated with

- They are a growing developing organisation with future potential
- They have a large market share and influence
- The supplier market is very competitive

Meanwhile sellers have power where:

- There are barriers to entry for other suppliers into their market, for example, requirements for specialised research and development
- They have "unique" products. For example, OEM spare parts
- They are a monopoly or oligopoly; the association of power to monopoly or competition markets is shown further below:

Feature	Monopoly	Oligopoly	"Perfect" competition
Supply & Demand Control	Statutory	Fewer companies, with the possibility of market collusions	No controls, all open
Barriers to entry	Retained and look to maintain "status quo"	High costs to enter the market for "new" suppliers	Few to no barriers and low costs to enter
Market view	Focus and concentrate.	Large and valuable markets. Possible cartels	Customers can easily "switch." Continual search for providing what is required and needed.
Customers view	No really considered as the customer has no choice	Sometimes considered	Customer "rules"
Prices	Can charge "What the market will bear"	Stable and related to costs and desired profits. Possible price fixing.	Demand driven, possible cost plus provision.
Examples	Some oil companies	UK Supermarkets	UK Car assembly

The relative power dominance, between buyers and suppliers, can L
follows:

With the buyer dominant:
- There is often a small number of big buyers who buy a large percentage of a seller's output
- It is easy for buyer to switch as there are many sources of supply
- Low transaction costs
- "Take it or leave it" approach.

With seller dominant:
- Then there is often a small number of big sellers who supply to many buyers
- It is difficult for buyers to switch as there are few sources of supply
- High transaction costs
- They can "enforce" a deal

With such relative levels of dominance, then this leads to unequal power distributions; these can be seen as a foundation for the forming of adversarial relationships. Sharp-eyed and experienced readers will also see the connection to the Kraljic portfolio where for example, the buyer's behaviour may be as follows:

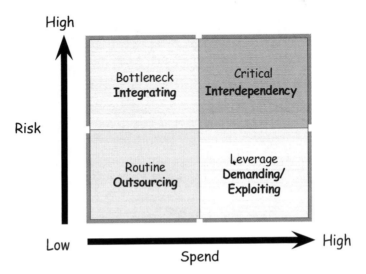

In turn; the link to more collaborative approaches may be seen:

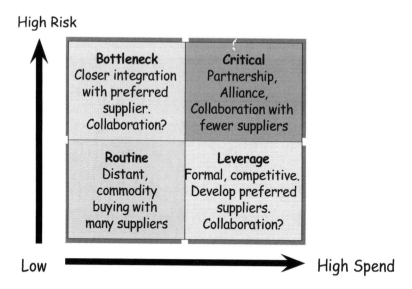

In turn, related to risks, then we can see a strategic and tactical approach to procurement forming, as follows:

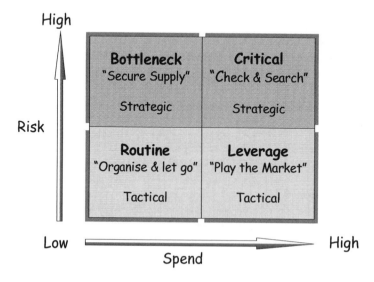

From this we can then see that there are actually varied levels of trust, openness and information exchange that results in varied types of relationships involved:

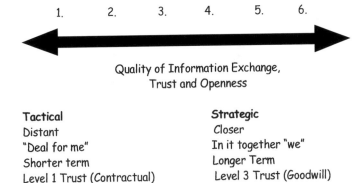

We can expand this further when considering how to deploy procurement staff:

Tactical procurement uses the new trainee and junior buyers and has the following types of relationships:

1. Adversary relationships; "Take it or leave it"
2. Transactional relationships; Normal ordering
3. Single Source relationships; Exclusive agreements usually at fixed price for a specific time

Strategic procurement uses the more senior buyers with the following types of relationships:

4. Strategic alliance relationships; Working together for a specific purpose
5. Collaborative relationships; Commitment with shared risks/benefits
6. Co-destiny relationships; Interdependency

Relating this back to Kraljic, the following gives us a typical perspective: (diagram overleaf)

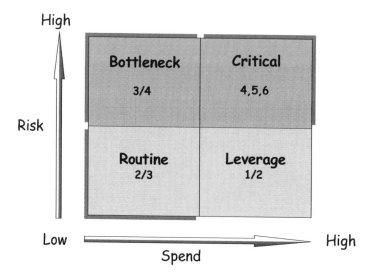

In allocating work between the buying team we may also consider personal style along with experience and seniority – some members of the team may be more comfortable with adversarial relationships than others and therefore be ideal for managing Leverage based purchasing relationships. Others may have a preference and skills for collaborative relationships and be better at managing Critical purchasing relationships. Most buyers are practiced at varying their preferred style to the one most appropriate for the particular purchase, but may still be most effective when using their preferred style.

Keeping in our ideal-typical view, then we can recap on the following stereotypes between transactional and collaborative approaches.

Transactional relationships have the following characteristics:
- Short-term
- Separated/arms length
- WIIFM - What is in it for me?
- "One off"
- Low contact/closed
- Little trust
- Price dominates
- "One night stand"
- Power based
- Win/lose

- One-way (customer demands sensitive data)
- Customer keeps all cost savings
- All risk with supplier, customer risks zero
- Power based "spin"
- Adversarial and inefficient
- Hierarchical/superior subordinate
- Blame culture
- High formal controls
- Rigid contracts
- Alienated employees
- Predatory
- Technical Performance specifications "rule"

Whereas **Collaborative relationships** are typified by the following:
- Long term
- Close/alliance
- WIIFU (us)
- "For ever"
- Shared vision/open
- Trust/risk/benefits
- Shared destiny
- "Marriage"
- Equality based
- Win/win
- Two-way exchange of sensitive data
- Mutual to reduce costs, times and waste
- Shared risk and benefits
- Pragmatic trust
- Challenging to implement and continue with
- Equality
- Problem solving culture
- Self controlled
- Flexible contracts
- Motivated employees
- Proactive
- Work beyond just "one" technical view

These differences are shown very clearly in the following case study on contracting

Case Study: Contracting: Adversary or Collaboration?

The £757 million UK's Wembley National Stadium is one of the largest, most costly and complex construction schemes in the UK. Like all mega-projects, it poses enormous technical and logistical challenges. How a project is procured has a huge bearing on whether problems arise, and whether disputes break out between different parts of the construction team.

The stadium, was due to open on 13 May 2006, was built under a design-and-build contract. This is a modern procurement method under which the main supplier (Multiplex at Wembley) in effect becomes the agent for the client, as well as being responsible for building the job.

This is a departure from the norm as traditionally; clients would deal independently with a designer, quantity surveyor and main supplier. Under design-and-build, however, the main supplier becomes the client's single point of contact, managing all other contractual relationships and the associated construction risks. The contract was also let on a fixed-price, lump-sum basis, shifting project risk to the supplier.

Dumping risk

Simon Murray, chairman of supplier Geoffrey Osborne and former director of major projects at Railtrack, says that in principle, "having a single party who you deal with and who takes responsibility is good, but it shouldn't be absolute. It's naive to put all risk onto the team doing the project. And if you are doing something of national significance, the idea that you can dump risk is absurd."

Risk dumping happens when companies pass responsibility for danger or problems that may occur during construction to firms they hire to do work for them.

"Main suppliers' relationships with the supply chain are very patchy," Murray says. "There are some who want to get the lowest possible price and dump risk on the people they hire to do the work. Yet those who really know how to do things are the suppliers and specialist suppliers."

He contends that lowest price generally offers a false economy, since it forces suppliers to compromise on the quality of their technical solution.

Graham Edgell, group procurement director at supplier Morgan Sindall, agrees: "A lot of clients are after a quick process — they just want the job done, without any added-value. Because we make such a stupendous effort for such small reward, and our guys are under such pressure to deliver for the sum agreed, there's no opportunity of letting your guard down. You've tied yourself to a price and then you've got to go out and do it."

Despite the UK construction industry tradition of firms "buying work" — taking on projects at cost, simply to keep its people and plant active — British firms walked away from Wembley. Multiplex, however, claimed it could deliver the job for the price offered, and told its shareholders it would turn in a profit.

Adversary relationships

Wembley's great technical challenge was the structural design, construction and erection of its signature arch. Multiplex awarded steelwork firm Cleveland Bridge a lump-sum, fixed- price subcontract to fabricate, supply, deliver and erect the arch and roof.

However, this deal has encountered problems. In a claim against Multiplex for non-payment, Cleveland Bridge alleges that "by spring of 2003 there were serious problems arising from late and incomplete design by the civil and structural engineer, and delays in providing design information. The design changes and late information caused substantial costs increases, and delays and disruption to the subcontract works." Though Cleveland Bridge and Multiplex agreed a plan for accelerating work, plus compensation for the resulting change in the subcontract terms, a legal row then broke out, over alleged non-payment and contract breaches.

Despite the integration that should have been achieved by using a design-and-build contract, "Wembley is a graphic example of old-style adversarial contracting," according to Bob White, chief executive of Constructing Excellence, who have the task of improving performance in the construction industry.

Despite the problems construction consultant Frank Griffiths says, "Wembley thought that a fixed-price, lump-sum contract could be the solution to all its problems. But that is only fine if the supplier has all the resources, time and money required for the project."

For such a contract to work, he adds, there has to be a rigorous work programme in place, and the client also needs to understand how the work is going to be subcontracted. "Through using a design and build contract, Wembley thought it had offloaded risk to Multiplex, but it hadn't."

BAA and Collaborative approach

Other such mega-projects have taken a different approach. British Airports Authority (BAA), which is building Heathrow's Terminal 5 and they have enormous in-house procurement and project management teams, which supervise and reduce risk at all stages of design and construction.

"BAA has spent a fortune on ensuring they're informed," says Gil Howarth, founder of project management company Howarth Associates. Both have elected to work in partnership with their suppliers, using the same offices, sharing information and resources, and, crucially, any savings or overruns.

BAA ditched conventional, reactive contracts, in which one party claims against another for delays or extra costs, in favour of creating incentives for proactive behaviour that would pre-empt problems. This tactic was guided by study of other major construction schemes, which revealed that, as a client, pushing risk to arm's length offered no real protection. "The client is always accountable in the end, on cost, time and health and safety — everything," says Riley. If the project were to go wrong, its failings would have an impact on BAA's reputation in the industry and on its standing in the City."

BAA took the radical step of accepting all risk, and took out £4 billion worth of insurance. "By doing that you take away negativity, allow space for innovation and create the opportunity for people to perform at levels they haven't been allowed to before," explains Riley.

A special contract, the Terminal 5 Agreement, was produced for the project, requiring totally integrated teams, including principal sub-suppliers up through main suppliers and designers to BAA itself and British Airways, Terminal 5's end user. Suppliers are paid on a cost- reimbursable basis, with performance encouraged by offering bonuses for beating target costs and completion dates; conversely, they share some of BAA's "pain" when schedules and costs overran. The agreement engaged all the key players early on to identify risks well before they come into the construction programme, leading to highly evolved risk-management strategies.

Cost efficiencies

The style of collaborative project management practised by BAA grew out of the North Sea oil and gas industry 30 years ago, and was being adapted for the construction sector by BAA and other clients more than a decade ago. But partnering only grabbed attention following the publication of two government-sponsored reports in 1994 and 1998 respectively, "Constructing the Team", authored by Sir Michael Latham, and "Rethinking Construction", by Sir John Egan.

Egan calculated the UK's £58 billion a year construction sector could achieve cost efficiencies of 30 per cent, reduce defects by 20 per cent and increase profitability from 2 per cent to 5 per cent by developing better leadership and greater focus on customer needs, by integrating processes and teams, and by adopting an agenda driven by quality rather than cost.

For clients, this meant releasing large volumes of work in a steady stream to give suppliers more continuity, and adopting them as preferred suppliers. For suppliers, it meant breaking the practice of paying sub-suppliers late and of casually hiring and firing labour.

Egan urged: "Industry must replace competitive tendering with long-term relationships based on clear measurement of performance and sustained improvements in quality and efficiency."

Source: Extracts from "A Game of Two Halves" in Supply Management 6 October 2005 by Andrew Mylius (the features editor of New Civil Engineer).

Changing procurement

This move towards more collaborative relationships can completely change procurement in some organisations, as the following indicates:

Old Procurement	New Procurement
Select lowest cost	Select on best value
Late involvement of key suppliers	Early supplier involvement
Defensive and confrontational contracts	Collaborate, cooperate, trust, honesty and sharing
Costly risk transfers leading to low profit margins	Open allocation of risks with auditable decisions and improved profits
High costs due to duplications, delays, disputes and defects (all are waste)	Time and cost savings without compromising quality
Poor H&S record	Improved H&S
Low rates of production/construction	Shorter lead in times speeds production/construction
"Silo" working practices	Cooperation and longer term views foster training schemes and shared learning
No whole life costing	Focus on Asset management
Every contract is a steep new learning curve	Learning transferred from project to project and continuous improvements
Dissatisfied users/customers/tenants	Increased satisfaction and wider community benefits

Source: After "Partnering Works" The Housing Forum Report (2003)

Making the change

What fundamentally will have to be changed when following a collaborative approach? This topic has been more fully covered in *The Relationship Driven Supply Chain* (2006) by Emmett & Crocker, but to briefly note here: a simple answer is "people first" – also consider the following:

- Contracts to simple flexible approaches
- Intensive management involvement
- Periodic performance monitoring

- Internal controls for confidential information
- Problem-solving procedures
- Supplier is seen as a customer = "reverse customer service" as what suppliers do affects what happens to the customer
- Cross functional supplier/customer teams
- Hub (supply chain managers) and spoke (suppliers/customer) organisations?
- And people last...as "people change one at a time".

It is people that change an organisation and it is the people who make the relationships in and between organisations. In the changing of culture ("what is down around here"), then this will need to pass through the following stages:

Aspect	"Stormy/Blame" Culture	"Steady/Sane" Culture	"Sunny/Gain" Culture
Goals	Announced	Communicated	Agreed
Information	Status symbol and power based	Traded	Abundant
Motivation	Manipulative	Focused on staff needs	A clear goal
Decisions	From above	Partly delegated	Staff take them
Mistakes	Are only made by staff	Responsibility is taken	Are allowed as learning lessons
Conflicts	Are unwelcome and "put down"	Are mastered	Source of new innovation
Control	From above	Partly delegated	Fully delegated
Management Style	Authoritarian/ aggressive	Cooperative	Participative/ Assertive
Authority	Requires obedience	Requires cooperation	Requires collaboration
Manager	Absolute ruler and feels superior	Problem solver and decision maker	Change strategist and self-confident

Once the culture has been defined, this will require the examination of all internal and external relationships. Trust will often remain a major barrier; however, without trust, there will be no relationship.

It is clear that partnerships with suppliers can be effective in the UK Public Sector, as long as the partnership does not have the effect of reducing competition or changing the market. Partnerships between UK Public sector bodies in order to achieve more efficient and effective procurement can also be successful, and again would be permissible as long as they do not distort the supply market (by becoming in effect a dominant customer).

Case Study: Effective partnership working

The UK Audit Commission (1998) use the term 'partnership' to describe a joint working arrangement where the partners:

- are otherwise independent bodies;
- agree to co to achieve a common goal;
- create a new organisational structure or process to achieve this goal, separate from their own organisations;
- a plan and implement a jointly agreed programme, of-ten with joint staff or resources;
- share relevant information; and
- pool risks and rewards

The key points are:

Deciding to go into partnership

1. Does this organisation have clear and sound reasons for being involved in its current partnerships?

2. Where new partnerships must be set up to meet national requirements, what groundwork is being done locally to maximise their chances of success?

3. Are changes in behaviour or in decision-making processes needed to avoid setting up partnerships with only limited chances of success?

Getting started

4. Have all the partnerships in which the organisation is involved been reviewed to evaluate whether the form of the partnership is appropriate to its functions and objectives?

5. Do all the partnerships have an appropriately structured board or other decision-making forum?

6. When setting up a new partnership, how are prospective partners identified?

Operating efficiently and effectively

7. Do partners share the same main objectives for the partnership?

8. Are the partnership's objectives consistent with those of the partnership organisation?

9. If an outsider watched a partnership operate, would they be able to identify the partnership's main objectives?

10. Do the partners know where the boundaries between the activities of the partnership and of their own organisations lie?

11. Do the members of partnership steering groups have sufficient authority to commit their organisations to decisions?

12. Are partnerships prepared to delegate responsibility for parts of their work to particular partners?

13. Do large partnerships have an executive group that all the partners trust to make decisions on their behalf?

14. Are project-planning techniques used to ensure the separate agreement of all the partners to a course of action in good time, when necessary?

15. Do the partnership's decisions get implemented effectively?

16. Are partnership staff selected for their technical competence and for their ability to operate both inside and outside a conventional public sector framework?

17. What actions are taken to build and maintain trust between partners?

18. If members have dropped out of a partnership, what lessons have been learnt about how to maintain involvement in the future?

Reviewing success

19. Does each partnership have a shared understanding of the outcomes that it expects to achieve, both in the short and longer term?

20. What means have been identified for measuring the partnership's progress towards expected outcomes and the health of the partnership itself?

21. Has the partnership identified its own performance indicators and set jointly agreed targets for these?

22. Are the costs of the partnership known, including indirect and opportunity costs?

23. Are these costs actively monitored and weighed against the benefits that the partnership delivers?

24. What steps have been taken to make sure that partnerships are accountable to the individual partners, external stakeholders, service users and the public at large?

25. Are some or all of the partnership's meetings open to the public?

26. Is information about the partnership's spending, activities and results available to the public?

27. Does the partnership review its corporate governance arrangements?

28. Has the partnership considered when its work is likely to be complete, and how it will end/handover its work when this point is reached?

Source: The Audit Commission: A Fruitful Partnership: effective partnership working, 1998

Outsourcing

"Virtual" companies give testimony to the fact that just about everything can be out sourced. In the supply chain, common candidates for outsourcing are distribution, production and as shown below, increasingly procurement.

It should be noted that outsourcing procurement does not necessarily mean that the procurement provider will be outside the scope of the EU directives – it is possible that they will be constrained to act in accordance with those directives.

Procurement outsourcing

The following summarises what one procurement service provider says how they go about the outsourcing of procurement:

What is involved?

- The transfer of selected services/activities to a third party, not the transfer of control
- Enables concentration on core business
- Normally multi-year agreements
- Contractually linked to targets, such as minus cost, plus service etc.
- Geared to set/step performance improvements

Levels of outsourcing

- Migration of infrastructure (people, technology, systems, supplier management)
- Assume responsibility for some process
- Offers added value functions such as strategic sourcing, supplier relationships
- Formulation of strategy

Why outsource procurement?
- For same reasons as would outsource anything
- Enables core concentration by the business
- Increase efficiency due to economies of scale of people, systems etc.
- Reduces, commonly, costs by up to 15%
- To drive change and to introduce new technologies more easily
- Connect to a larger supplier base

How does it work?
- Aggregate spend by pooling requirements
- Access higher levels of expertise
- Tap economical labour sources in transactional processing by "off shoring"
- Operations after the transition are more "self-service"
- Adjustments needed to now being more automation intensive
- More centralised purchasing contact
- More use of operating performance matrices
- More formal service level agreements (SLAs)

Going forward
- Needs a careful consideration of current circumstances - it may not suit everyone
- Is service provider bound by EU procurement directives? Need to take advice.
- Executive team decision is due to: need for change, merger activity, urgency for cost reduction, ability to change, reducing fixed costs
- Scope for savings/need for capital/prioritisation/sharing of benefits
- Future vision/capability/investment needed/strategic nature

Organisations who outsource will have taken the basic decision of "Buy in" rather than "DIY". In the public sector there are often political considerations involved in the decision whether or not to outsource a given service. There are often arguments about efficiency and cost saving on hand, and quality and accountability on the other. In this section we are concerned purely with the processes and possibilities rather than recommending the extent of outsourcing that should be undertaken by any public sector organisation.

Many aspects of outsourcing are common ones and this section will therefore look at these common elements of outsourcing.

The secrets of outsourcing have been identified in *Supply Management* (29 June 2000) as follows:

- Concentrate on what organisation does well and allow specialists in other areas to handle the non-core services
- Adapt to new ideas and developments- what was acceptable in the past, may not be so in the future
- Choose a provider who understands all your needs
- It is crucial to fully know the current costs and service levels
- Ensure outsourcing delivers planned benefits such as cost/service/time targets
- Acknowledge that information equals power in areas such as service level requirements
- Develop a strategic alliance with the provider based on mutual trust
- Start with a phased controlled service with monitored cost/service levels at all stages
- Develop the right culture which supports outsourcing
- Monitor the outsourced function with regular performance measurement

The important questions an organisation will need to consider, before outsourcing, are:

- Is it a non-core activity?
- Can we release some capital?
- Will we retain some operations in house? If so, which?
- Will we retain management expertise?
- What increased monitoring will be needed?
- What are the risks of committing to one supplier?
- Will flexibility be increased?
- Will costs be reduced, whilst service is increased?
- How will we account for future changes?
- Are there any implications on the Transfer of Undertaking, Protection of Employment (TUPE) legislation?
- Are there political concerns that need to be managed?
- How does this fit with EU Procurement directives?

The suppliers of the outsourced service will have to be determined as being "capable".

Outsourcing is classic activity for procurement to be involved and the following **supplier criteria** can be studied:

- Financial Stability/Ownership/Turnover/Profitability
- Size/Equipment/Systems/Methods/Capacity
- Management Skills/Industrial relations/Contracts
- Referrals/Other Customers/Similar business handled
- 'Feel good factor'/Understanding/Easy to deal with
- Dependable/Reliable/Accreditation by an internationally recognised quality management standard

If it is then decided to examine outsourcing further, then the financial, operational and strategic advantages and issues will be raised; for example:

Financial Issues

- Capital released
- Off balance sheet finance is available
- Asset Utilisations change
- Economies of scale
- Planned/Known costs are available
- Cost comparison must be comparing "apples with apples", for example by using Total Acquisition Cost(TAC)

Operational Issues

- Flexibility in 'spreading' peaks/troughs
- Response to special requests
- Management role changes
- Specialist knowledge is brought in
- Control (Management control must remain a core activity)

Strategic Issues

- After outsourcing, will some "in-house" expertise be retained so there is there still the ability to make changes?
- Internal implications
- Spreading of risk
- Customer reactions (customer contact must remain a core activity)
- Fair and complete comparisons
- The outsourcing may assist in any internal change/new strategies/expansion

- Are there political factors that would raise issues (e.g. involvement by councillors with the service provider, anticipated government policy etc.)

Finally, with any outsourcing, management must ensure that control is retained. Management needs to recall again here that the management cycle not only involves planning, organising, directing but also, controlling; outsourcing of control can cause problems, control must remain "core".

Meanwhile a case study covering the NHS outsourcing of procurement follows:

Case Study: NHS Supplies
As reported in 2000

The problem
- Standards of purchasing vary. There are some excellent departments with high-calibre individuals who are imaginative and skilled in a wide range of modern purchasing techniques. But there are also some buyers, who are less imaginative, having lower skill levels and are often more interested in filing than in doing a good deal.

- There are too many petty controls, for example, far too much emphasis on paper pushing and very little real added value; for example, if a buyer wanted to know how much was spent with a particular supplier in the previous year, what else was bought from them, how they had been performing recently or how their prices had moved, it was difficult and time consuming to access the data.

- If they want to ask more fundamental questions, such as by how much a supplier's performance was improving or declining, whether any of its main competitors were also supplying the trust, or how many different users in the trust had dealt with that supplier, it was virtually impossible to find the answers. Yet, access to information like this is the first step in a purchasing improvement programme.

- One reason for these problems is the culture of suspicion and blame in which the function operated. Good staffs with imagination and intelligence either leave through frustration, or gradually become disenchanted as in some organisations, keeping your head down and blaming others when something goes wrong, is the only way to survive.

The result

- They miss the chance to save money by not taking a more commercial approach to agreeing and awarding contracts.
- They miss opportunities to encourage suppliers to improve their quality of service, product, and delivery.
- They also miss opportunities to drive down internal costs through efficient processing, and to drive down external costs through managing and removing the "extras", which so often creep in and can sometimes add as much as 25 per cent to a price.
- Service levels can be substandard. While there could be a high level of stock available, for example, it could take up to seven days to get that stock to the ward, or office, that needs it. World-class organisations get stock items delivered in minutes, rather than days.

What Trusts like this need is a three-fold programme

First they must change the structure of the purchasing department, promote the best staff and encourage new employees to adopt modern ideas and gain experience of up-to-date buying techniques.

Second, they must improve their purchasing systems, so that administration is more streamlined and information is more accessible.

Third, and perhaps most importantly, they must embark on a scheme of attitude and culture change, so that everyone with supplier contact – not just those in purchasing –understands the main implications of their behaviour and how their actions affect the way their suppliers respond and behave towards them.

Other ways forward

Taking a professional approach to purchasing is crucial. Not only does it add value, through the achievement of bought-in cost savings, better supplier relationships and quality improvements, it also helps organisations to minimise most of the commercial and legal risks that can accompany the sourcing process. It is vital that NHS trusts' purchasing staff are well resourced, trained, and supported. There must be the procedural and organisational backing in place to allow departments to operate effectively and really add value.

One technique that is currently being adopted in many industries is supply chain integration. True integration provides the ability to balance long-term future capacity and forecasted demand throughout the supply chain. It also helps to identify potential bottlenecks arid constraints, and to find solutions with partners.

If applied throughout a trust, it would offer substantial benefits. It would mean that all processes were properly aligned, operating relationships were streamlined, and trouble free and key suppliers were seen as part of the overall process of service delivery.

Supply Chain Integration is an emerging and powerful method of purchasing that uses e-commerce and a range of other management tools to integrate and streamline the whole supply chain to produce significant, sustained advantage.

It has recently been described as "an alignment of the end-to-end supply chain and the creation of an integrated and high-performance entity that will deliver superior end-customer value". Examples of organisations exploiting SCI in the consumer electronics and automotive industries show leading firms offering customised products, while achieving significant savings and efficiencies. This involves breaking down barriers and building trust and collaborative relationships with users and suppliers.

Conclusion

It is clear that purchasing in the NHS is under scrutiny and unlikely to remain unchanged. The new Purchasing and Supply Agency (PASA) has a mission to save money and make buying in the NHS more efficient. The changing market place and the demands facing the health service will force a re-evaluation of the whole supply chain. Only by integrating the supply chain can the full benefits be realised. I only hope that purchasers grasp these with both hands.

Extracts from Source: Supply Management 15 June 2000. Will Parsons

However, the above mention "saviour" PASA did not last long and a revolutionary change was announced on the 6 September 2006 that dismantled part of PASA.

NHS selects DHL for £1.6bn procurement outsourcing deal

DHL, the logistics unit of Europe's leading postal company, Deutsche Post AG, announced that it had won an outsourcing contract to run a part of the UK-based National Health Service's (NHS) procurement and delivery function.

DHL would take over operations currently controlled by NHS Logistics and NHS Purchasing and Supply Agency (PASA). According to the contract, DHL will manage a minimum of £22 billion in spending. DHL will deliver procurement and logistics services to 600 hospitals and other health providers in the UK.

The deal is expected to generate savings of approximately £1 billion, or about 5% of turnover, for the NHS over the period of the contract.

Goods and services supplied by DHL will include food, bed linen, cleaning products, surgical and medical equipment and stationery.

The move is the biggest example of what some regard as creeping NHS privatization.

Source: Press Release 6 September 2006

A wider view of this change follows:

The Department of Health (DH) yesterday officially announced it had signed a 10-year deal with DHL Logistics for the outsourcing of NHS Logistics and the consumables purchasing function of the NHS Purchasing and Supply Agency (PASA). DHL will run a division called NHS Supply Chain on behalf of the NHS Business Services Authority.

The contract, which comes into effect on 1 October 2006, will cover the supply and delivery of 10 categories of products including catering supplies, clothing, stationery, bed linen, office equipment, cleaning products, patient clothing, dressings and provisions, and medical and surgical equipment.

David Bennett, vice president for DHL Healthcare, said DHL "will look at purchasing medical equipment as high up the scale as linear accelerators and patient monitoring equipment but not technology as advanced as MRI scanners, which will remain in PASA's domain".

The NHS currently spends a total of around £3.7bn a year on products in these categories, £1.1bn of which is accounted for by NHS Logistics and NHS PASA. The rest is delivered through locally negotiated contracts.

Under the agreement, DHL will be required to reduce prices to hospitals. The company has set a target of over £1bn savings for the NHS during the life of the contract. Bennett says DHL, as a private sector company, is not bound by the short-term annual budgeting cycles of the public sector, so will be in a better position to negotiate deals that reduce total cost over the longer term. In addition, Bennett says the company will be able to negotiate better prices with suppliers by making a commitment to buy an agreed amount of a product, taking on the commercial risk that government bodies like PASA are unable to assume.

"By applying commercial experience and procedures to core logistics and procurement functions, and working very closely with the supplier community, we now have a unique opportunity to deliver innovative, high quality products to support public health in England," said John Pattullo, chief operating officer for DHL Exel Supply Chain, Europe, Middle East and Africa.

The company intends to set up 'product councils' based around clinical areas similar to those set up by general purchasing organisation (GPO) Novation in the US, with representation from clinicians and suppliers in order to inform the purchase of products. Novation will be subcontracted by DHL to "play a role in procurement" and it is expected that the American company will provide three to four senior managers with expertise in public health procurement to work with the staff that transfer to DHL from PASA.

The Association of British Healthcare Industries (ABHI) has some concerns about Novation – and about the way the contract has been negotiated. "This whole deal has been conducted in virtual secrecy with minimal consultation or parliamentary scrutiny, and with no evidence produced on how this new regime will benefit patients or the taxpayer," John Wilkinson, ABHI director general said. "There are also serious concerns over the role of the US giant Novation in this deal. In the US, group purchasing organisations such as Novation have come in for strong criticism for alleged anti-competitive practices and financial secrecy, and are the subject of an ongoing US Senate investigation."

Bennett says DHL investigated the allegations before entering into an agreement with Novation. DHL chose to work with Novation in order to take advantage of its expertise as the largest buyer of healthcare products in North America, overseeing $28bn (£14.8bn) of spend in the US healthcare sector. He says the company was only one of the GPOs investigated by the US Senate, as a result of complaints from a number of small suppliers, and now participates in a self-regulated monitoring scheme reporting to a Senate subcommittee.

Both DHL and Novation will be bound by public procurement rules in the UK which, according to the Department of Health, "will allow a range of companies to provide products to the NHS".

The contract with DHL represents 45% of total current Department of Health spend in England.

Source: Kathleen Armstrong, editor of HES dated 6 September 2006

Meanwhile suggestions were made by the Association of British Healthcare Industries in a parliamentary briefing note, which saw that the role of procurement was as follows:

One of the principal barriers to achieving the efficiency and productivity savings and patient benefits available through the adoption of new technologies is the NHS procurement landscape. Procurement lies at the heart of effective service improvement. Steps should be taken to ensure that the goals of the procurement teams in the NHS are effectively aligned with the goals of the broader organisation in order that the desired shift from people-intensive care pathways to quality and cost driven pathways will be delivered.

Specific barriers to innovative adoption include:

- Buying solely on cash saving targets ignores the wide range of other benefits which flow from using innovative technology. Buying yesterday's technologies at the lowest price has an impact on both total cost and quality of care.
- Use of a 'one model fits all' mind-set for procurement. The large contracts favoured by NHS Purchasing and Supply Agency (PASA) may be entirely sensible for high volume, widely distributed and mature technologies. For other, often more specialist, technologies the value proposition involves elements of service that are highly valued by users. Clinicians and managers should therefore be contracted regionally or locally and often on the basis of more dynamic contracts which reflect the pace of technological change.
- Following the outsourcing of NHS Logistics, the high-volume model of procurement may be extended to products ill suited to this model. This may stifle innovation by prioritising older/cheaper products and by blocking smaller companies with new technologies from selling to the NHS.

In order to create a more innovation-friendly and yet efficient landscape for the future it is essential to involve key stakeholders from the clinical community, NHS management, industry and procurement professionals, together with patients.

We need to develop sustainable models of procurement which address the critical innovation issues and bring about lasting behavioural change from all parties. This is consistent with the recommendation on procurement agreed by Government and industry jointly at the end of the Healthcare Industries Taskforce (HITF).

ABHI key suggestions

1) Supply chains should be encouraged to evolve according to the nature of the products and the distribution of users. National procurement contracts which attempt to cover all products are unlikely to deliver the quality and diversity clinicians and patients need, or the cost savings envisaged by the government. Procurement should be set up to secure a wide range of benefits, including long-term value and innovation, and this is supported by NHS PASA.

2) Collaborative Procurement Hubs (CPH) are a key element of the procurement landscape and should be developed in order to:
- Facilitate truly collaborative behaviour between members.

- Allow effective interaction with clinicians and managers charged with redesigning and developing new patient pathways which improve productivity and quality. A range of benefits needs to be targeted to deliver value, not simply cash-releasing savings.
- Allow an effective market to operate by creating enough independent transactions to encourage and reward both innovative suppliers and innovative buyers. The structure should also facilitate the development of business in manageable increments for small and medium sized enterprises.

(The Association of British Healthcare Industries (ABHI) is the lead trade association for the medical devices and systems industry (manufacturers of medical devices, equipment and consumables and other suppliers to the medical community).

(For further details contact 020 7960 4360 or visit www.abhi.org.uk)

One year on the following was reported:

SM News, 5 July 2007: NHS Supply Chain saves £6.3m

NHS Supply Chain has announced a £6.3 million saving, made within the first five months of its procurement contract with the NHS.

This is the first audited saving to be reported and was audited by the NHS Business Services Authority.

It was achieved on behalf of more than 200 NHS hospitals in England with the procurement of foetal scanners in February. The NHS Antenatal Foetal Anomaly Ultrasound Screening Programme was allocated £12 million in 2006 to replace old equipment, and approached NHS Supply Chain for procurement support.

The saving resulted from the first national imaging e-auction in the NHS and was achieved through volume purchasing, with some suppliers also providing extended warranties and extra software.

NHS Supply Chain, managed by DHL Logistics, was created last October when the NHS outsourced its buying. It claims it will generate £1 billion savings over the 10-year contract on the purchase and delivery of more than 500,000 products.

The first meetings of the NHS Supply Chain's Product Councils – made up of procurement experts, clinicians and nurses – will take place in the next few months to discuss products that could save NHS money.

And another year on reported the following:

SM Features, 8 May 2008: A clean bill of health

The decision to outsource NHS Logistics and much of NHS PASA was met with controversy. Twenty months on, Helen Gilbert finds out how the new organisation has fared.

It's early in the morning and Roger West is listening to Radio 4. His ears prick up. New figures have revealed that incidents of NHS staff being abused by patients are increasing and the Department of Health (DH) plans to invest in alarm systems for employees to combat the problem.

West is procurement director of NHS Supply Chain, the organisation formed in October 2006 when the NHS Logistics Authority and parts of the NHS Purchasing and Supply Agency (Pasa) were outsourced to DHL in a 10-year deal. Within minutes he is on the phone to his team, instructing them to find out more details. What type of alarm is required, how many, and what can NHS Supply Chain be doing to support this initiative?

West joined the body in March 2007. His mission is to help deliver £1 billion of savings by 2016 by offering a wider range of goods to NHS Trusts at lower prices. And, so far, his organisation looks on course to do so.

In the first year of the new contract around £9 million in savings were delivered back to frontline NHS services – £8 million above the initial target. According to West, this has been achieved through a combination of effective contracting - "working with customers to bring contracts to market quickly" – investing in the right people, buyers and, in time, clinicians, and developing an extensive online catalogue.

However, he admits the original target was low. "Transferring an organisation that has long been run on a not-for-profit mindset to a with-profit cap and looking at how we grow the scale of the organisation is the biggest challenge. In 2007 our work plan covered about 90 contracts with a spend value of £250 million. This year we are looking to do 150 contracts, covering £2 billion. That's nearly a tenfold growth in value."

Meanwhile, West has been investing in people. Last year he recruited 30 buyers and the procurement department has grown to 130 staff in 12 months. Back in 2006, he says, procurement would have been made up entirely of NHS Pasa staff, but by the end of 2008 it will be 50 per cent former NHS staff and 50 per cent new recruits.

"We are bringing in people with backgrounds in Tesco and Asda as it's important for us to increase the commerciality of procurement. I've got three trading directors who report to me that are managing the buying and selling of products. "This is one of the differences about us. We are buying but also responsible for selling as well. The end-to-end responsibility for pricing and profitability is embedded in procurement."

Last year, NHS Supply Chain sales grew by 7 per cent and it is investing in a new warehouse to meet increased demand for 2008.

Framework agreements

Over the next eight months there are plans to generate more value from the contracts inherited from NHS Logistics and Pasa, and branch out into new areas including capital, joint replacement and pathology.

Identifying new opportunities is essential. A new national framework agreement for medical imaging was launched towards the end of November 2007. It enables trusts to buy equipment, such as MRI and CT scanners and flexible endoscopes, and supports government strategies to expand digital mammography in a bid to improve cancer diagnosis and treatment.

According to West, the health service spends approximately £200 million each year on medical imaging. His plan is for NHS Supply Chain to service half of that in the first contract year. And in only four months, more than £40 million of sales had been generated through the framework, resulting in significant savings for trusts.

"It's a rapid means for them to access supplier contracts and suppliers are not inundated with lots of different OJEUs. This has been positively welcomed by customers and suppliers alike."

Andy Harris, head of procurement at the University Hospital Birmingham NHS Trust, which requires some £25 million of diagnostic imaging equipment for its new hospital project, has used the framework.

Previously, he says, major diagnostic imaging equipment would have been purchased either by individual trusts, as and when required, or co-ordinated by Pasa if included as part of a national initiative to take advantage of economies of scale. "For a trust procurement team to have the detailed market knowledge and technical expertise to procure an MRI scanner, as an example, is rare.

"The creation of the framework agreement allows trusts to tap into expertise. NHS Supply Chain has provided a dedicated resource to this project, which is working directly with our clinicians and project management team."

Shared information

Elsewhere, "product councils" have been established where clinicians can talk about the type of products they require. At present, NHS Supply Chain has created three councils for nursing, theatres and, more recently, rehabilitation, which was launched in April. It invites a number of specialists in the field to take part in these forums. Meanwhile, buyers can share information about the latest innovations on the market.

Clinicians also feed into product taskforces, which help NHS Supply Chain with tender processes. "They [the clinicians] tell us what products they want, help us to find the specification and evaluation criteria and work with us to do the non-price evaluation," West explains. "There might be a workshop in a hotel, the products are laid out and they say what is best for the patient. We also ask clinicians to trial products in hospitals to ensure they fully meet the need. It is critical we have this input as procurement people can't effectively determine what a clinician needs and how a product is used."

Council representatives

But not everyone is convinced. Mario Varela, director of procurement and e-commerce at Barts and The London NHS Trust, describes himself as a "supporter" of NHS Supply Chain, but says the answer is not only to get "half a dozen people round a table". He fears not enough views are taken into account and questions how well represented the councils and taskforces are.

"A cardiologist from Manchester can't speak on behalf of other leading cardiology centres," he says. "The people they [the councils and taskforces] might attract might not be the leading lights. A professor in cardiology's main purpose is to look after the patient. He might only be around at 7am or 7pm. These are not the people NHS Supply Chain is going to attract for an away day in Manchester."

Varela is also concerned that NHS Supply Chain and the regional procurement hubs – which enable trusts to collaborate and buy items in bulk – are fighting against each other in some respects, and need to identify how they can work together in the future. He says NHS Supply Chain needs to win the commitment of trusts. Procurement hubs continue to be popular because trusts feel their local requirements will be listened to, whereas their views on a national basis might not be.

Varela also warns NHS Supply Chain may lack the relevant experience to tackle highly complex areas. "The major challenge is in areas where NHS Logistics was never involved. Cardiology and orthopaedics were traditionally managed at local level by individual hospitals or where hospitals have collaborated in a geographical area. To aggregate that on a national basis is difficult.

"In many of those areas it [NHS Supply Chain] hasn't delivered anything... Some of these people [NHS Supply Chain staff] have never tackled these complex areas or these commodities because they have always been tackled at local level."

National collaboration

So what's the solution? Varela believes NHS Supply Chain should be working more closely with collaborative outfits. He heads a medical and surgical work stream for an organisation, which bears the collaborative hallmarks of a hub. This negotiates on behalf of all cardiology centres in London on items such as pacemakers and defibrillators.

"I have said [to NHS Supply Chain], 'Why don't you become part of my programme team and support how we might deliver this in London? Then you stand a better chance to use that as a learning process, a lever to negotiate on a national basis.' It [NHS Supply Chain] can then engage with hubs and the rest of the NHS to get the commitment to negotiate from a position of strength with suppliers." His request has not been answered.

Meanwhile, there has been a drive to support other DH initiatives. In September 2007 Prime Minister Gordon Brown announced all hospitals would undergo a deep clean programme to tackle healthcare-associated infections such as MRSA. Earlier this year, NHS Supply Chain launched a contract for steam cleaning products, to enable trusts to buy items on a national basis and help them to achieve cost savings. In addition, a new national contract for MRSA screening products will go live in May.

West's strategy is clear. "It's [about] making the procurement team more effective, growing what we do, bringing those things through to market quickly, being more efficient, and how we can use data and knowledge and connections with the DH to get good practice procurement."

Helen Gilbert is a freelance business journalist.

More info

NHS Supply Chain at a glance

On 1 October 2006 NHS Logistics, part of NHS Pasa and DHL joined together to become NHS Supply Chain.

DHL runs NHS Supply Chain on behalf of the NHS Business Services Authority (responsible for managing core public sector support services).

NHS Supply Chain has a core customer base of 450 NHS trusts in England and also supports a number of private healthcare organisations.

NHS Supply Chain employs around 1,600 people in eight locations, who include a combination of staff from the former NHS Logistics, Pasa and DHL Logistics. NHS Supply Chain provides services in procurement, logistics and e-commerce across the following product category areas: theatre and surgical services, medical, food, facilities (including office supplies), clinical markets and capital equipment.

The deal is expected to save £1 billion over its 10-year lifetime by offering a wider range of goods to NHS trusts at lower prices.

NHS-CAT= the new online catalogue

In October 2007 a new online catalogue called NHS-CAT was launched. Some 500,000 items are listed, compared with 50,000 products previously under NHS Logistics.

Products ranging from medical supplies to food and stationery items can be purchased online using a shopping basket facility linked to NHS Supply Chain's ordering systems and trusts' own purchase order systems.

A new e-sourcing and supplier management tool called Intenda is expected be the primary business software in procurement for managing the tender process and will do all the sourcing. Suppliers will also post tenders to it. A new regional distribution centre in Rugby is a stockholding hub for food and other products. It will also cater for increased sales and help to provide an efficient service to customers.

In the above case studies it should be noted that Primary Care Trusts (PCTs) are being replaced as commissioning bodies from 2011, and procurement of both services and treatments and medicines will be delegated to GPs. The structures that will deliver this commissioning and the procurement routes to be used were still in development at the time of writing.

PFI – Private Finance Initiative

The Private Finance Initiative is a scheme developed as a way of funding public infrastructure projects using private capital rather than public funding. PFI schemes were originally developed in Australia in 1990, and are now used in a variety of other countries, including EU states such as France, The Netherlands, Spain and Portugal, and further afield, includes the USA and Japan.

The scheme has been controversial from its inception in the UK in 1992, and attracted particular criticism following the 2008 global credit crunch, and the associated public sector funding and debt problems. Indeed at the time of writing (2010) the future of the scheme in the UK is uncertain. The PFI secures private funding for public projects in return for part-privatisation; this transferring responsibility for the delivery of public services, but not accountability, to private companies. The private sector will then operate the facilities as well as providing finance, and may also take some public sector staff into the private sector. Each PFI arrangement being developed to meet the unique requirements of the project, with the Competitive Dialogue process being commonly used as the procurement process.

The PFI is commonly used for infrastructure projects such as roads, railways, hospitals and schools. In return for funding the initial construction project, the operator is guaranteed future revenue streams. By October 2007 the total capital value of PFI contracts in the UK was £68bn, committing future spending of £215bn over the life of the contracts. The PFI scheme can be used by central government and the NHS trusts and local authorities. A few examples are given below:

Project	Authority	Cost
University Hospital Coventry	Coventry and Warwickshire NHS Trust	£410m
Medway Police HQ	Kent Police	£30m
National Physical Laboratory	Department of Trade & Industry	£122m
Skye Bridge	Scottish Office	£93m
Balmoral High School	Belfast Education and Library Board	£17m

Procurement issues with PFI

Clearly PFI schemes are designed to create funds for investment, in return for a long term return for the suppliers/operators. To ensure that this is reasonable deal, it is essential for procurement to consider a number of issues:

- Specification of the requirements including forecasting requirements over the life of the project
- Design of the procurement process and/or Competitive Dialogue process
- Financial planning including discounting of future cash flows
- Engagement with potential bidders
- Future cash flow management

A particular concern is the temptation, in times of a lack of readily available credit, to agree to particularly generous repayment terms in order to secure funding for projects. This can lead to inappropriately large returns on investment. It can also allow projects to go ahead that in other circumstances would not have been funded; there being a risk that these have only gone ahead because of the availability of PFI funds.

Another concern is whether risk is effectively transferred to the public sector, or whether in reality the risk remains with the public sector. In the case of the National Physical Laboratory a cost overrun was carried by the building supplier who when bankrupt as a result. However the brunt of the cost was not incurred by the public sector, but by the private sector company which lost an estimated £100m.

The length of the commitment to the supplier can be an issue, the Balmoral High school project cost £17m in 2002, but the school closed in 2007 because of a lack of pupils. The contractual obligation however continues until 2027. These large capital projects may require a 20 to 25 year commitment, but it is very difficult to anticipate requirements over such a timescale. It is worth remembering that 25 years ago few people were anticipating the imminent demise of the Soviet Union – and yet in 2010 countries from the Soviet bloc are now part of the European Union.

On the other hand, the involvement of public sector suppliers can have benefits in terms of ensuring completion of projects on time and budget. HM Treasury and the National Audit Office reported in 2003 that the only deals that were over budget, in a sample of projects studied, were those where the public sector commissioner had changed their minds after the initial commissioning.

A key consideration should be whether a project would be simpler as a standard procurement exercise, and whether there is a real value with improved risk management by involving suppliers in the operation of the project.

Use of the Competitive Dialogue for PFI

CD should only be used for procuring particularly complex contracts, and PFI contracts are identified as suitable candidates for this route, as shown in the illustration below from *Supply Management* (2 September 2010):

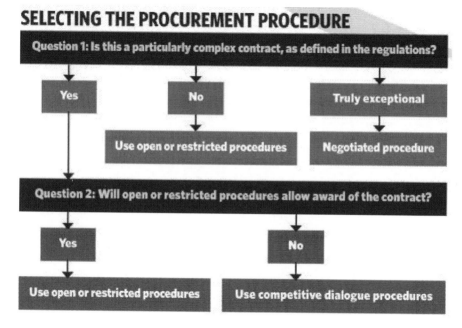

SELECTING THE PROCUREMENT PROCEDURE

Question 1: Is this a particularly complex contract, as defined in the regulations?

Yes — No — Truly exceptional

No → Use open or restricted procedures

Truly exceptional → Negotiated procedure

Question 2: Will open or restricted procedures allow award of the contract?

Yes → Use open or restricted procedures

No → Use competitive dialogue procedures

For a successful PFI Competitive Dialogue, the guidelines are the same as for a standard CD, with additional success factors specifically for PFI; for example:

- Be prepared to walk away from the CD ; a weakness of PFI procurements is that there is often "no plan B" which weakens the position of the buying authority
- Recognise the process will be complex, with multiple stakeholders on both sides
- Provide adequate project management and team resources for the process
- Allow adequate time for the process; several months, and potentially years
- Consider use of Project Management tools such as Prince2

- Treat suppliers as partners in the process; their inputs must be seen as real and valid rather than just sales proposals
- Define the requirements as accurately and completely as possible; focussing on the desired outputs and outcomes rather than the inputs by the suppliers
- Focus on both the immediate and long term financial implications
- Carry out frequent reviews, taking the "devil's advocate" role of why continue rather than just driving to completion
- Conduct a dialogue with 4 to 6 suppliers rather than 1 or 2, or more
- Utilise the opportunity to reduce the successively reduce the number of participants in the dialogue
- Recognise that significant costs are incurred on both sides, but do not fall for the "sunk cost" fallacy and throw good money after bad.

Information, Communication Technology (ICT) & E-business/e-procurement

All parts of the supply chain rely on ICT in the planning, operational, administrative and management processes. ICT provides integration, co-ordination and control mechanisms across a supply chain between all internal and external players. Information is required therefore at every stage of the supply chain and for all levels of supply chain planning.

Electronic business refers generally to commercial transactions that are based upon the processing and transmission of digitised data, including text, sound and visual images and that are carried out over open networks (like the Internet) or closed networks that have a gateway onto an open network (Extranet). Meanwhile, the CIPS definition of e-Procurement is; *"E-Procurement is using the Internet to operate the transactional aspects of requisitioning, authorizing, ordering, receipting and payment processes for the required services or products."*

E-procurement has been proven to provide a return on investment (ROI) of anywhere between 5% and 15% for many organisations and time savings in the procurement process of up to 75%. With these kinds of benefits, the impact on profitability can be immense as procurement savings drop straight to the bottom line. With e-procurement now available across the internet many companies and not for profit organisations are evaluating the available solutions for the first time and trying to assess the scale of benefit that will accrue to them.

The adoption of the internet as a medium changed everything. With a network that is instantaneously available world wide, 24 hours a day, and is inexpensive to access, it also requires no specialised training to use.

Moreover, unlike the proprietary Value Added Networks, it is owned by nobody and is governed by standards for access, transferring and using data integration. The emergence of these standards – FTP, TCP/IP, XML and others provides for the first time a cost effective convergence of computing and communications to allow many buyers and many suppliers to interact electronically: the birth of the electronic, or "e"-procurement market.

E-Procurement therefore includes a range of technologies that apply the speed and uniformity of computer processing and the connectivity of the Internet to:
* accelerate and streamline the processes of identifying and selecting vendors of goods and services;
* placing, receiving and paying for orders;
* assuring the application of purchasing rules, guidelines and discounts;
* consolidating purchasing to achieve lowest prices;
* reaching customers and offering goods and services for sale

Procurement encourages and facilitates procurer-provider visibility and collaboration that move both toward the ultimate organisational goal of Supply Chain Excellence. Good e-Procurement also requires a strong sense of collaboration that helps build stronger partnerships in which both sides prosper.

E-business applications

Some of the E-business applications are classified as Business to Business (B2B) and Business to Consumer (B2C):
* Business to Business (B2B) trading exchanges provide a two way on-line link between buyers and suppliers; they are now often referred to as a "marketplace". Suppliers can advertise their products and services through electronic catalogues; buyers can order from supplier catalogues, take part in auctions, or conduct tendering online. In industries with large numbers of buyers and suppliers, third parties generally organise and manage online forums. In industries with few buyers and a large number of sellers, the buyers often own and run the on line marketplace.
* Business to Consumer (B2C) where individual consumers and any system user

can get up to-the-minute information, make enquiries, place orders and payments can be made on-line. Information about the current position and status of orders services can also be obtained.

Meanwhile some E-business applications follow:

Supply Chain aspect	Buying	Ordering	Designing products	Post sales
Information	Sharing with Suppliers	Visibility	Sharing with suppliers	Customer use records
Planning	Coordinating when to replenish	Forecast sharing/ agreements	New product launching	Service planning
Product flow	Paperless exchanges	Automated	Product changes	Automatic replacement of parts
KPIs	Compliance monitoring	Logistics track and trace	Project monitoring	Performance measurement
Business changes from "E"	On line "reverse" auctions, market exchanges	Click on ordering	Mass customisation	Remote sensing and diagnostics, download upgrades

It should be noted that buying on line, as with any other from of procurement, should still be subject to the assessment of risk. Additional risks with E procurement methods may come from paying for an expensive E procurement/reverse auction that does not produce commensurate savings, and if using an on-line E marketplace, it is necessary to check and verify who has undertaken the prequalification of suppliers. With reverse auctions, the emphasis will be on clear simple specifications that tend to be more on a price decision, as for example is found with leverage and routine items. MEAT or "best value" is more difficult to access with reverse auctions, therefore requiring the use of more traditional procurement methods.

Costs and benefits

In a paper-based, manual system, the cost of procurement is significantly higher than most people realise. For example, the average administrative cost of a simple purchase order can be between £75 and £125. Therefore, a purchase order for the purchase of a product priced at £10 actually costs more than £85. E-Procurement uses refined business processes and supplier relationships supported by technology to automate processes, eliminate the paper, and reduce errors, and it ultimately can cut the administrative cost of a purchase order by more than 75 per cent. The purchase order that once cost a company £75 in administration now costs only £18.75 – a saving of £56.25.

"Industry Week" magazine published the following research results in its "E-Procurement Explosion" article in May 2002:

- *Hewlett-Packard (HP) saved more than 30 per cent on advertising and $220,000 per quarter on electrical power. They claimed 20 per cent to 25 per cent increased efficiency due to a reduced number of purchase orders and administration.*

- *Lucent claimed 60 per cent to 70 per cent reduction in transaction costs.*

- *Texas Instruments reduced the cost of a purchase order from $80 to $25, Deere & Co. from $97 to $22. 3M report costs went from $120 to $40 and errors from 30 per cent to 0 per cent.*

- *Owens Corning used auctions to cut negotiation time from two to three months to less than 90 minutes.*

Case Study: IBM and E-Procurement

E-procurement is an area in which IBM is actively engaged. It says it has become a strategic necessity because so much business advantage can be gained. However, it does not feel that even after several years, it has tapped the full potential that e-procurement has to offer. The primary operational benefits that come from e-procurement are around catalogues, requisitions, approvals, purchase orders, delivery, invoices, payment and asset management.

Automating this procurement flow is critical to reducing expenses in the procurement process and minimising the cost of acquiring goods and services.

Most purchases go through IBM's SAP system. The goal is for 80 percent of purchase orders to be "hands-free."

Results

The collective transformation process for procurement at IBM has paid off. The activities, beginning in the 1990s to today, have yielded tremendous improvements, including:
- Savings of more than $6 billion
- Maverick procurement reduced to less than 1 percent
- Client satisfaction improvement from 40 percent to 86 percent
- 99 percent of purchasing transactions are "hands free"; and 98 percent is conducted electronically
- Purchase order lead time down from 30 days to 1 day

IBM estimates that operational efficiency alone contributes to approximately 10 percent of its cost saving efforts.

E-sourcing

The CIPS definition of e-Sourcing is:
"E-Sourcing is using the Internet to make decisions and form strategies regarding how and where services or products are obtained."

E-sourcing covers the parts in the buying process, which are at the discretion of the specialist buyers, which include knowledge, specification, requests for quotation/e-tender/e-auction and evaluation/negotiation contract. Good e-Sourcing practice is essential to making e-Procurement work. If you do not make the correct strategic decisions you will create a poor operational process. E-Sourcing also provides a platform for delivering on promises of social responsibility; it provides accountability and visibility on why a company makes a decision to source products from their chosen suppliers.

E-Sourcing systems should therefore enable the sourcing team to:
- Easily analyse and model complex decisions in real time

- Automate the contract lifecycle management including awards, rejections, amendments and renewals
- Collaborate with the supplier, using a central system enables people to collaborate easily

E-Sourcing should deliver the following visible benefits:

- Real-time information; the sourcing team get visibility on contracts and spending patterns. Any planned improvement must ensure reliable up to date information for analysis purpose. A system can provide pre-qualified information about suppliers.
- Integrated process automation; taking time out of the sourcing process by reducing the amount of paper involved in the system. Typically such systems can distribute all requirements electronically.

E-sourcing can also be defined as providing accountability and visibility on why a company makes a decision to source products from its chosen suppliers. E-sourcing covers the decision and strategy of how and where a service or product is obtained. It therefore covers that part of the buying process that is implemented and controlled by the specialist buyer, including specification, requests for quotations, e-tenders, e-auctions and so on, up to the award of the contract. E-auctions should be part of the e-sourcing toolkit. If they are used to only drive down price, they will only have an effect in the short term.

E-sourcing in e-procurement is then, is the process and operation of deploying these sourcing decisions and strategies within the organisation, typically by devolution to local users. E-procurement would then cover processes such as requisition again contract, authorisation, ordering, receipt and payment.

Too many people have tried to implement E-procurement without having an underpinning e-sourcing strategy in place first. The benefits of e-sourcing should therefore include:

- Real time information giving visibility on contracts
- Spending pattern and supplier performance
- Integrated, largely paperless, automation of the sourcing process
- Capability for analysis and modelling of complex decisions in real time
- Automated contract life cycle management
- Enablement of collaboration with suppliers.

E-sourcing software and tendering

The e-sourcing software on the market is split into four loose categories.
The first is the tendering software that handles drawing up a contract within the buying organisation, as well as communication and negotiation with suppliers. This includes electronic reverse auctions or e-auctions.

Second, collaboration software helps organisations work with suppliers to draw up more efficient tenders, as well as publicizing changes in a tender.

Third, evaluation software helps users to trawl through competing bids, some of which may be thousands of pages long.

Lastly, contract management software reminds buyers when completed contracts are due for renewal.

All sourcing software should in turn be linked to the e-procurement part of the buying process, the actual buying, ordering and delivery of goods that takes place after a contract is signed.

One multinational drugs company finds 90% of its goods through e-sourcing and ran 2,500 auctions in 2005. It estimates the average saving at 19 per cent. They firmly believe that the major share of savings do not come from auctions or competitive bidding techniques. Supplier collaboration is where the long term benefit is from. Lengthy relationships with suppliers rarely start well if they are preceded by an aggressive round of price cutting e-auctions.

The automation of administrative tasks, in the tendering process, for example, reduces process cycle times and the cost of tendering.
Professor Andrew Cox, from the UK's Birmingham Business School, says that the real e-sourcing prize lies in improving supplier's process efficiency over a number of years, rather than simple reductions in the costs of goods and services.

E-procurement and Supplier Management

Whilst reverse auctions are successful, the real test for e-procurement is its ability to improve supplier relationships, according to a pronouncement from a senior US procurement figure, Daniel Enneking, vice-president of global operations and chief procurement office at NCR Corporation.

He told the Conference Board's 2003 Electronic Procurement Conference in Chicago not to get carried away with the success of e-auctions. He stated that the biggest challenge is expanding the use of electronic capabilities in the supply chain to improve supplier performance and management.

Robert Waugh, chief sales and marketing officer at software supplier Bze Markets, also said that using software for supplier management was the next big step for companies after reverse auctions.

Enneking continued by warning that while e-procurement allowed greater tracking of costs, it was just an enabler for efficiencies. Suitable processes and people skills must be in place before electronic systems were implemented.

E-procurement within NCR, which has an annual procurement budget of about $3.6 billion on revenues of nearly $5.6 billion, had freed up his staff for more strategic work. NCR, well known as a maker of cash machines was working on extending e-procurement to include the sharing of manufacturing and design information.

E-procurement options

E-procurement automates the internal and external processes associated with buying, with added value increasing in line with the extent and sophistication of the electronic communication.

Catalogues

At the basic level, staffs are given access to web based catalogues, with goods and services are delivered direct to their desk.

Electronic versions of existing supply catalogues are good for buying and selling commodity items from stock. Buyer and sellers can now have a one-to-one direct relationship. Efficiencies come from moving from paper based post contract process to electronic message passing. Implementing the capability to use electronic catalogue also facilitates participation in marketplaces.

Marketplaces

Whereas catalogue commerce is good for post contractual message passing, marketplaces are mainly good for pre-contract searching and negotiating for partners and prices. There are however some misconceptions about marketplaces. They do not help you manage the internal transaction processes better, but, they do support them by providing an excellent source of information about suppliers and access to multiple catalogues. They do not just provide auction facilities as 90% of the business going through them will be normal contracts based on improved collaboration.

Vertical marketplaces are electronic exchanges providing a range of capabilities (auctions, reverse auctions, dynamic bid and exchange, trade directories) within an industry. Horizontal marketplaces are electronic exchanges, usually offering a combination of information, contacts and the opportunity to buy and sell, based around either a community of users or a class of goods and services.

Marketplaces may be private, available only to invited players, and/or public, open to any organisation (normally subject to some entry rules). Public marketplaces are good for buying and selling where there is no advantage from sustained buyer–supplier relationships. Private marketplaces are good for closer collaboration across the supply chain.

In all cases, the budget management, requisition authorisation and goods received paperwork (and even payment) is electronic. In many cases, tendering, contracting and opportunities for on-line auctions also feature. Buying is aggregated and management information is collected and processed centrally.

E-procurement: success factors and challenges to implementation

The following have been put forward as perceived barriers to electronic procurement:
- A "wait and see" attitude among firms in selecting e-marketplaces and procurement service providers;
- Concerns over security and confidentiality of the data needed to be exchanged in electronic environments;
- Reluctance of share data with trading partners;
- The "non-feasibility of custom made products" for pooling initiatives;
- Lack of standardisation; and

ainty over trust and commitment among trading partners.

Moreover, both small buyer and seller firms which the authors have talked to considered the following prohibitive and discouraging:

- The costs and development time required to set up online procurement systems, enabling these systems, and meeting workforce requirements of such systems;
- The lack of adequate security measures to protect data; and
- Trust issues between buyers and sellers.

In the same vein, managers of the seller firms also cited attitudinal resistance to change stemming from a number of concerns:

- The uncertainty over its ability to gain the expected return on investment to cover development costs;
- The work required to enforce business process changes called for by these systems; and
- Worker apprehensions about being replaced by automated procurement systems.

E-Procurement Legislation

E-procurement has been such a revolution for purchasers that uncertainty has been growing about which laws apply in cyberspace. However, e-procurement is still governed by existing law and purchasers should not forget good procurement/purchasing practices.

Apart from the laws that apply to purchasers in what may, guardedly, be called the 'real' world, there are key pieces of legislation that they need to be aware of. The Data Protection Act 1998 is principally concerned with information held about individuals, and so may have some relevance if purchasing from sole traders. The Freedom of Information Act (FoIA) 2000 also makes a wide range of information held electronically available to individuals and organisations on request.

Regulation of Investigatory Powers (RIP) Act 2000

This controversial piece of legislation in now in force and the act gives the authorities the right to intercept and/or monitor e-mails and internet communication data. They would also when circumstances required, be able, to demand that the sender or recipient of an encrypted message hand over the code or decode the message.

Among the provisions of the act are:

- A maximum two year sentence for failure to comply with an order to disclose encrypted information.
- That the authorities can require public communications providers to allow e-mails to be intercepted and internet messages monitored (this will usually require a warrant).

The act has been widely seen as interfering in the private transactions of businesses and individuals and has faced a barrage of criticism.

EU Electronic Signature Directive 1999/93

This was affected as part of the Electronic Communications Act 2000. The directive has three parts.

The first section relates to the establishment of a voluntary register of cryptographic support services providers. These services include the certification of signatures, key management and the time stamping of documents.

Part 2 provides for electronic signatures to be legally recognised as evidence in court proceedings. In the future, legislation is likely to be altered to allow the use of electronic communication in place of hard copy in a wide range of circumstances. The conveyance of public records and company reports and accounts are specifically under consideration.

The third part of the act contains a number of provisions, one of which is that users of encryption are under no obligation to deposit copies of their encryption keys with third parties. This appears to contradict the RIP Act, which says they are.

E-Commerce Directive 2000/31/EC

The directive sets out to remove barriers to the availability of information society services (ISS) within the European Union. (The word society here is an EU description of the new digitally driven ways of doing business).

There are 5 main areas. The first is electronic contracts. Provision must be made for drawing up and concluding contracts electronically. Detailed procedures are set out to follow, although business to business partners can, if they agree, not adhere to them.

The second is transparency. ISS providers will have to make their basic business details readily available to customers and the relevant authorities.

The next area is commercial communications. These are defined as e-mail or web based advertising and marketing. They must be identifiable as advertising and their sourced named.

Codes of conduct are the fourth area. These are encouraged by the directive and also, when disputes arise between trading parties, it is recommended that they resolve their arguments outside the courts, rather than resorting to litigation.

The most contentious part of the directive concerns intermediary liability. It is made clear than an ISS provider will not be liable for the content of third party information that it transmits when:

- It is simply a conduit for such information (i.e., the ISS provider neither initiates it nor selects its recipients),
- It merely stores the information on a temporary basis for the sole purpose of subsequent transmission,
- It merely stores the information at another party's request.

Distance Selling Directive 97/7/EC

This came into force in the UK as the Consumer Protection (Distance Selling) Regulations 2000 and covers business to consumer rather than business to business transactions. Under the directive, website designers and developers acting on behalf of suppliers must make certain information easily available to potential buyers, including:

- Identity and address of the supplier
- General terms and conditions of business
- Delivery costs
- Details of the terms applying to the return of goods
- The period for which the price or offer remains valid
- In most cases, the buyer has a minimum of seven days to cancel the contract.

Draft EU regulation on jurisdiction and judgments

EU ministers have come to an agreement on this proposal and the legislation will decide which laws apply to a given transaction, enable aggrieved web purchasers to seek redress through their local courts and set up local arbitration.

Companies using the web for buying and selling should always remember that e-commerce legislation supplements existing sale of goods acts, such as the Supply of Goods and Services Act 1982 and the Unfair Terms in Consumer Contracts Regulations 1994. It should not be regarded as a replacement.

Supplier Relationships and E-Sourcing

As we have seen above, organisations are increasingly looking at e-sourcing and reverse auctions as a means by which to reduce their procurement expenses and provide bottom line savings to the organisation in a relatively short time. However, this has sometimes led to resistance among suppliers who believe that e-sourcing results in commoditization of goods and services, lack of appreciation of value added services, and in negative impacts on buyer-supplier relationships.

Whilst E-Sourcing and reverse auctions can provide benefits to buyers including process cost savings, reduction in search/information costs, and a more efficient procurement process; there is a potential that suppliers, especially those incumbent, will resist sourcing and reverse auctions in the belief that they lower profit margins and overlook value added services. Newer suppliers are more likely to view e-sourcing as an opportunity to expand their existing businesses without corresponding increase in their sales expenses.

We therefore discuss below the various strategies that buyers can employ to maximise supplier participation in the reverse auction process as well as strategies suppliers can use in the short and long term to ensure that they are active participants in the strategic e-sourcing process.

Buyer Strategies

Buyers have a choice of working with a third party as an e-sourcing provider of licensing software or to conduct e-sourcing in-house. Companies in the initial stages of their e-sourcing efforts are more likely to benefit from going with a third part e-sourcing service provider to speed up their learning curve. Also, utilising a third party provider also helps to reduce conflicts of interest because most third part providers have a set of rules that must be followed by both buyers and sellers. These include rules about buyer intent to award the contract, the buyer bidding against suppliers to create artificial competition etc.

Choosing the right e-sourcing service provider is an important step in initiating an e-sourcing programme. In addition to strategic sourcing and reverse auctions expertise, technology and staying power, fit with company size and culture should be considered. A buyer should consider the provider's familiarity with the nuances of spend analysis, the identification of the right categories for e-sourcing, supply market analysis, the design of the right RFP, the ability to train suppliers, and the ability to provide operational support during the bidding event. The buyer also should consider the service provider's experience with similar buyers. A service provider with a client base of FTSE 500 companies may use an approach that is not well suited to the needs of the public sector with more limited resources. Finally, the buyer should understand the process by which service providers choose suppliers and ensure that appropriate suppliers are chosen. For example, some service providers may choose poor suppliers who do not match client needs, such as geographic proximity, regulatory requirements, ability to timely deliver a certain volume of goods or services etc.

Once the right partner has been selected, buyers can improve supplier participation in the reverse auction process by being proactive in the process. Close buyer participation that helps set the stage for a full fledged e-sourcing programme include spend analysis, identification of categories that are better suited for the e-sourcing process, proper timing of the events, appropriate lot and bidding strategies etc. Typically, indirect categories, MRO/spares items, computers, office supplies, may be better suited for e-sourcing than direct materials. Buyers should improve supplier participation (particularly incumbents) by explaining:

- The goals and objectives of the e-sourcing programme,
- How the process will differ from the traditional process,
- What the evaluation and selection criteria will be and
- The time line for decision making.

Suppliers also should be notified if only pre-qualified vendors have been invited to participate. This is likely to be viewed positively by the suppliers and increase participation, especially if pre-qualification has been achieved through site visits to manufacturing locations or other audits. E-sourcing does not preclude establishing strategic relationships with select suppliers, but can be used as a first step in establishing such a partnership with competitive suppliers.

Supplier Benefits

E-sourcing can provide benefits to suppliers. These include a more transparent purchasing process, increased market reach, reduced customer acquisition costs and competitive pricing information. The e-sourcing and reverse auction process forces buyers to spend more time upfront in creating and communicating specifications, contract specifications, and delivery requirements, thus providing better information to the suppliers prior to the bidding process.

The e-sourcing process also tends to level the playing field for smaller companies with limited number of sales resources. Some suppliers have used reverse auctions to benchmark themselves against the competition and, if necessary look at approaches to obtaining more competitive pricing without compromising quality of products or services. As long as the cost of participating is less than the potential benefit from participating, a supplier will benefit from participating. There is clearly no benefit from not participating.

Supplier Strategies

Suppliers should be proactive in the e-sourcing process as well. They need to know the rules upfront that can include criteria for evaluation and award (lowest price versus best value), weights for each of the criteria, a timeline for decision making, and the reserve price (if any).

Incumbents may have an advantage when they participate due to their previous relationship with the buyer. They also may have a better idea of the buyer's needs and requirements. Suppliers will generally find it advantageous to participate in the auction, because participation provides potential profit and additional information. Not participating generates no profit and no information. Suppliers should communicate issues and concerns in a timely and appropriate manner. For example, if there are anti trust concerns due to few suppliers of certain products, buyers can modify auction types to prevent revealing pricing information.

Suppliers should be careful not to get carried away in the reverse auction process by submitting a bid at a price at which they cannot supply the product/service profitably. For the long term, suppliers should attempt to differentiate their products/services in some way and ensure that this value is effectively communicated.

Collaborative commerce

Many buyers and sellers should be able to leverage e-sourcing to reduce their costs without negatively impacting the existing buyer-supplier relationships. After identifying the appropriate e-sourcing partner, effective communication is key both among buyers and suppliers.

The marketplace enables information sharing and process synchronization in a true e-business context, delivering seamless integration across the supply chain. Collaborative commerce has arrived.

Case Study: Higher Education E-Procurement

The University of Salford has developed an e-procurement marketplace primarily for the University Sector. The marketplace, known as HEeP, uses internet technology, is innovative and facilitates collaborative e-procurement in the Higher Education Sector.

The HEeP marketplace is a low cost solution which in time will provide major benefits in improving the effectiveness of University purchasing and in reducing the costs of transactions.

The HEeP project's aim is to be the primary internet marketplace for e-procurement activity in the Higher Education Sector.

The UK Higher Education Sector comprises in excess of 170 institutions (Universities and Colleges) with a combined annual spend on goods and services in excess of 4.5 billion pounds. In recent years the Sector has improved its purchasing arrangements and has collaborated through seven regional purchasing consortia to develop contracting.

A myriad of national, regional and local contracts exists to cover the majority of supplies and services but contract compliance by institutions is generally unsatisfactory. Existing procurement processes are typically manual and paper based and transaction costs are estimated to be between 35 pounds and 50 pounds per purchase. Such costs can be significantly reduced by avoiding the need to repeatedly key in the same data to different systems.

A number of e-procurement systems have been tried by individual institutions but no single solution, prior to HEeP, has generated widespread support.

The HEeP marketplace provides significant benefits to the Sector by delivering a marketplace to support real time electronic trading between institutions and their suppliers. HEeP's "thin" marketplace delivers real efficiency gains by streamlining the procurement and transaction process which in turn reduces costs and enables both institutions and suppliers to make financial savings.

Another feature of HEeP is that it provides much needed management information regarding the acquisition of different goods and services. This purchasing information will in due course enable the Sector to improve its contracting arrangements further for example by identifying opportunities for more local contracts to be combined into regional contracts and for more regional contracts to become national contracts, thus delivering economies of scale.

The HEeP marketplace is designed to facilitate and automate the processes by which institutions procure goods, namely:
- Identify suppliers who are contracted to supply them particular goods and services
- Locate the appropriate areas on those suppliers e-commerce websites
- Raise purchase requisitions on their own finance systems so that the purchases can be awarded formal approval
- Send confirmed purchase orders to suppliers' back office systems to initiate dispatch of the goods
- Receive supplier invoices and upload them into their finance systems so that payment can be made.

E-auctions and the procurement of services

A common misconception of e-auctions is that they are chiefly suited to the sourcing of material "products" and preferably, commodities.

While commodities undoubtedly lend themselves to sourcing via online bidding, there is now very clear evidence to indicate that e-auctions can, and do, produce excellent results in the purchasing of services. Indeed, it is in the area of services purchasing that the most explosive growth in the adoption of this process is being seen. E-auctions are becoming such a popular tool for the sourcing of these categories for the following reasons.

First, every substantial organisation has a need to buy general services, from car fleet management to security to cleaning to office supplies. For some organisations these purchases are "core"; for the majority they are not considered strategic. The levels of spend are, however, often quite considerable. With any large spend, the supply base will be very keen to compete for business.

Second, there is invariably considerable scope to improve the services procurement processes and thereby to deliver surprisingly large savings. For many organisations, direct procurement was initially far more sophisticated and controlled than was the case for indirects. This is still true for many.

Third, the fact the demand for purchased services is so broad has lead to the development of significant supply base capability. In many services sectors, the supply bases are still extremely fragmented. This invariably means that the supply market is highly competitive.

A further essential ingredient is the fact that, with professional input, services requirements can be extremely well specified. Indeed, selecting online bidding for the negotiation phase of the tender exercise often drives greater clarity in specification. It is vital that suppliers participating in an e-auction are clear about what they are bidding to supply.

With a commodity, specification is relatively straightforward, the only major differences often being the packaging and delivery arrangements. But even purchases at the other end of the "complexity spectrum" can be well specified and successfully auctioned.

Indeed, the specification can legitimately vary from bidder to bidder. For example, when Ford bids to supply a medium sized car it is probably a Mondeo, whereas Vauxhall would offer an Insignia, each with a specification list pre-agreed with the buyer.

Another charge sometimes levelled against e-auctions is that "they're all about price". This is not the case. Whether or not a tender project involves the use of e-auctions, an optimum result will only ever be delivered in non price factors are given due consideration alongside the price elements.

After an e-auction, the buyer is left with a series of written "best bids" from suppliers. In the vehicle example cited above, the buying company will be left with a decision probably based on weighted parameters, but within which price (or whole life cycle costs) have been determined via a highly rigorous process – the e-auction.

The experience of many of the author's clients as users of e-auctions, then it quickly becomes clear that without unlimited resources, a traditional tender process could not possibly enable parties to make as many revisions during the negotiating process as they can within an e-auction. The process saves significant resources as well as driving a better deal.

Finally, there is the hard evidence. Thousands of separate projects have seen e-auctions deliver fantastic results in the sourcing of services. Not only have buyers been able to discover new suppliers and price levels, but it has opened the way for vastly improved levels of quality and service.

In many ways e-auctions achieve many of the same aims as conventional tenders, and are similarly open, transparent and encourage competition. The difference lies in their ability to deliver lower prices through the competitive bidding of potential suppliers rather than each putting in a one-off best offer.

The case against e-auctions

An e-auction is a good way to buy commodity goods and some commodity services. But it is an unsuitable way to buy a service that cannot be simply described and instantly delivered. Every problem can look like a nail when on e is armed only with a hammer and it is not just complexity, but a series of factors, that limit its use.

Other dimensions that make services less suitable for e-auctions include intellectual property and switching costs, as well as the fact that service contracts are not covered by any equivalent of the Sale of Goods Act or the concept of "fitness for purpose".

Services frequently require ongoing definition and negotiation. Improved efficiency is often reasonably expected and buyer and seller have to achieve continued savings through some form of gain share. This dimension of a purchase can be negotiated competitively but it seems hardly suited to the frenzy of an auction.

Imagine, for example, the purchase of a facilities management service in which the vendor must invest months trying to understand the local situation. Many will take a lot of time working to develop proposals. But this becomes more difficult to maintain if the final stage is a dog eat dog affair after the buyer has absorbed all of the supplied know-how. Opportunities for continuous collaboration on cost reduction and benefits sharing are ruled out.

The relationship between a vendor and customer goes through a power shift during the procurement process. The buyer's power is greatest at the start and declines as commitment increases. The e-auction delays this, until power shifts suddenly and completely. Some vendors are getting expert at exploiting this by bidding low to get the business and then cashing in through extortionate charges for changes.

Better suppliers may even refuse to enter a tendering process that ends in a gladiatorial contest. The cost of preparing proposals and bids can be high. Risking everything in a sudden death may simply not be worth it. And those vendors that do take part and face the prospect of an e-auction at the end are likely to hold positions in reserve, protecting their information and their best and final offer until the endgame. This may reduce the worth of any requests for information and requests for proposals that precede it.

Competition is not always perfect, especially in services, and bidding process can be more rigged than a wrestling match. In one case, a buyer of a temporary staff agency service went straight to auction on the total mark-up, missing the fact that local agencies had got used to margins for overheads and profit that were three times the norm.

We should not lose sight of where most value is added in service buying. Research shows two thirds of all potential savings come from persuading the internal client that a standard service will do the same job as the specified exclusive one. More than two thirds of the remaining potential can be achieved through traditional means, with a real time bidding process.

De-skilling of purchasing, by going straight to auction, helps to leverage scarce resources but it also contributes to the exclusion of purchasing from the big decisions of the day. There are few examples of e-auctions for outsourcing HR or finance services and, unfortunately, not even many cases where purchasing is consulted about such strategic outsourcing.

Case Study: BA and E-Procurement of Services

British Airways has cut its European public relations spend by 25 per cent after holding an e-auction.

Previously, the airline's PR work for 28 European countries was shared between three agencies. Two agencies retained the business, on three year contracts; a departure from the previous annual rolling basis.

There was some concern by PR people at first in that an e-auction would take that human contact aspect out of dealing with suppliers; an antithesis to PR and marketing people.

The process made them extremely focused on their specifications. They had to be, because PR services are not like cleaning or catering where the job is tangible and can be clearly defined. It also saved them probably four to five days work that would have been meeting suppliers to negotiate deals.

A mock e-auction was run two days before to get people used to it.

BA's procurement director, said the e-auctions are part of the airline's purchasing strategy, established in 2003 to save 300 million pounds from its 4 billion pound procurement budget.

They have met the target for reduction in suppliers to 2,000 which is about right for a company like BA with an 8 billion pound turnover. Three years previously they had around 14,000 suppliers.

Case Study – Shell

Oil giant Shell is expecting to process 90 per cent of its global spending electronically.

This is a huge undertaking and is forcing many of their suppliers and competitors to rethink their own procurement strategies.

As the costs of implementation have reduced greatly over the years, this has made it very difficult for Shell's suppliers to resist the development.

For Shell, currently a leader in its industry in e-procurement development, a possible 1.5 – 2 per cent saving in its global procurement cost has provided the main thrust to the business case.

Further efficiencies will come from increased contract compliance, lower supply chain costs, increased global reach and the removal of 'non-value adding steps' to the internal procurement process.

Shell have said that positive changes for Shell's suppliers will include quicker payment, vendor maintained catalogues that allow suppliers to own and maintain their own data, further integration and collaboration within the supply chain and an increased profile with other companies that can support e-procurement.

Mini Case Study – Shell Nigeria

SPDC Nigeria in pushing for online bidding, the company aimed to, as much as possible, cut out the human element in handling bidding processes and give a level playing ground for suppliers in a manner that was quick, convenient and unwaveringly transparent.

They were faced with key questions:
- which product(s) do they select for bidding?
- how do they align the online bidding activity with current Tender Board approval processes?
- how do they get the buy-in of local suppliers?
- how do they manage the bandwidth and internet accessibility problems?

The team zeroed in on products with the following attributes:

- Availability of many suppliers
- Ease of specification
- High spend/value
- Possibility of significant savings

For the local suppliers to buy in into the process, an awareness session was conducted showing the potentials of online bidding for them. They were also able to use an "internet café" set up in the Shell offices.

The gains of online bidding showed up the very first day. The savings in the final bid price translated to 9% when compared to the historic price offered for the same goods in the conventional Tender Board process.

A second session for another product was held along the same lines in which 10 suppliers participated. The savings was 40.6%.

Another nine suppliers took part for a third product, which made savings of 14.2%.

E-auctions; some other reported savings

E-auctions can cut the cost of council goods and services by an average of one quarter, according to figures from the Regional Centres of Excellence.

Results from the first wave of the national programme of e-auctions show they delivered an average saving of 27 %.

The nine e-auctions held in 2005 – 2006 generated savings of 12.9 million pounds from set up costs of 137,000 pounds, a gain of 94 pounds for every pound spent.

ICT Project Procurement

IT Project Procurement has often been severely criticised in the media for cost over runs and project delays. New major ICT project announcements are therefore often greeted with great scepticism about the costs, the duration and the likely benefits of any proposed schemes. It is commonly expected that such projects will take longer, and cost more than budgeted by a factor of 2 or more.

The Department of Health established a £12.7bn project to modernise the 5,000 computer systems used by the NHS.
The project, known as the Care Record Service, is by any measure a major project and may be anticipated to experience some problems. However it has been reported to be 4 years behind schedule, and two of the original suppliers (Accenture and Fujitsu) have walked away from the project.

The Department of Justice abandoned its National Offender Management Information System (C-Nomis) in 2007 after £155m of investment when the projected costs doubled to £690m.

With the planned National Identity card scheme, the main criticisms were that it would either not work or cost too much, rather than any question of civil liberties. With a projected budget of £5bn the potential costs of failure would be significant.

ICT problems are not limited to the UK. The Swedish Social Security agency had a number of IT projects audited by the Swedish National Audit Office, who found multiple projects. Not only had the Agency bypassed standard procurement processes, they also produced Requests for Proposals that were both complex and lacking in clarity on specification and additionally, gave suppliers little time to respond. As a result, a number of suppliers declined to submit proposals. The lack of competition forced the Agency to accept much of the risk in contracts. For one SAP implementation project (Customer self-service) the project was delivered by Logica a year late at a price of about £7m against a proposal price of nearly 5 times the original estimate.

Difficulties with ICT procurement

There are a variety of reasons for the ICT procurement to be uniquely complex and fraught:
- Speed of development and innovation within ICT
- Complexity and Size of the projects e.g. ID card database
- Limited number of potential suppliers
- Rapid change of ownership of ICT firms
- Political and public sensitivity about the role and purpose of projects.

- Obsolescence of current platforms leading to limited time windows
- Essential nature of ICT
- Off the shelf vs. tailored products.

We shall examine these further below:

Speed of Change

Some examples follow:

- In 1969 NASA flew to the moon using less computing power than most of us will have in our mobile phones.
- The Space Shuttle computing power has increased relentlessly and follows Gordon Moore's predictive law that computing power doubles every eighteen months. To replace the installed systems with the latest technology would be a never ending and impossibly expensive, therefore in 2010 the final flights of the Space Shuttle still used computers built with Intel 8086 chips in 1980.
- At home, we are used to the fact that our four year old laptop will have to be replaced because it no longer has the memory or capacity for the latest software, games or applications.
- Mobile phones change with the seasons, or at least annually.
- At work, some are used to accessing a twenty year old mainframe database through a ten year old PC. Or at least trying to, but increasingly failing.

The relentless pace of change is the enemy of all ICT projects. No sooner is a product or service specified than it is on the way to becoming obsolete. New technologies and concepts are emerging rapidly, and for the public sector it is expensive to keep up and also difficult. The difficulty of forecasting future ICT requirements is then combined with a high degree of publicity and criticism if a mistake is made. However, history tells us that the phone companies did not predict the massive demand for text messaging. Similarly few people predicted the massive demand for social media like Facebook and Twitter.

The one issue that is common is that the larger a project, and the longer it takes, the higher the likelihood that it is going to appear to have the wrong specification on completion. Many legacy ICT systems are kept limping along by ICT support staff because of the huge cost of replacing the existing system, and the risks involved in a change project.

Size and complexity of projects

The UK public sector spends some £16bn each year on ICT and ICT services. The scale of this in a country of some 60 million people imposes some huge requirements. Any project, for example, to standardise recording of NHS data, would require a database that might need to provide access at 100000 points to 60 million records, each containing hundreds or thousands of pieces of information.

Inevitably the desire to centralise, standardise and share information creates the potential for projects of considerable size and massive complexity. Even at a regional or local level, local authorities and other public sector bodies have requirements for ICT that could hardly have been imagined a decade or so ago.

Consequentially the average ICT procurement of a services contract takes between 55 and 77 weeks. With complexity comes increased risk. The challenge for Buyers is to balance the need for project management of that risk with the need to deliver projects quickly and to budget.

ICT projects need to include clear terms and conditions to clarify the consequences for the project if there are changes in technical specification, or the potential for upgrades, and how these will be managed and costed.

Dominance of key suppliers

There was an old saying "no one gets sacked for buying from IBM". This reflected the truth that in the 60s and 70s IBM were the world leader in mainframe computers and with little competition, were able to price high. Alternative suppliers were around, but in justifying a major capital purchase buyer were asked if they wanted to take a (perceived) risk with relatively unknown and untested organisations. If the project was unsuccessful then the Buyer would have to defend their decision, whereas IBM were well known and the installation was likely to be successful; the technical merits of the ICT system itself may not therefore have played a strong role in the decision making process.

This situation persists, with a small number of key suppliers dominating particular sectors of the ICT industry; examples include Microsoft, SAP and Oracle. In any situation where there is a dominant supplier (which are Kraljic's Bottleneck or Critical items) it is difficult for new entrants to establish a position, but it is particularly so in the ICT industry. Despite the efforts of some individuals to establish open source technologies such as Linux Operating Systems, and Open Office software packages to rival Microsoft Windows and Microsoft Office, the majority of buyers will find that they are looking at a very restricted number of suppliers.

The number may be further reduced if the technical specifications are focussed on the technological implications of the purchase to the exclusion of any commercial considerations.

Although there are a number of routes to market for Microsoft products, public sector buyers would be unduly optimistic if they anticipated a greatly discounted price for their products.

With ICT services there is more competition, but a relatively few providers have strong positions in the market and with particular niche approaches. These further limit completion and the options of public buyers. This can put them suppliers in a strong position in developing contracts with the public sector. Buyers therefore must pay particular attention to the terms and condition of contracts so that they can ensure that they are properly protected from the consequences of cost or time overruns and the introduction of new technologies.

Changing ownership of key suppliers

In any industrial sector there are many mergers and acquisitions, but within the ICT sector this is a regular part of the landscape. Large software companies such as Microsoft, Google and SAP regularly complement their own R&D efforts by buying companies with new technologies. In the service sector, companies regularly buy other companies to increase their scale, to access their staff and widen the client base, an example being the acquisition of EDS by Hewlett Packard to form HP Enterprise Services.

The consequences of these changes for large projects are that it can be difficult to ensure the contracted supplier will exist in the same form at the end of the project and with the same skills and resources. This can mean that projects could have to be redesigned during the execution phase and Buyers need to ensure that this is anticipated in both the selection criteria and the contract conditions. A particular concern is to ensure continued access to source code through escrow agreements (the deposit of the code with a trusted third party who holds the code securely pending changes to agreed circumstances).

Political sensitivities

The UK Public Sector not only spends a considerable sum on ICT each year, it uses ICT to interact and engage with the people in many ways. As examples, organisations have online registration at Companies House, employers receive online notification of job vacancies through the Department of Work and Pensions, and the general public purchase of tax discs online from the DVLA.

This means that the public sector has strong ICT visibility, where any errors or examples of poor performance will be immediately identified and given a high media profile. A consequence of this for Buyers is that there can be a stronger than usual focus on making a purchasing decision that is defendable in the event that anything goes wrong, rather than one that creates the greatest value if everything goes well.

Obsolescence

A standard joke in ICT procurement is that whenever anyone asks "when is the best time to buy a computer?" the answer is always the same, "in six months".

The rate of change in the industry means that newer and better technology solutions will be available in the relatively near future; therefore any technology solution developed now, has only a limited life before a better solution is available. The challenge is to avoid keeping the obsolete struggling on at increasing cost with increasing failures, while waiting for new solutions to be available, whilst not yet to purchase systems that will need to be replaced within the predicted lifetime of the system because they better technologies are available.

These decisions can only be made by Public sector managers from different departments working together to form a shared views and a common strategy. This team should include Procurement manager and ICT managers, but also the functional and delivery team managers who will be aware of the environment in which the ICT will be used. Decisions on technical specifications can also be made by the technical people for all the right reasons without considering the mechanics of how to buy, such as the route for engaging with the market and ensuring a competitive element to the procurement. Next, ICT projects need to include clear terms and conditions to clarify the consequences for the project if there are changes in technical specification or the potential for upgrades, and how these will be managed and coasted.

Increasing ubiquity of ICT

There is no aspect of modern life in the public sector that does not involve ICT, for example, from having access to internet systems and telephones. The growing interconnectedness of the technologies means that this is only likely to increase for the foreseeable future. This means that ICT solutions being developed now have to consider potential future changes in use and demand, such as access to information on mobile phones, to the use of social networking technologies to engage with the community. This places a requirement on Buyers to keep abreast of the latest technology concepts and ideas so as to be familiar with the developing ICT environment.

Use of tailored solutions rather than off-the-shelf solutions

The UK government in 2010 in the strategy paper Smarter, Cheaper, Greener, identified the use of open standards as a means of improving ICT effectiveness (rather than having standards tied to one supplier or group of suppliers). The aim here is to establish a common infrastructure, with common standards and common capabilities. In this way learning and capabilities can be shared across the public sector and help to deliver the targets identified in the paper title, e.g. smarter (better) ICT solutions, lower prices and improved environmental performance.

The ownership of any solution developed by a supplier should be identified in the terms and conditions; if the buyer pays for system development, then they should own the intellectual property or at least share in any commercial exploitation of the solution by the supplier. If the supplier is to have sole exploitation rights for the software or solution, then that should be appropriately reflected in a low price.

Counterfeits and Security

Probably no other industrial sector is as rife with counterfeiting as the software industry. With any knowledge based industry, the actual means of sharing of the intellectual property is a tiny percentage of the cost of the product. Software can be easily and accurately forged and it is therefore essential to ensure that the procurement channel is understood and trusted.

Software also provides the potential for security risks, with hidden elements of the code potentially providing hackers the capability to gain access to confidential information.

Hackers often exploit vulnerabilities in code written for other purposes, and so it is essential to ensure that any software commissioned has appropriate security testing, with any purchased software is assessed for security risks.

Best Practices in ICT procurement

The OGC has published ICT Services Model Agreement and Guidance note. As with all guidance it is subject to revision with changes in government policy, but it highlights the key areas for consideration in any ICT services agreement:

* Milestones and payment for reaching milestones
* Service Levels to be delivered
* Due Diligence in the appointment of the supplier
* Change or Variance control
* Ownership of Intellectual Property
* Key project personnel
* Financial distress of the supplier (including escrow)
* Termination criteria, rights and compensation
* Step-in rights (i.e. when the authority can step in to take control)
* Liabilities
* Remedies
* Indemnities and insurance
* Taxation

In developing and then operating ICT procurement, it is important to recognise that this is likely to be a project requiring a large and continuing contribution from procurement right through from the initial definition of the requirement, to the project sign off on completion. A topic that is fully covered in a companion book ***Excellence in Supplier Management*** (Emmett and Crocker 2009), where we attempt to safeguard organisations from situations where procurement place the order and then wave it goodbye, meaning then there is know one left to manage the implementation and the supplier.

Because of the highly technical nature of the technology many organisations therefore have ICT procurement as a specialist role, where it is vital to ensure that the appointed people have both the technical skills, commercial skills and the knowledge needed to be able to conduct the role. A number of best practices can be identified for ICT procurement, identified as follows:

* Focus on outcomes rather than inputs; that is the use of performance

specifications that cover what needs to be done, rather than, using a technical or conformance specification covering the equipment or the definite approach

- Get the expert input of the market into the specification; what is possible, and what might be possible in the near future?
- Consider use of a competitive Dialogue rather than a standard tender
- Involve users and buyers in a real team with shared views and aims; most importantly ensuring everyone remembers they are on the same side (rather than some siding with the suppliers).
- Define priorities such as cost, delivery, outputs in terms of critical success factors (these are essential) and measures of success (that are desired but are not essential outcomes).
- Leave lots of time to prepare and to make corrections throughout the procurement process.
- Try to develop alternative solutions at all times and stimulate competition
- Work hard on the Ts and Cs as these need as much consideration as the specification
- An Escrow agreement is essential, even if the solution is open source. (Escrow referring to a third party holding source code, so that a customer can have access under certain pre-agreed conditions such as the bankruptcy of the supplier, but without impinging on the IP of the supplier, it has similar arrangements applying to money)
- Use Project Management tools and techniques
- Define your exit points and step in points; such as at what point do will intervene to take ownership or cancel the project along with the implications
- Have a worst case scenario plan, for example, if you have to cancel the project what will you do instead
- Think about full life costs and life expectancy of project; can you really forecast requirements more than 10 years ahead?
- Off the shelf or bespoke solution? Which approach adds value, reduces cost and controls risk in a given situation

Corporate Social Responsibility (CSR)

There are many views on what constitutes CSR. The narrowest view is the classical view proposed by the economist Milton Friedman that the corporate responsibility of business is to increase its profits. The owners of the company, who are supposed to be interested in profit maximisation, are the turning point of the decisions made by the company. Social responsibility is considered here, to be primarily the responsibility of the government and other parties such as the voluntary sector.

A broader approach is stakeholder perspective; here, companies are not only accountable to the owners of the company, but also to the stakeholders such as staff, suppliers, the local community and customers. The argument is that stakeholders influence the activities of the company and/or are influenced by the activities of the company. Companies are, for example, accountable to politicians who can curb the activities of the company by introducing a bill.

The broadest approach is the societal approach in which companies are considered to be responsible to society in general. The view is that companies are part of society. They need a "licence to operate" from society. Today companies representing this approach are characterized as "good corporate citizens".

Carroll focuses in on the essentials of the above three approaches. He considers the role of companies today as a role which includes four dimensions:

- economic
- legal
- ethical
- philanthropic

Carroll also focuses on the stakeholders of the company as he sees that social responsibility is a diffuse and almost non-operational concept, unless organisations learn to "unfold stakeholder thinking".

The European Commission also links CSR to the stakeholder approach. CSR is a concept whereby companies integrate social and environmental concerns in their business operations and in their interactions with their stakeholders on a voluntary basis (EU Commission, 2001, p.6). The definition is used by leading companies in Europe and is considered as the basis of the European CSR policy.

One of the most referred to definitions is by the World Business Council for Sustainable Development (WBCSD, 1999) that defines CSR as "the continuing commitment by business to behave ethically and contribute to economic development whilst improving the quality of life of the workforce and their families as well as of the local community and society at large".

The CSR concept is still developing and has not reached the maturity stage. It consists of a number of free standing and competing ideas that have not been sufficiently integrated into a broadly accepted and robust theory. In particular, there is an absence of consensus regarding the elements (steps) underpinning the processes of corporate social responsibility. Therefore, the analysis presented in this section is to seen as work in progress and subject to change as the CSR concept climbs the maturity curve.

In the public sector there can be an explicit, as well as implicit, obligation to consider the broader issues of CSR. This is encapsulated in the requirement to evaluate proposals on the basis of the Most Economically Advantageous Tender, which can incorporate a range of social factors, rather than just the lowest price. In a broader sense the use of public funds will require a broader and explicit consideration of the public good, rather than just financial profitability. In doing so public sector bodies should consider not just their own activities, but also those of their suppliers – who may have a supply chain with wider implications for CSR including overseas sourcing, employment practices and policies, and environmental considerations.

Other CSR Definitions

There are many definitions of Corporate Social Responsibility (CSR).

One such definition is as follows: *"the organisation's consideration of, and response to, issues beyond the narrow economic, technical, and legal requirements of the organisation to accomplish social benefits along with the traditional economic gains which the firm seeks."*

Another definition offers the following: "An ethical organisation is one that is able to reflect appropriately and evaluate its actions in the context of an ethical domain, within the process of organisational decision making. In attempting to do so, the organisation must grapple with the problem of multiple agency-constituency roles".

Many correspondents argue that pressure for CSR emanates from multiple stakeholder groups including customers, employees, suppliers, community groups, governments and institutional shareholders. CSR here is concerned with treating the stakeholders of the organisation ethically or in a socially responsible manner. Stakeholders exist both within an organisation and outside. The aim of social responsibility is to create higher and higher standards of living, while preserving the profitability of the corporation or value for money, for its stakeholders both within and outside the organisation.

This is pragmatic and acknowledges the importance of economic performance, it recognises that organisations serve a broad range of stakeholders, and it highlights the importance of striking a balance between economic performance, meeting the stakeholders expectations and responsibility towards society. CSR can only flourish if its protagonists recognise the importance of economic performance.

CSR values

The following values underpin the CSR concept:
- Seeks to understand and meet the needs of stakeholders including that of customers, owner, employees, suppliers, and the society at large;
- Integrity of individual and collective action;
- Honour;
- Fairness;
- Respect;
- Participation;
- Individual and collective responsibility to others.

Waddock and Graves (1997) empirical research showed a positive association between corporate social performance and financial performance. The outcome of studies examining the link between CSR and financial performance is however indeterminate with other studies in identifying this positive link and finds no link and in some cases, a negative link.

Martin-Castilla (2002) argued that CSR serves the long term interest of the organisation by aligning the interests of the organisation with those of its' stakeholders.

Elements of CSR Process

Elements of CSR Process	Description
No-Harm	This principle draws upon the rights philosophy by demanding that the organisation should not engage in any action that leads to harm.

Transparency	This principle draws on the liberty and informed choice theory. That is full disclosure and provision of information to all parties so that they are able to take decisions that do not compromise their welfare
Voice	This principle requires that stakeholders' interests are protected through visible and active participation in the decision making process at all levels.
Equity	This is derived from the theories of rights and justice and its aim is to ensure that there is perceived equity in the actions of business.
Benefit	The need to examine the benefits of an action, that is to say, if a certain act is carried out, who wins, who stays the same and who loses from it? What are the gains and losses?
Integrity	This requires integrity of action in all forms
Liberty	This is based on the liberty theory of ethics by stressing the right of the individual freely to engage in or disengage from transactions with the firm.
Care	This is focusing on protection and promotion of positive rights by the firm.

Source: Table Adapted from Ahmed and Machold (2004)

Checklist: Drivers behind Corporate Social Initiatives

- Gaining a competitive advantage
- Emerging morals and ethics – although some people still believe that an organisation exists solely to maximise shareholder value, many more have come to the conclusion that this should not be at the expense of the environment, community or society in general
- Thinking in terms of engagement and not speedy solutions – for example, acting with only the shareholders in mind will create a gap in commitment between employees and investors

- Understanding that society and economics are inextricably linked – just as social situations impact upon the economy, the economy also has an effect on society. This is the view of Mintzberg who vehemently opposes the argument that a company exists purely to create profit for its shareholder; he believes that companies must accept the part they play in society.

Critical Success Factors
- Connect with your organisation's core values and competencies
- Respond to moral pressures – although your response may not be completely to the liking of any pressure groups, it will demonstrate that you are prepared to listen and, in most cases, compromise
- Measure your success

Case Study: CSR and Business in the Community (BITC)

Twenty five years ago a group of British companies decided to improve the way that business affects society. They set up Business in the Community (BITC), an independent charity to inspire, engage, support and challenge companies to continually improve the impact they have on society. It now has 750 member companies, including 71 of the FTSE 100, and its combined membership represents 12.4m people in 200 countries.

The creation of the Corporate Responsibility index began in 1998 when it was decided that companies needed a way to measure and report on responsible business practice. The purpose of the Corporate Responsibility Index is the only index that measures the impact businesses have on the staff they employ, and the societies in which they operate and on the environment.

Business in the Community (BITC), emphasises that corporate responsibility is not just a "feel good" exercise but is of strategic and financial importance to every business and is vital that the momentum behind CSR is maintained.

Companies that do not keep a grip on working conditions, the activities of their suppliers or pollution are more likely to be prosecuted, shut down by the authorities or boycotted by the public. Overall, there has been a substantial increase in the number of companies with policies and targets in the public domain, especially on hum rights, standards in the supply chain and in the work place.

The companies in the CSR Index are committed to measuring and controlling their social and environmental impact. Companies that have taken part said it led to business advantages, including cost savings, an improved corporate image, better recruitment and greater efficiencies.

But there are still some of Britain's biggest businesses who do not take corporate social responsibility seriously.

Companies are recognizing that a genuine commitment to responsible business can be a source of innovation that produces new opportunities. BITC's Company of the Year – Marks and Spencer – has made sustainability and corporate citizenship an integral part of the M&S brand as well as a key part of its commercial recovery.

Environmental issues as a CSR driver

Environmental concerns are reflected in reducing waste. It has been estimated that most companies underestimate the true costs of their waste by a factor of 20. True costs can equate to 4% of turnover of which about 1% could be saved by waste minimisation, for example, one company, specializing in the management of industrial fluids converted from steel storage to plastic drums. With plastic drums used over and over, the company saved approximately $1.8 million annually and significantly reduces the volume of discarded containers. This demonstrates that good environmental policy can also be good business practice, rather than a financial burden.

The "making waste work" initiative has identified the Four "R's" for the reduction of waste. These are:
- Reduce the amount of waste
- Reuse items i.e. plastic reusable packaging rather than cardboard
- Recycle items i.e. at recycling depots or recycling companies
- Repair items, i.e. increase maintenance and avoid scrapping

The Procurement Department is often most suitably placed within the organisation to contribute to overall environmental performance. It is unlikely that a local authority or other public sector body can make significant progress towards environmental targets such as reduced Green House emissions without engaging fully with the supply base. Green issues have to filter down from the organisation to its suppliers to be effective and there are at least three good reasons for organisations to try to influence their suppliers to improve their environmental performance:

- Obtaining better service or reduced prices from suppliers
- Responding to life cycle demands from end customers
- Maintaining or enhancing the organisation's image.

Many larger organisations have already seen benefits (cost avoidance, cost minimisation and environmental liabilities) from waste minimisation. Key to the success of a waste minimisation programme is supplier involvement.

This means that suppliers are not faced with unreasonable demands and puts a proportion of the innovation in the hands of suppliers who have the greatest technical knowledge of their product.

Checklist: common considerations for procurement professionals undertaking waste minimisation and pollution control:

- Purchase of recycled products; increases market for recycled products and strengthens the developing infrastructure
- Purchase of recyclable products: products with greater percentage of recyclable materials or more easily recycled materials increase post use recycle value and encourage recycling.
- Purchase from suppliers with preferred environmental status; provides impetus for suppliers to pursue environmental initiatives
- Purchase products manufactured with renewable resources; minimise depletion of non renewable natural resources
- Specify or purchase reusable packaging; reuse on site, at other facilities, or return to the original supplier for reuse
- Purchase materials that are environmentally friendly or neutral
- Purchase products that are manufactured with environmentally superior processes; for example, powder coating versus spray painting reduces air emissions

- Reduce the number of different or incompatible materials; facilitates recycling, coloured paper reduces value of recycled office paper, labels/stickers that are difficult to remove inhibit recycling

Environmental evaluation criteria

What are the likely criteria to be applied in assessing a supplier's environmental performance? It is not possible to be too specific, as it will depend on the precise nature of their activities, but there are some general headings, to be analysed and supplemented, which can be given.

There are likely to be four main headings which provide a high level taxonomy in relation to environmental issues. These are as follows:
- Regulatory compliance
- Environmental effects and performance measures
- Existing environmental management procedures
- Commitment to management and process improvement

The first heading will encompass the various legislative and regulatory issues. Some will be mandatory conditions for supplier approval. Other criteria under this heading, though not mandatory, may nonetheless have a high weighting, both within this high level category and for the overall evaluation. For mandatory criteria, it is likely that buying organisations would withhold approval/negotiation until such time as the supplier did fulfil the mandatory conditions.

The second category of environmental effects heading covers the various effects and performance measures, such as ecotoxicological information, volatile organic compounds records, etc.

The third category heading covers the existing management procedures relating to the existing set of products and processes. This will involve environmental effects register maintenance, energy conservation policy, etc.

All of the above headings will relate to specific products or sets of products and bout in materials and components relating to the transformation processes involved in the business covered.

The final category covers the commitment to continuous improvement in both management and transformation processes. These will apply to the supply company irrespective of the various product and materials which are supplied.

It should also be noted that the Environmental impacts of activities are being constantly reviewed and revised in the light of new scientific evidence. In some cases this revision remains controversial, or at least subject to considerable debate. As an example, Atomic energy was previously seen as a major environmental threat but is seen by some as a "greener" alternative to oil, coal and gas power stations.

A smaller scale example is the use of recyclable PET bottles rather than reusable glass bottles – both of which have proponents amongst environmental experts.

Case Study: Nissan UK

Nissan manufacturing UK's environmental journey began several years ago and, initially, was brought into focus by a need to comply with legislation. Achieving this soon brought all functions, including our suppliers, together on activities designed to meet requirements but at no on cost.

They set out to look at it from the total business need. Foremost was the instruction to meet environmental legislation but at no cost. Achieving this requires savings to be made elsewhere to offset against legislative demands. First, they had to identify and understand all the drivers of the activity. A list was compiled including total detailed costs expended within each category. This involved collaboration with suppliers of components and packaging in order to detail and calculate all costs, including secondary costs.

For example, if they received the components in cardboard box packaging from a supplier and the intention was to delete the cardboard and use a returnable stillage, it took not only the cost of the cardboard versus the cost of the new stillage but included such issues as time saved on decanting the cardboard box to present the components to the assembly line versus the ability to present the new stillage direct to line side. Also, by working with the supplier of the component, they calculated any benefits in their manufacturing and used those to reduce the piece cost.

Also, eliminating decanting operations improved the welfare of employees by reducing heavy lifting operations. This reduces potential for industrial sickness which is a cost to the company.

A further example is dealing with the safe transportation of airbags. An airbag contains explosives which are subject to handling and transportation legislation. There are also environmental issues should there be an incident in transit. The initial packaging was aimed at meeting those issues. However, it was expensive and created waste from the protection involved. The new method for delivery was developed jointly with the supplier. The benefits it will bring are:

Benefits
- Elimination of supplier packaging (environmental waste)
- Reduction of disposable packaging (wastes)
- Improved compliance with legislation on transportation of hazardous goods (environmental issues)
- Elimination of decanting operations (safety and cost)
- Prevention of dust ingress (quality improvement)
- Reduced handling requirements (safety, employee welfare)

They have also worked on other issues with suppliers, such as recycling (for example, of plastic fuel tanks); reduction of process waste; paint technology and elimination of environmentally unsound materials. All achieved reduced costs. The environment is best dealt with not as a specialised activity, but as a natural part of business. It is not an obstacle to performance but an important driver in obtaining business advantages. The public do not buy items solely because they are green; they buy them because they are better quality and lower cost as well as green.

Nissan's Waste Strategy
- Conform with all government and European legislation
- Adopt proactive introduction of strategies to conform with future legal requirements
- Introduce and maintain cost reduction exercises aimed at achieving waste elimination and improving effective waste management
- Monitor and control current day to day waste stream activities
- Adopt a programme of continuous improvement.

CSR and the Supply Chain

Think of a typical existing supply chain. The products are conveyed from suppliers to original equipment manufacturers (OEMs) and then on, via various other intermediaries, to the end user, who finally disposes of it.

This concept is changing and those involved in supply management arena are witnessing the dawn of the "closed loop supply chain". The most obvious example of the closed loop model is the disposable camera. A customer buys the camera, which can only be used once, with a film already inside. The customer returns the camera for developing; the manufacturer retrieves the camera and then either services it and repackages it for further use or disassembles if for reusable components.

Today, makers of printer sand refrigerators, are arranging their supply chains in similar ways, coming full circle to reap economic and ecological benefits. Undoubtedly, these benefits and pressures have been the main forces behind the closed loop shift.

In EU, the Waste Electrical and Electronic Equipment (WEEE) Directive aims to reduce waste by promoting reuse, recycling and other means by which products can be salvaged to minimise the impact on the environment.

The Green Supply Chain

Procurement managers are entrusted with the task of procuring a wide variety of services, raw materials, components, consumables and packaging materials. They have a vital role to play in giving their organisations environmentally sound policies and practices. Purchase decisions, alongside other considerations, must be environmentally sound and every link in the supply chain tuned to this philosophy.

They must impress upon their management that in the present climate of increasing public awareness of environmental issues, a proactive approach will be beneficial. Adoption and use of environmentally sound technologies and use of eco friendly products will lead to overall reductions in cost.

For a proper appreciation of the ecological soundness of a purchase decision and its likely impact on environment, an in depth study and analysis of the complete life cycle of the product needs to be carried out. This concept, called the "cradle to grave" approach, must examine the cumulative impact on the environment that the product generates, right from the stage of extraction of its raw material up to its final disposal after completion of economic life cycle. It must be noted that this is a complex and extensive calculation, and is therefore sometimes open to debate and disagreement about both the procedure and the conclusions.

This cradle to grave analysis will study and assess the environmental impact of:

- The raw materials used
- Manufacturing/production methods/processes employed
- Energy consumed
- Modes and quantum of transportation used
- Pollutants and wastes generated by the manufacturing process
- Type of packing used, scope of its reuse/recycling
- Final disposal of the product after expiry of its useful economic life

To be able to carry out such a life cycle analysis, the procurement manager must study and understand the entire manufacturing and use cycle and discuss the subject with the manufacturer and/or supplier of the raw material/component.

The supplier of a component or service must be taken into confidence and the objectives of the exercise explained to him. It needs to be conveyed to the supplier that the proposed study will be equally beneficial to him and will in no way affect his business prospects. On the contrary, it will help him improve quality and consumer acceptance of his product and reduce overall cost by minimising energy consumption, reducing waste and generation of pollutants and reuse/recycling of hitherto discarded products. With the introduction of partnership sourcing and the reduction supplier base, it should be possible to have a proper interaction with the suppliers to obtain the requisite details for life cycle analysis.

Checklist: Elements for Life Cycle Analysis (LCA)

The following are the important elements that need to be considered in LCA and details gathered about them from the supplier or other source of information.

Raw materials

What are the raw materials used in the manufacture of the product and is their consumption optimal? Is the raw materials derived from a renewable or a non renewable resource and how can its impact on environment be minimised? Use of raw materials such as lead, mercury, and nickel, found to be carcinogenic or otherwise hazardous, must be avoided where possible.

Energy consumption

Is the manufacturing process energy efficient? Presently most of the energy is produced from non renewable resources. It is therefore imperative that use of energy is optimised and non renewable resource conserved.

Manufacturing process

Is the process of manufacture efficient in use of raw material/energy/labour and does it employ environmentally sound technology. Does it create excessive pollution and generates toxic wastes? Manufacturing technologies have been a major source of environmental degradation. Manufacturing processes using potentially harmful ingredients such as cyanides, chlorine and asbestos need to be avoided. It is better to use clean technologies to reduce pollution rather than using cleaning technologies, to remove pollutants which have already been generated. Use of clean technology will prove to be cost effective besides being environmentally friendly.

Another important point to be examined is whether the technology employed permits use of recycled raw materials. This is an important consideration as it will reduce the need for virgin raw materials and lead to cost reduction and other benefits.

Waste reduction

Waste during manufacture is very costly and must therefore, be eliminated or minimised. It not only represents poor quality but is also a source of employee demoralization.

Reuse/recycling of by products of production process

Are the wastes and by products of production process recycled or reused so as to recover material and energy, thereby minimising down stream pollution? Reuse of reclaimed water, oils and lubricants etc can lead to considerable savings and also reduce environmental contamination.

Packaging

Primary and protective packing contributes substantially towards total cost and their disposal presents problems. Use of reusable or recyclable packing needs to be encouraged. With the advent of partnership sourcing and limited supplier bases, the use of reusable and returnable packing can be expanded, resulting in cost reduction and minimising the need for disposal of packing materials. As far as possible, use of recyclable and or bio-degradable packing needs encouragement to reduce the mountains of packaging rubbish.

Final disposal

Recycling and disposal of the product at the end of its useful economic life is the last stage in the cradle to grave approach. Can the product be recycled for use as raw material? If not, is it bio-degradable? Will its disposal by dumping pollute the environment? All these aspects need careful evaluation as there is an emerging concept that producers are liable for final disposal of their products even after they have been transferred to others. Such concerns arise from the difficulties experienced in disposal of products such as nuclear wastes, used auto tyres and certain on recyclable plastics which can not be easily disposed of in an eco friendly manner.

The result

Having carefully examined the important parameters, based on the data obtained from the manufacturer and/or supplier, the parameters which have a predominant environmental impact can be identified. The importance and role of these can then be discussed with the supplier to enable him to incorporate the necessary changes in the raw material, manufacturing process, packing to make the final product more environmentally friendly. The procurement manager will have to act as a guide and facilitator to enable the manufacturer to incorporate various changes and derive full benefits from the life cycle analysis.

For more details, this topic is fully covered in ***Green Supply Chains - an action manifesto*** (Emmett and Sood, 2010)

CSR in Global Supply Chains

Corporate Social Responsibility (CSR) in a general sense reflects obligations to society and stakeholders within societies impacted by the organisation. To illustrate the increasing importance of CSR with respect to supply chain management, consider the case of Wal-Mart and the Kathie Lee Gifford line of women's clothing. Despite the fact that items with the Kathie Lee Gifford brand carried a "made in the USA" label, news items started appearing in 1996 suggesting that the garments were actually being produced in Honduran sweatshops. This news about its suppliers damaged the Wal-Mart brand name and tarnished its reputation. The Wal-Mart case is not an isolated one.

However, recently, Wal-Mart has been aggressively pursuing a variety of environmental strategies that have profoundly impacted its highly integrated global supply chain. The company will invest $500 million in sustainability projects that already involve its vehicle fleet, energy usage, packaging, agribusiness, organic clothes and food, and eco stores themselves.

This example shows that there is considerable interest in the supply chain, and public sector bodies should not assume that this attention will be directed entirely towards private companies or multi-nationals. Pressure groups, individuals and the media will be interested in understanding how the local authority spends public funds, and as a result of new openness initiatives introduced in 2011 will be able to establish this with some accuracy. If money is being spent with suppliers who are failing to pay attention to CSR standards this is likely to be identified, and publically reported. The trend towards embracing CSR has become so significant that Hau Lee, a global authority on supply chain management (SCM), claims that socially responsible supply chains are, indeed, a new paradigm.

"...implementing CSR initiatives within supply chains effectively (involves) ensuring supplier compliance"

Many issues are involved in implementing CSR initiatives within supply chains effectively, not least of which is ensuring supplier compliance. Recently, firms have come under pressure to raise the level of supplier monitoring as a means of increasing such supplier compliance. For instance, the International Labour Organization (ILO) initiated the Better Factories Program to raise working conditions in Cambodia's garment factories. Relying on unannounced visits to factories, it monitors a 500-item check list, notes progress made in remedying problems and reports its findings publicly.

Its success is attributed to the fact that all factories are involved and share a similar set of objectives, it is transparent and credible to foreign buyers, and meets the needs of the workers.

High levels of monitoring may also carry unintended consequences relating to managing the exchange relationships that make up a supply chain. Research suggests perceived fairness can improve commitment and trust within buyer-supplier exchange relationships, which have been repeatedly shown as important to achieving the level of interaction and knowledge exchange necessary for high performing supply chain relationships.

Several factors drive organisations to accept responsibility for managing supplier CSR, including customer and stakeholder expectations and the potential threat of legal liability.

Companies primarily use three instruments in implementing socially responsible behaviour among their sub-suppliers:
- Social labels
- Socially responsible investment
- Codes of conduct

Social labelling informs the public of the firm's compliance to an established set of criteria, and tends to be more effective in certain situations than in others. Labelling seems to work more efficiently in export markets involving the retail trade, and is often associated with niche products aimed at affluent consumers who are not price sensitive and are willing to trade price for support of the espoused social issue. For instance, Starbucks might label its coffee as being grown by producers who received a premium price because Starbucks negotiated directly with the source. That premium is then passed onto the consumer.

In the case of the public sector the use of socially labelled suppliers and/or products may be acceptable under the Most Economically Advantageous Tender approach if it is clear how this will benefit the community and does not eliminate competition. This may then have associated benefits in helping the authority to meet their environmental or other CSR goals.

Socially responsible investing arises when financial decisions are based on achieving a socially desirable end and acceptable economic returns. Where public sector bodies invest their revenues this does not usually come under the control of the procurement department. However, it may be appropriate for a local authority to support new start businesses through either agreement of long term contracts, or pre-funding of projects to allow for investment, particularly if the beneficiary is a disadvantaged group such as BME owned businesses, or Voluntary or Community Organisation (VCOs).

Codes of conduct are applied to corporate policies and actions rather than to goods, and imply that the firm observes and/or enforces the policy advocated. For instance, Levi Strauss' 1992 code stipulates that it will seek to do business with partners that do not use child or forced labour, do not discriminate, and do not use corporal punishment.

Cisco began the process of addressing both human rights and environmental issue in 2004. They adopted a code for suppliers that outlined standards to ensure safe working conditions, where workers are treated with dignity and respect and manufacturing processes are in conformance with stated environmental considerations. The code also includes the expectation of full compliance with host country's laws and regulations, as we as compliance with internally accepted standards.

Public Sector bodies frequently have a code of conduct for suppliers, and should seek to enforce those to ensure that suppliers behave in accordance with ethical and environmental best practice.

Codes of Conduct

Adopted in 1998, the International Labour Organisation (ILO) Declaration on Fundamental Principles and Rights at Work is an expression of commitment by governments, employers' and workers' organisations to uphold basic human values that are vital to our social and economic lives. The Declaration covers four areas:
*   Freedom of association and the right to collective bargaining
*   The elimination of forced and compulsory labour
*   The abolition of child labour
*   The elimination of discrimination in the workplace.

High monitoring levels lead to buyer/supplier conflict, militating against the trust and commitment integral to successful performance. A firm cannot manage its supply chain partners if it has not articulated precisely what its intentions are, what it is doing itself and what it expects from its suppliers and its suppliers' suppliers. Codes of conduct represent the efforts of each company to put into writing a statement or set of expectations regarding supplier corporate social responsibility.

There can be no ambiguity as to what the goals are, the penalties for those who violate the letter and spirit of the code, and resources are available to help suppliers (current or potential) become and remain compliant. Accuracy of information is essential as are consistency in criteria used in selecting and evaluating suppliers, as well as the need for objective (i.e. unbiased) application of the criteria.

Any action that encourages involvement or participation in supply chain issues will go a long way to building commitment and a common CSR vision.

To complete the circle, a corporate policy of statement of the buying company's commitment in the form of a corporate social responsibility report should be developed and endorsed. Companies such as Disney, Gap and McDonald's Corporation publish CSR reports that both illustrate their commitment to their codes of conduct, and also highlight the benefits they derive from their efforts. More important, they measure the effectiveness of those efforts, and embrace those supply chain partners whose behaviours epitomize CSR.

An Environmental Management System

An Environmental Management System (EMS) is defined as:
"A method of controlling and regulating the organisation's environmental concerns"

The International Standards Organisation; ISO 14001: Environmental Management System standard states:
"The EMS includes organisational structure, planning activities, responsibilities, procedures, processes and resources for developing, achieving, reviewing and maintaining the environmental policy".

In turn the standard then clarifies that the following is involved:
- Aspects covered are: Activities, products or services that can interact with the environment.
- Impacts are: Any change to the environment adverse or beneficial
- Objective: Overall goal arising from the environmental policy – quantifiable where applicable

- Performance: Measurable results related to the control of environmental aspects, based on policy, objectives and targets.
- Policy: Statement of intentions and principles – provides a framework for action and for the settings of objectives and targets.
- Target: Detailed performance requirement that arises from the objectives
- Interested party: Individual or group concerned or affected by the performance of an organisation
- Pollution prevention: Use of processes, practices, materials or products that avoid, reduce or control pollution.

Checklist: the benefits of EMS

- Avoiding fines and prosecutions
- Reduced operating costs
- Reduced wastes
- Compliance with environmental legislation
- Reduced insurance premium
- Increased public/customer relations
- Satisfying stakeholder demands
- Integration of improvement efforts

ISO 14001 is an Environmental System Standard and when adopted by an organisation can be assessed by an independent third party who will check conformity to the standard.

If the organisation achieves certification the EMS has been independently verified and attained a recognised level of environmental Management.

ISO 14001 sets out the following five principles for a successful EMS:
- Commitment and policy
- Planning
- Implementation
- Measurement and evaluation
- Review and improvement

Checklist: Initial considerations for Implementing EMS

Commitment from management is a key factor to the success of an EMS who needs to develop awareness and understand of:
- Why the organisation needs an EMS
- The benefits
- The goals and objectives
- The links with other objectives

Senior management has the responsibility for:
- The environmental policy
- Environmental reviews
- Appointment of an environmental representative and team
- Ensure adequate resources are available to support them

Undertake an Initial Environmental Review (ER), this ER helps the environmental team to:
- Compile a register of significant environmental aspects and impact (Cause & Effect)
- Prepare an environmental policy
- Develop objectives and targets

An ER typically covers:
- The significance of the above
- Quantifies emissions, discharges, wastes, energy usage
- Identifies cost saving opportunities
- Identifies the "must do's" for legislation and regulation (law)
- Provides an overview of site activities
- Reviews current environmental system documentation

The Environmental policy should state:
- A commitment to compliance with environmental legislation
- A commitment to continual improvement
- A commitment to preventing pollution

It must be:
- Written and communicated
- Specific to the organisation
- Signed and approved by the person with the highest authority and responsibility for the site
- A controlled document

The responsibility of the Environmental representative is important, as ISO 14001 states: "An organisation should establish and maintain a procedure to identify and have access to legal and other requirements that the organisation subscribes to that are applicable to the environmental aspects of its activities or services".

This is usually satisfied by a register of legislation which typically includes:
- The main law or code
- Secondary legislation
- Guidance on the legislation
- Summary of requirements
- Implications for the organisation
- Who are the regulatory authority or equivalent

An Environmental Management Programme is usually in two parts:

1) Outlining the environmental controls:
- Operational procedures that affect environmental performance
- Risk assessments (R-Probability x Consequence)
- COSHH register/controls
- Emergency preparedness procedures
- Organisation/responsibility charts
- Environmental policy

2) Setting Objectives and Targets
- Objectives are set out in reference to initial environmental review, register of legislation, assessments of significance and the environmental policy.
- Targets are the clear and concise operational requirements relating to the objectives.

- Targets should be realistic and measurable, time scaled and assigned to an individual or team.

Senior management of an organisation must review the effectiveness of the EMS and whether action is required to take into account.

- Changing environmental legislation
- Modified customer expectations
- Stakeholder pressures
- Failure to achieve objectives or targets
- Required changes to operations
- The results and recommendations of audits.

Monitoring and measurement of activities that can have a significant impact on the environment must take place. This is documented and carried out by trained operational personnel.

Adequate awareness and training must be delivered to communicate and support the environmental management system policy, goals, management of objectives and targets. Training must be relevant to the management of significant aspects and impacts at all levels and positions that affect the system performance and should be delivered to support the Environmental Management System.

Environmental Audits

There are three levels of audits:

- Internal audit, the self assessment
- Customer audit of your organisation and vice versa
- Independent

The first two audits use experienced and trained auditors with appropriate knowledge experts when required. They have a schedule to audit and document the audit process by checking check at all levels, for example:

- policy
- objectives/targets
- operations
- documentation
- ISO 14001 compliance/implementation

Finally they give feedback to managers responsible and management meetings.

The third and independent audit is called the certification audit and is conducted against the requirements of ISO14001. It uses completely independent assessors and a certificate system that provides proof of compliance to a standard. They are usually conducted twice per year.

Summary

The Procurement and Supply Chain functions are most suitably placed within the organisation to contribute to overall CSR and environmental performance. Many larger organisations have already seen benefits (cost avoidance, cost minimisation and environmental liabilities) from waste minimisation.

Key to the success is supplier involvement. It means that suppliers are not faced with unreasonable demands and puts a proportion of the innovation in the hands of suppliers who have the greatest technical knowledge of their product.

Buying from the Third Sector

The Third Sector is sometimes known as the voluntary sector or the non-profit sector, and comprises a range of bodes that are neither the public sector nor the private sector. It includes Voluntary and Charitable Organisations (VCOs), Social Enterprises, not for profit organisations (NPOs), and community organisations. It has been the focus of considerable attention and support from governments of all political persuasions, including Tony Blair's "Third Way" and David Cameron's "Big Society".

The attraction of the sector to government lies in the potential benefits that this sector can deliver such as:

- Engagement with communities
- Understanding of local needs
- Investment without the need for public spending
- Efficiencies compared to public sector programmes
- Delivery of social aims such as inclusion and training
- Lower cost than private sector solutions
- Avoidance of political issues over profits for providing services

Types of Third Enterprise Organisations

The sector is very diverse, with a wide range of operators and types of organisations involved.

Charities have to be registered for charitable purposes with the Charity Commission of England and Wales (or the Office of the Scottish Charity Regulator or HM Revenue & Customs in Northern Ireland), and all of their activities must be charitable in nature. They are governed by the Charities Act 1992.

Social Enterprises in turn are those that have the following characteristics:
- Are not for profit organisations that have social goals at their heart
- Are democratically managed
- Are users of surplus income (profit) for social aims
- Are funded through a combination of grants, donations and business activities
- Have mixed business and social objectives

They often consider themselves as delivering a triple bottom line of social, financial and environmental benefits. There is however no single definition of a social enterprise, and they include companies limited by guarantee, and industrial and provident societies, but also, companies limited by shares, unincorporated associations, partnerships and sole traders.

There are believed to be more that 62,000 social enterprises in the UK with a turnover of £24bn. The average turnover of about £400 000 of course conceals a wide range of scales and sizes of organisations. The John Lewis Partnership and the Co-operative Society are both social enterprises on a very large scale, but so are the many small local organisations who are working within and for a small community.

Community interest companies (CIC) are a type of limited company designed specifically to operate for the benefit of the community rather than for the benefit of the owners of the company. This means that a CIC cannot be formed or used solely for the personal gain of a particular person, or group of people. Legislation caps the level of dividends payable at 35% of profits and returns to individuals are capped at 4% above the bank base rate.

Legal Structures

There are a wide range of legal structures covering the third sector, and it can be difficult to determine whether a particular body is or is not a third sector organisation. The additional forms including:

- Industrial and Providence Societies
- Co-operative Societies
- Community Benefit Societies
- Community Interest Companies (CIC)
- Charitable Incorporated Organisations (CIO)
- Limited Liability Partnerships (LLP
- Registered Charities

Buying from Third Sector Organisations

Public sector procurement objectives of open competition can be offset with a community interest clause (explained in Part 3). Whilst this does not give Public Sector buyers a free licence to "buy local", it is appropriate to have local community benefit clauses in many of the tender notices and give as part of the selection criteria such considerations as providing training to local people, or taking people off the long term unemployment register. These activities are often the province of third sector organisations, and so there are opportunities for them to establish a track record and income stream.

The Third Sector organisations themselves often experience many of the same problems in selling to the public sector as other more conventional SMEs such as, the need for a track record, robust accounts, a high level of insurance and a lack of understanding of the commercial processes used for procurement.

The OGC has therefore issued a number of guidance notes on the subject including "Think Smart… Think Voluntary sector" and "Buy and make a difference".

Problems with buying from Third Sector Organisations

Third sector organisations are often the recipients of grant funding as well as undertaking commercial activities. This means that they may well be in receipt of grants and awards from a local authority, whilst at the same time, bidding for work with the authority. This can lead to a lack of clarity on both sides as to whether a particular project is a commissioned project funded through a grant, or it is a commercial project for which there should be an element of competition.

The confusion can arise because in both cases there may be elements of writing proposals to meet a specification and rounds of interviews and selection. The local authority commissioning team may themselves be confused as to whether a project is a purchase or a commission, and whether the procurement department need to be involved; they sometimes will seek therefore to make sure that the procurement department are not involved.

A third sector organisation used to grant funding, though experienced in completing proposals and forms, may also find it difficult to understand the commercial environment and the element of competition in procurement run processes.

Lots of social, little enterprise

Many, but by no means all, third sector organisations are established and run by people with a strong focus on a social issue or agenda. This remains the vital core of the organisation and the management will naturally tend to emphasise social skills and experience rather than commercial skills. In some organisations the only tradition commercial role will be accounts and finance.

Because of this focus on social issues, some Third Sector Organisations are sceptical about commerce and be reluctant to engage in commercial activities. Some may see commerce and capitalism as part of the "problem" rather than the "solution". This leads to difficulties with the concept of making a profit for reinvestment in the organisation, as "profit" is associated with big business and "exploitation". In these situations it is often necessary to refer to profit as "funds retained for investment", which could arise from commercial activities or grant funding.

As the economic climate has tightened since 2008, many third sector organisations are becoming more aware of the need for a mix of funding streams (grants, donations, and commercial activities) and therefore are becoming more open to enterprise. Not all of them though have yet acquired sufficient commercial acumen to give the organisation commercial strength that is needed.

Of course, there are also some third sector organisations that have excellent commercial managers, bid writers and sales teams. In some cases these teams have been transferred from public sector authorities, for example from housing departments into housing trusts. These are the organisations most able to benefit from the third sector rather than those with a purely charitable status.

Size and ability/willingness to grow

Third sector organisations (3SO) come in all shapes and sizes, but like standard businesses are dominated by smaller organisations. This means that they share many of the problems of SMEs in engaging with the public sector.

3SOs that are based in a particular community can find it difficult to expand without outgrowing that community they have existed to support. This can create a real tension between the primary focus of the organisation and the need for scale as a credible supplier to the public sector.

There can be the additional issue that these often recently established organisations, may be both small and lacking three years accounts, although because they draw on established and experienced personnel, they may be perfectly capable of delivering a contract.

Primacy of focus

The prime focus of social enterprises is often a particular community or social issue. The commercial side of the organisation is therefore sometimes seen as a "necessary evil" rather than the core of the organisation. There can sometimes therefore be a conflict of interest and priorities between delivering a contract and delivering the support/services to their target community.

Volunteering and continuity of key personnel

Many, but not all, third sector organisations rely on volunteers and/or part time staff to deliver their activities. Others deliver management training or apprenticeships to people as part of their core activities. This means that there can be real issues about the continuity of key personnel.

All organisations rely on key personnel. When that person is a volunteer it is difficult to ensure either that they will continue to make the required commitment of time and effort, or that it will be possible to replace them with a person of a similar calibre if they decide, through changes of circumstances, to not continue volunteering for the organisation. Volunteers are often exceptionally dedicated, but there are occasions when they may decide to reduce their involvement.

Grant funded staff is also vulnerable to the ramp up and ramp down processes where for example, someone funded through a one year grant funded project may naturally be looking to secure a future role on another project any time from 6 months before the end of their current project. The longer the project, the less significant this factor is, but it does mean they key staff may move more rapidly and frequently than is desirable.

Some organisations train and develop people as part of the core of their activities. In these cases it is likely that personnel will move on having come to the end of their funded training.

If the turnover of key personnel is significant, it may have an impact on the ability of the social enterprise to deliver the contract.

Legal entity

As was identified earlier, there are a wide variety of forms of organisation that can be applied in the third sector. These have different advantages in terms of taxation, income and accountability. Often organisations have a historical charter or similar founding document that limits or bounds their activities. The accounting and reporting requirements for these can be very different. These can all prove a problem for organisations that are by nature not standard commercial organisations, but in competing for contracts are often judged as if they were through requirements to account for parent companies, trading accounts, and legal form etc.

Best practices in buying from Third Sector Organisations

Best practices for buying from third sector organisations are similar to those for buying from SMEs of similar size.

Engaging with the sector enables them to be aware of the requirements of the public sector, and the opportunity for mutual benefit. The creation of a "How to sell to the Council" guide is an appropriate first step, but in reality will achieve little unless effort is made to meet with the third sector and through training, coaching, mentoring and feedback, help them to improve their capabilities.

Communicating with the sector is obviously part of the engagement process, but there can be an additional element of making sure that third sector organisations are aware of tender and other procurement opportunities. They may not be looking at standard channels for advertising tenders, and may not consider themselves as suppliers to the public sector. Community teams and other public sector workers engaging with the community groups may be a more appropriate way of making them aware of the opportunity. Consideration should also be made for the fact that they may need more time to respond than standard commercial organisations, and so projects deemed suitable for third sector involvement should have longer deadlines than usual.

Third sector organisations are by definition not fully commercial enterprises, and can be lacking in some of the commercial skills and accreditations that would be possessed by a similar sized private sector.

To encourage them to bid it is therefore appropriate to consider whether a lower than usual level of capacity, experience, and insurance would be acceptable for a project. The requirement for high levels of insurance, financial resources, and accreditations are often seen as off putting by third sector organisations, and lower the requirement for these for all bidders might allow them to compete more easily than otherwise. If the project *requires* the usual standards, then of course they should not be lowed or the project may be put at risk.

Supplier development

As a business's needs, supplier goals and objectives change constantly, it is unlikely that the capabilities of a supply base and the requirements of a buyer organisation will naturally align for any prolonged period of time. Supplier development aims to create and sustain alignment between a buyer organisation and a supplier for the benefit of both parties.

Supplier development has been described as supporting the supplier in enhancing the performance of their products and services or improving the supplier's capabilities. An amalgam of various definitions produces a definition of supplier development as:

"A long term cooperative effort between a buying organisation and its suppliers to upgrade the suppliers' technical, quality, delivery and cost capabilities and to foster ongoing improvements."

Supplier development is meanwhile defined here as::

"Any effort of a buying organisation with a supplier to increase its performance and/or capabilities and meet the buying firm's short and/or long-term needs."

Portfolio analysis

Clearly when a typical supplier base can consist of thousands of suppliers, effort should be focused on those key categories of spend that are most likely to delivery significant additional value to the organisation, as developing current or potential suppliers can be resource intensive. Using portfolio analysis, such as Kraljic, to segment spend it is relatively straightforward to determine the most appropriate categories and, therefore, identify those suppliers to engage in a supplier development programme.

At this stage, some other factors should also be considered, such as the expected benefits from supplier development for the buyer organisation and the supplier's ability to develop and change. Also, another consideration is the cost of development for both the buyer and supplier to ensure that there is an acceptable return on investment for both.

There must also be a consideration of the need to protect market competition, and not to discriminate against other potential suppliers. The safest areas for supplier development are therefore those where there is a clear market failure, and there is no existing competition between suppliers.

Buyers need to protect themselves from supplier power, and long term relationships built up through supplier development programmes may be a way of achieving this. This is because the expenditure is large enough to encourage supplier participation and the category's supply market is difficult to buy in, so the relationship tends to be seen as long rather than short term.

The stated commitment to a supplier development initiative means that is highly likely that the relationship between buyer and supplier will progress and migrate "up" the relationship spectrum towards partnership. A well-structured supplier development programme should link the achievement of specific performance deliverables to discrete "steps" in this relationship migration, where suppliers receive benefits for delivering on their commitment to change and develop.

Added-value supplier development

A number of different offerings can add value to the relationship and could help to compensate for any price increases or offset them. Examples include:

- Joint focus on identifying and solving the shared problem together
- Incentivised performance and shared risk and rewards
- Product innovation, assistance with research and development or even outsourcing responsibility for development
- Scheduling delivery in order to support product availability
- Consignment stock or simplified ordering and invoice processes
- Packaging waste reclamation, reduction or both
- Improvements and developments in product yield
- Higher quality levels.

There are many ways to increase the value that suppliers can deliver. Active participation internally from teams identifying whole life cycle advantages, which are linked to strategic needs, is one of the best ways to ensure the supplier development programmes work.

One of procurements basic objectives is to maintain a network of capable suppliers. Yet many purchasers view their suppliers' performance as lacking in critical areas of quality and cost improvement, delivery performance, new technology adoption, and financial health.

As public sector organisations focus on their core activities and reducing cost, they become ever more dependent on their suppliers to provide high quality goods and services at fair prices. To ensure this buying organisations need their suppliers' performance, capabilities and responsiveness to constantly improve. Therefore, many organisations actively facilitate supplier performance and capability improvements through supplier development.

In practice, supplier development activities vary significantly, ranging from limited efforts that might include informal supplier evaluation and a request for improved performance, to extensive efforts that might include training of the supplier's personnel and investment in the supplier's operations (particularly if the supplier is a VCO).

The focus of many supplier development activities has been short term, targeted at improving suppliers' product or service performance, instead of being a long term focus on improving suppliers' capabilities.

Supplier development activities

Buying organisations may use a variety of activities to develop suppliers' performance and/or capabilities. These activities include:

- Introducing further competition into the supply base
- Supplier evaluation as a prerequisite to further supplier development activities, raising performance expectations
- Recognition and awards
- Training and education of the supplier's personnel
- Secondments of personnel between the buying organisation and the supplier
- Direct investment in the supplier by the buying organisation (in rare situations).

It is a fact that the success of supplier development efforts varies. This raises the question; what factors are responsible for supplier development success? Further, what factors may inhibit successful supplier development? Supplier development is often a manifestation of a buying organisation's proactive stance or attitude towards supply base performance.

Lack of buying power, measured in terms of the percentage of a suppliers output purchased by the buyer, has been cited as one reason suppliers seem to be reluctant to participate in supplier development efforts. If the public sector, or an individual body within it, is only a small part of the supplier's overall business then they may lack a drive to better understand how best to supply the public sector. Lack of effective communication has also been cited as a barrier to supplier development.

Do organisations that engage in greater supplier development efforts reap greater benefits? The answer is overwhelmingly yes.

Supplier Development Practices

Supplier development is becoming increasingly important when supplier switching (i.e. searching for alternative sources of supply and sourcing the product from a more capable supplier) is not viable due to unavailability of alternative suppliers or due to excessively high switching costs.

The basic notions of supplier development can be traced back to 1943, when Toyota joined a supplier association (renamed thereafter Kyoko Kai) to assist a number of sub-suppliers in the Tokai region in improving productivity. From then on, supplier associations within the Toyota supply network and collaboration between Toyota and its suppliers grew constantly. With some exceptions, such supplier development played little part and was not widespread in the Western economies until the 1990's. Since then, firms in the automotive industry have pressed ahead with this practice and turned it into a popular and powerful approach to improve supply chain performance.

Other chronicled examples of supplier development practices applied subsequently by firms outside the automotive industry are, for example, Harley-Davidson, Digital Equipment Corporation, Motorola, and Marks & Spencer.

Reactive and Direct supplier development

Organisations taking a 'reactive approach' measure a supplier only when there are known to be poor supplier performance, and therefore only try to eliminate existing. By contrast, with a strategic approach organisations try to actively improve supplier performance before performance problems occur.

Supplier development can be identified by the role the buying organisation plays and by the resources committed to developing suppliers. In the case of "direct" or "internalised" supplier development, the buying organisation plays an active role and dedicates human and/or capital resources to a specific supplier. Direct supplier development includes activities such as on-site consultation, education and training programmes, temporary personnel transfer or secondments, as well as the provision of equipment. As discussed above in carrying out these activities the public sector body must ensure that it is not distorting the existing supply market, and is treating all potential bidders equally.

The buying organisation commits no, or only limited, resources to a specific supplier in the case of "indirect" or "externalised" supplier development. Instead, the organisation offers incentives or enforces supplier improvement and hence makes use of the external market to encourage performance improvements. This is frequently done by assessing suppliers, communicating supplier evaluation results and performance goals, increasing a supplier's performance goals, instilling competition by the use of multiple sources or alerting to future business. These practices can easily be performed for a wide range of current and potential suppliers, and therefore are less likely to unfairly distort the supply market whilst still improving the quality of supply.

> ### Checklist: Supplier Development Practices
>
> - Buying from a limited number of pre-qualified suppliers per purchased item (where such qualification is appropriate)
> - Supplier performance evaluation and feedback
> - Parts standardisation
> - Supplier certification
> - Supplier reward and recognition
> - Visits by suppliers
> - Training of suppliers
> - Intensive information exchange with suppliers (i.e. sharing of accounting and financial data by the supplier and sharing of internal information such as cost, quality levels, by the supplier)
> - Collaborating with suppliers in materials improvement and development of new materials
> - Parts standardisation complements sourcing from a limited number of suppliers by increasing the volume orders with specific suppliers.

Supplier development and purchasing performance: a structural model

Proper management of supplier relationships constitutes one essential element of supply chain success. As we have mentioned above, buying organisations faced with problems of deficient supplier performance and/or capabilities can implement a wide range of supplier development practices such as supplier evaluation and feedback, supplier recognition and supplier training, in order to upgrade the performance and/or capabilities of the weakest links in their supply chain.

We can view supplier development at three levels, basic, moderate and advanced.

1) The basic supplier development model applies to those supplier development practices that require the least involvement and minimum investment of resources (i.e. personnel, time, and capital) and are thus likely to be implemented first in an effort to improve supplier performance and/or capabilities.

These basic supplier development practices include providing information about public sector requirements and processes, evaluating supplier performance, providing feedback about bids and contracted work. These are also the practices most easily made available to a wide range of potential suppliers.

2) Moderate supplier development practices are characterised by moderate levels of buyer involvement and implementation complexity, therefore requiring comparatively more resources (personnel, time and capital) than basic supplier development practices. The supplier development activities considered to have moderate levels of involvement and implementation complexity include visiting suppliers' plants to asses their processes, reward and recognition of supplier's achievements in quality improvement, and supplier certification.

The collaboration with suppliers in the improvement and development of new materials and components completes the moderate supplier development construct. This practice contrasts with the involvement of the supplier in the buyer's new product design process which is considered in the advanced supplier development construct. Hence, the moderate supplier development construct includes measures of visiting suppliers to assess their facilities, rewarding and recognising supplier's performance improvements, collaborating with suppliers in materials improvement and certification of suppliers through ISO 9000.

3) The advanced supplier development model pertains to those supplier development practices characterised by high levels of implementation, complexity and buyer involvement with suppliers, therefore, requiring a greater use of resources (personnel, time and capital) than moderate and basic supplier developments. These are practices that are mostly likely to have a distorting effect on the supply market, and therefore should only be conducted in the event of market failure or when it can be demonstrated that they will improve the overall level of competition rather than discriminate against some suppliers.

Advanced supplier development practices include training suppliers and involving suppliers in the buyer's design process.
Supplier involvement in the buyer's design process is also linked to other supply practices, in particular, a collaborative atmosphere. A cooperative climate between suppliers and buyers can be achieved by intensive information exchanges such as suppliers releasing internal information (e.g. costs, quality levels) and buyers having access to a supplier's

accounting and financial data. This type of communication with suppliers requires a high level of involvement.

The advanced supplier development model includes measures of training provided to suppliers, supplier's involvement in the buyer's design process, sharing of accounting information by the supplier, and sharing of cost and quality information by the supplier.

Checklist – Supplier development phases

1. Basic supplier development
- Suppliers are informed of their performance (quality, delivery, cost, etc)
- We use standardisation of raw materials and parts.
- There is a procedure for supplier quality qualification.

2. Moderate supplier development
- We visit suppliers' factories to assess their facilities.
- Purchasing collaborates with suppliers in improvement and development activities for new raw materials and parts
- Suppliers are recognised and rewarded for materials quality improvement.
- Suppliers are certified ISO 9000.

3. Advanced supplier development
- The company provides training to its current and potential suppliers.
- Suppliers participate in the buying organisation's design and planning process.
- Purchasing has access to suppliers' internal information (production costs, level of quality).
- Purchasing has access to suppliers' external information (accounting information).

Relationships among supplier development activities

Supplier evaluation allows the buyer to identify what supplier performance indicators and/or capabilities need to be improved. Using this information enables the buyer to make a better decision about the kind of supplier development activity that needs to be implemented.

For example, if the quality of materials needs to be improved, the buyer could collaborate directly with suppliers in materials improvement, or provide training on quality management to suppliers. Similarly, if the focus is to improve on-time delivery, the buyer could share detailed information about requirements with suppliers. Additionally, the reward and recognition of supplier performance improvements is not possible without continuous supplier performance evaluations.

Empirical research has shown that the evaluation of suppliers through site visits, and the use of a supplier reward and recognition system, improves supplier performance.

Supplier Development Methodology

Some public sector organisations have addressed the development of local supply chains through a structured development programme. During this sort of programme selected local suppliers are initially termed associate suppliers. These 'associate' suppliers work alongside established suppliers to gain experience and technical know-how. They are then incrementally able to take on increased volumes of contracts as their technical and logistical capabilities increase.

Existing suppliers may be willing to take part in these exercises, despite the apparent increase in competition, as it will gain them competent locally based sub-contractors and suppliers. In addition it may also allow them to demonstrate an economic advantage element to their proposals. Developing the capabilities of local suppliers should not however be confused with giving them an unfair advantage over suppliers based outside the region.

The development of associate suppliers approach is based on three major stages, namely:
- Technical development
- Capacity development
- Logistical development

Firstly, the technical capabilities of the company are developed prior to concentrating on their capacity and logistical capabilities.

The second stage of the development process aims at ensuring that the associate supplier can meet the increased volume requirements required of full suppliers whilst maintaining quality at every stage. For instance, the associate supplier may be given a subcontract of between 5 and 10 per cent of the volume requirements of the established supplier in order to test the process capability and logistical capacity of its system – it may also be encouraged to bid for small contracts of such as size (although no preferential treatment should be given). Working with the established supplier, the company will be given increased product volumes as and when the system is capable of achieving the volumes under repeatable quality levels. They will then be able to bid for business themselves without support, but may continue in a partnership or sub-contracting relationship with the established supplier.

Finally, the logistical system is refined. What is particularly interesting is the ability to continually drive costs down year by year and to improve on the company's supply flexibility and delivery frequency. The company can become a fully fledged potential supplier when there is suitable technical and logistical capacity within the company.

Contract Management

The worst way to 'manage' any contract is simply to leave it to take its course; it will then more than likely go wrong and leave an incomplete audit trail. Let's be very clear here, control cannot be outsourced and management control must remain a core activity. Effective contract management therefore provide for the handling of contractual, commercial and collaboration aspects:

1) Contractual: Performance to a required standard and compliance with the contract conditions; for example, costs and services supplied are in accordance with the requirements of the contract and its terms and conditions. Contract control involves actively keeping the supplier's performance to the required standard.

Participation by both parties is needed if this is to be successful so that any problems can be quickly identified and resolved. It is therefore important that a sound working relationship is established.

If monitoring indicates that a supplier's performance has deteriorated, action will need to be taken. The nature of the action will depend upon the level of the under- performance or complaints. If regular monitoring is effectively carried out problems will be spotted early and the degree of any disruption from corrective action will be minimised. In most cases a discussion on the problem, will be all that is required to secure agreement on remedial action.

2) Commercial: Clear and documented records with evidence where necessary, to invoke any non-compliance procedures, for example, recording complaints received from customers of the service and recording customer satisfaction with the service. It is important for contract managers to have clear and documented evidence if contracts do not run smoothly. Records of all meeting and telephone conversations should be held on file. The supplier should be notified in writing of all instances of non-compliance, and a written timetable for rectification, should be drawn up. It is likely that the supplier will also be keeping records of the problems incurred with the contract.

If the supplier continually fails to perform, this may constitute a breach of contract. The severity of the failure and the cost to the organisation will need to be assessed. Legal advice may be required before any further action is considered. Below are examples of where default in a contract may arise from a failure to:

- Perform any part of the services
- Provide financial or management information
- Employ appropriately qualified, experienced, skilled or trained staff
- Comply with legislation
- Make payment to the supplier on time (clearly both parties must fulfil their contractual obligations)

3) Collaboration and relationships between the parties, the way they regard each other and the way in which their relationship operates, is vital to making a success of the arrangement.

Although it is sometimes difficult to predict accurately where problems may arise, good contract management with regular dialogue between the supplier and customer will help to identify early, potential problems. This will enable problems to be dealt with swiftly and effectively and so prevent major disputes.

Active contract management therefore requires efficient two-way communications between both parties which will anticipate problems, so that these are dealt with quickly and corrective action is taken to prevent similar problems from arising in future. This requires established lines of communication and an overall approach that will jointly and seamlessly manage and control change, for example making joint improvements

As identified by the OGC (2002), good contract management goes much further than ensuring that the agreed terms of the contract are being met - this is a vital step, but this contractual step is only the first of many. Whilst a successful relationship must involve the delivery of services that meet requirements and the commercial arrangement must be acceptable to both parties (such as offering value for money for the customer and adequate profit for the provider), the collaboration between the parties, the way they regard each other and the way in which their relationship operates, is what is really critical in making a success of the arrangement.

No matter what ever is the scope or the terms of the contract, there will always be some tensions between the different perspectives and perceptions of the customer/buyer and the supplier/supplier. Contract management is about resolving such tensions and to do this, there must be an effective collaboration with the supplier/supplier that is based on mutual gains, understanding, trust and open communication.

Control of change

Contract requirements are often subject to change throughout the life of the contract. We live in a fast changing world with a future of "stable turbulence" and it is not therefore always possible to predict such changes and variations in advance, or, at the specification stage.

It may therefore be decided during the course of the contract, that a slight change to the requirements are needed.

Such changes to the requirements will often affect the cost and so will need to be recorded. Changes to the contract may also affect the following:
- The initial specification can be now out of date
- The cost and service, for example, changed delivery times, locations
- The nature of the services being provided

It will normally be the role of the contract manager to ensure that any need for any contract variation is recorded and the contract changed to be line with the newly agreed procurement procedures, where the variation, is clearly tied in with the main contract so that a clear audit trail is possible. Audit trails being especially important for those organisations in the public sector who find it essential to keep records of dealings with suppliers whether written or verbal as such records are required for:
- Information if problems arise,
- Reviewing meetings and re-negotiations

- Audit purposes
- Planning for any subsequent re-tendering processes

End of Contract/Completion Reports

It is good practice at the completion of any contract to review and place on record what went well and what lessons can be learned for any future contracts, for example with a Supplier Evaluation Report. The information on this report will be used to evaluate and monitor the effectiveness of the organisations suppliers. This essentially covers the outcome and extent to which the expected benefits (deliverables) were achieved.

A Paradigm Change

Through the decision to use suppliers or suppliers, an organisation moves from a focus on protecting the "how" to managing the "what". This means changing the organisational structure from a focus on internal competencies in the higher risk/strategically important zone to the external sourcing of lower risk/non-strategically important competencies. This requires a paradigm shift in the organisation's management from being process operationally minded managers towards becoming contract managers. There may be considerable attention paid to such changes in the activities of a public sector body, but these are outside the scope of this book which is focuses on the practicalities rather than the political implications. The key attitudinal changes required as follows:

- **Respect** the supplier. Often, there are clashes as two different cultures come together. For example, the supplier is now the "expert", and will have different ideas of how to carry out a contract that standard public sector practices.
- **Develop Rapport.** A longer term contractual arrangement is an opportunity to move away from adversarial/transactional relationship to a collaborative/ partnering supplier relationship. This requires the development of rapport between all of the key players.
- **Focus upon Project Milestones.** Regular meetings are required to report on transition, optimization and process improvements. The supplier must be regularly accountable but must also receive regular clear guidance.
- **Clear Statements of Deliverables.** There should be no doubt about the deliverables of the supplier. They should be stated in the agreement but also clearly understood by the key players and regularly reviewed by them at an appropriate forum.
- **Staff Interaction.** Interaction is vital at both the management level and the

working level. Contract management should always be on the lookout to facilitate interaction to head off potential problems and to encourage innovation and synergies. There may be problems because of perceptions of the differences between public and private sector staff practices, which may lead to tensions if not quickly identified and resolved.

Any eventual gap between planned and actual benefits of using a supplier and the non achievement of the expected performance will not be caused only by the external supplier; but also by internal barriers, such as resistance and failure to change attitudes. Consequently the required support to the new ways of working together has been stifled and prevented.

Best Practice Contract Management

We can identify the following aspects of good contract management. This can be summarised as follows:

1. **Good preparation**. An accurate assessment of needs/requirements helps to create a clear technical and/or performance based specification. Effective tender evaluation procedures and selection against the right specification criteria will ensure that the contract is awarded to the right supplier.

2. **The right contract**. The contract is the legal foundation for the relationship. It should include aspects such as allocation of risk, the quality of service required, and value for money mechanisms, as well as procedures for communication and dispute resolution and the contractual obligations of the customer/contracting organisation. This may mean more than simply using standard terms and conditions.

3. **Empathy and understanding**. Each party needs to understand the objectives and business of the other. The customer must have clear public sector objectives, coupled with a clear understanding of what the contract will contribute to them; the supplier must also be able to achieve their objectives, including making a reasonable profit.

4. **Service delivery management and contract administration**. Effective governance will ensure that the customer gets what is agreed, to the level of quality required. The performance under the contract must be monitored to ensure that the customer continues to get what they expect.

5. **Collaboration and relationship management**. The eventual success of a contract depends on mutual trust and understanding, openness, and excellent communications. These being just as important (and may be more so), then the fulfilment of the legal terms and conditions.

269

6. **Continuous improvement**. Improvements in price, quality or service should be sought and, where possible, built into the contract terms and the benefits shared.

7. **People, skills and continuity**. There must be people with the right interpersonal and management skills to manage these relationships at all the multiple levels in the organisation. Clear roles and responsibilities should be defined, and continuity of key staff should be ensured as far as possible. A contract manager (or contract management team) should be designated early on in the procurement process.

8. **Knowledge**. Those involved in managing the contract must understand the business fully and know the contract documentation inside out. This is essential if they are to understand the implications of problems or opportunities over the life of the contract.

9. **Flexibility**. Management of contracts requires some flexibility on both sides and a willingness to adapt the terms of the contract to reflect a rapidly changing world. Problems are bound to arise that could not be foreseen when the contract was awarded.

10. **Change management**. Contracts should be capable of change (to terms, requirements and perhaps scope) and the relationship should be strong and flexible enough to facilitate it.

11. **Proactivity**. Good contract management is not reactive, but aims to anticipate and respond to business needs of the future.

Budget Management

Organisation budgetary control

Financial budgets are used throughout all types of organisations. A budget is a plan and a forecast in financial terms, covering a specified period of time. Budgetary control involves the setting of objectives, in monetary terms, and enables managers to plan and control the resources they are responsible for. When regular comparisons are made between what was planned and what actually occurred, any variances can be remedied or the plans can be revised. Budgets as a management tool are therefore very important.

There is however no perfect budgetary control system. If it is to be effective, though, it should be tailored as closely as possible to the needs of the organisation. An effective budgetary system will be possible if the following points are adhered to:

- There must be a system in place for the efficient collection and processing of accounting data.
- All of the management team must be committed to and involved in the budgetary process.

- The will to act on budgetary information quickly and positively, must be encouraged.
- Managers must be trained in budgetary control and interpretation techniques.
- Good lines of communication must exist within the organisation.

Constructing a Budget

Two of the most popular methods of setting budgets are as follows:

1) Zero-Based

This way to establish budgets is to take a view that all forecasts are developed from a zero assumption basis about what costs or revenues might be for future periods. The budget is built up without any reference to previous periods. It is based upon what is likely to occur, derived from the forecasts.

2) Historical Costs

In this type of budgeting, previous knowledge of costs is used as a basis on which to formulate the forthcoming period's budget. For example, if postage and stationery costs equalled £20,000 last year, and the inflation rate is 5%, the budget for the forthcoming year would be set at £21,000.

This system can be fraught with difficulties, however, if those responsible do not take into account the many factors that affect revenues and costs over a year.

After making the above choice then the following process can be used to construct a budget:

- Determine the assumptions, for example, the sales forecasts, the future unit cost estimations etc.
- Specify the demand; for example, the daily number of orders to be placed
- Analyse the process and resources needed; for example, if 100 orders are to be placed a day and the known operative rate is 2 orders per hour, then 50 labour hours are needed
- Apply the financial factors, for example with order placing, 50 labour hours at a labour cost of £"x" per hour, gives the labour cost per day for order placing.
- Evaluate; to see if the plan looks realistic and conforms to expectations from others in the organisation. This may mean iteration is then required.
- Finalise the budget/forecast plan.

Variance Analysis

After the implementation of the budget forecast plan, eventually the forecasted levels will become actual levels. The actual and the expected or the forecast plan are compared and thereby enable the financial performance to be assessed.

On receipt of these figures, the next task is to explain the variances. These will be due to changes from the time when the budget was planned and the current time. Budgets are after all, a forecast and will rarely be 100% accurate in the months when the "actual time" later has come.

Changes may have been caused by one or a combination of the following:
- Volume; for example, order throughput was forecast at "x" orders, the actual was plus/minus "x"
- Mix; for example, spend was forecast at 80% low value and 20% high value, however the actual was 60%/40%
- Performance; for example, order placing rate was forecast at 2 orders per person hour, actual was 1.6; therefore more labour hours (and cost) were incurred.

The impact of the variances can then be assessed and adjustments, where appropriate, can be made; for example, to the physical activity/operations/KPIs and to the financial budget.

A budget therefore, enables performance to be monitored and controlled on a period basis; provided of course, the system for collection and allocation of the relevant data is an efficient one.

Advantages/disadvantages of budget control
The use of budgetary control systems has advantages as follows:
- Resources are controlled efficiently.
- Motivation of those involved can increase if they are included in the budgeting process.
- Decisions can be based on the examination of problems and corrective action.
- Plans can be reviewed regularly.
- The activities of the various functions, in the company, can be coordinated effectively.

Meanwhile the most common criticisms of budgets are:

- Budget setting and monitoring are time consuming and can prevent people performing their jobs.
- As mentioned above, planning is an inexact science and the results can be totally different from what was anticipated.
- Some managers may be happy to achieve only the budget targets and not push beyond this.
- The setting of budgets can de-motivate, if targets are imposed or set at levels that are felt to be unrealistic.
- Some budgets can actually constrain managers and prevent them from taking opportunities which may arise; these are also those people who believe they must spend the allocated budget; otherwise they will not get an allocation next year. Such people need to appreciate that a budget is essentially a plan in financial terms; therefore budgets must not be seen as being "fixed must happen". For example, an effective manager may actually make savings in year one, but is then penalised in the year two's budget for not spending the allocated money. This is truly a management form of insanity; and as someone not familiar with such ridiculous practices said incredulously to one of us, "you mean you can actually get penalised for saving money?" Clearly such fixed "must spend the budget" thinking should be an outlawed practice and be replaced with proper and correct budget practices.

Budgets in the public sector

Many Public sector projects are criticised for being delivered late, over budget or both. This is often attributed to both poor procurement and poor project management. The problem is by no means constrained to the public sector, but the fact that the public purse has to pick up the extra costs and means a much higher profile for such projects. The project management of projects is outside the scope of this book, but the related procurement processes are worth consideration.

Perhaps the most infamous recent case is the case of the Scottish Parliament building in Holyrood, Edinburgh. The building was eventually delivered two years late, massively over budget, and some of the problems can be identified as arising early on in the procurement process. Although undoubtedly an iconic building, the flaws in the procurement process began with very early the selection of a designer who did not have the required £5m of professional indemnity cover required of entrants to the design competition. They were allowed to "sort it out" later. Also, the impact of changes to the specification process was not understood or adequately project managed.

Case Study – The Scottish Parliament Building

- The original estimate was £34m
- The contract award value was £65m
- Final cost of the project was £413m (after deducting claims against the contractor – not allowing for that the final total would have been £432m)
- Project was over two years late
- A public enquiry revealed a lack of change control, or any realisation by the client of the impact of change on cost and delay

By contrast Heathrow Terminal 5 (which has already been referred to earlier in this book) was also a massively complex procurement and build project in the private sector, opened on time and on budget, although the success of the project was slightly marred by relatively minor people problems from the operator British Airways in the first days of operation. As noted by Matthew Riley, Supply Chain Director, BAA (in *Supply Management* 13th March 2008):

"What we found was that, if we were to apply the average outturn performance …..to Terminal 5, a five-year build programme would probably be about two years late, a cost target of £4.3 billion would probably be at least £1-£1.5 billion over budget, the quality would be variable and statistically 12 people would die on site."

Two of the key approaches taken at Terminal 5 were that BAA (the terminal owner and buyer) held all risk in the project in order to minimise the potential for delays caused by disagreements between the contractors. BAA also insisted on collaboration ways of working and a no blame environment with co-operation, transparency and joint problem solving being the preferred and only contractual approach.

Spending to budget

One problem frequently associated with public sector procurement is that of "spending to budget". This has two elements, both of which are understandable, but both of which are poor practice:

- Buying extra goods or services to spend up to a budget limit

- Paying for goods or services well in advance of delivery in order to take advantage of an available budget.

The problem often arises from a "use it or lose it" policy, whereby budgets are set relative to the previous year's expenditure. This creates an incentive for commissioning departments to ensure that budgets are matched exactly.

There can be a number of problems with this approach. Firstly, spend is often arranged at short notice when the budget surplus is clearly identified near the end of the financial year. This usually means that normal procurement processes are shortcut or even circumvented all together (often by issuing several small Purchase orders, which individually are below procurement thresholds but collectively are above the limit; this of course is not an acceptable way of avoiding procurement limits).

As a result, spend is usually with the existing suppliers and new suppliers are not able to compete for the business. This also exposes the authority to the risk that the appointed supplier is unable to fulfil the contract due to financial problems, although the cash flow benefit to the successful supplier is normally appreciated. However, for the upfront payment, a discount would normally be anticipated, which is usually not sought because of the time constraints.

Finally, this practice also creates a risk of paying for services or goods that are not actually required or, in the case of services, which are not delivered. Whilst the supplier may be willing to deliver alternative services instead, this is still not a proper process open to completion.

Tracking spend against budget

With large projects it is important to track spend against the budget progress. This is not only a case of ensuring that payments are made on time, but also that they are made against the appropriate project milestone. The original Invitation to Tender or supporting documents and the bid proposal should include a timescale for the project. This should include milestone, stage payments, and potentially any retention.

Overspend against budget timescales can be an indication of rising costs, or a faster than anticipated delivery. In turn, under spend could be due to the unanticipated efficiencies, or to a lack of progress. It is important to be able to distinguish between these two issues.

Other factors to be considered include:
- Accuracy of the original project plan
- Accuracy of the original cost forecasts and projections
- Changing of key circumstances, e.g. interest rates and commodity materials
- Supplier obligations to fixed fee or day rates for activities
- Variation charges and claims
- Disputes between suppliers
- Revisions to specifications
- Unforeseen and unforeseeable problems, e.g. weather, ground conditions, Icelandic ash clouds etc.
- Progress Payments
- Incentives for early completion
- Expiry dates for projected costs
- Long lead time items

In order to assess whether the project is on track it is necessary to look at not only how many of the work packages have been completed, and how much money has been spent but also to consider how whether the project is likely to be on budget, overspent or under spent. An under spend at any stage during the project might indicate purchasing effectiveness, or delays in the project. Similarly an over spend at any point on the timeline might indicate that the project is in fact progressing faster than anticipated, rather than costing more.

Halfway through a project, we might expect to have completed half of the deliverables. In the example below, only 40% of the work packages have been completed. Additionally the budget indicates that £525,000 should have been spent by this time (the BCWS – Budgeted cost of work schedule), but in fact £675,000 has been spent (ACWP – Actual cost of work performed). Clearly the project is over budget, but by how much? The additional £150,000 – or a larger amount?

As can be seen the true overspend is £275,000 (the cost variance, CV) reflecting the fact that the money spent has only been for 40% of the work packages, rather than the 50% planned – the Schedule Variance (SV). The whole project therefore can now be forecast to cost considerably more than budgeted (the Forecast at Completion FAC, compared to the Budget at Completion BAC).

Example of earned value of project completion

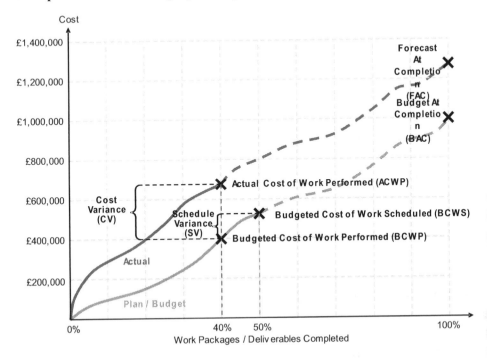

5: Public Sector Procurement: some conclusions

Size of the public sector

The number of commissioning bodies in the public sector is extensive and the details of these bodies will change over time along with central and local government reorganisation. The following is list of such bodies (that will no doubt be out of date between the writing, publishing and buying/reading of this book):

- 152 Principal Authorities in England (2 tier shire counties 27, Metropolitan District Councils 36, London Borough Councils 32, Unitary authorities 55, others 2)
- 32 unitary authorities in Scotland
- 22 unitary authorities in Wales
- 26 districts in Northern Ireland
- Plus the Isle of Man
- 9 Regional Development Agencies; most to be phased out by March 2011
- Other Central Government Public sector bodies
    - ACAS (Advisory, Conciliation and Arbitration Service)
    - DEFRA (Department for Environment, Food and Rural Affairs
    - BBSRC (Biotechnical and Biological Sciences Research Council)
    - The British Library
    - The Cabinet Office
    - Civil Service College Directorate
    - Central Office of Information
    - Council for the Central Laboratory of the Research Council (CCLRC)
    - The Court Service
    - Crown Prosecution Service (CPS)
    - DCMS (Department for Culture, Media and Sport)
    - HM Customs and Excise
    - Welsh Historic monuments
    - Ministry of Defence
    - DfES (Department for Education and Skills)
    - Employment Service
    - EPSRC (Engineering and Physical Sciences Research Council)
    - DTLR (Department for Transport, Local Government and the Regions)

- Export Credits Guarantee Department (ECGD)
- Foreign and Commonwealth Office (FCO)
- Department of Health
- Health and Safety Executive (HSE)
- The Home Office
- HM Inland Revenue

Reductions in the number of commissioning bodies are expected to be severe during and after 2010. Each of the bodies shown below has their own procurement processes and guidelines, which should be derived from the UK national guidelines and the EU Procurement directives. No surprises then that some suppliers become confused and will also make "customer supply decisions". Therefore we examine below the perennial strategic dichotomy and paradox of trying to be commercial, yet, a requirement to retain public accountability; coupled with the constraining bureaucratic process, yet, also a requirement to release supplier/buyer innovation.

Controversy: is tendering the best way?

This section is deliberately presented to be provocative, to provoke discussion and to give views of alternative best practices. It needs to be read with this in mind. The authors welcome discussion of these themes at the blog www.pawablog.blogspot.com

We were recently encouraged by a conversation with the head of one the UK's major academic institutions, who solely teaches on procurement in the public sector, and who observed that as a University they need to discuss more alternatives and options, so as to encourage thought and to challenge current thinking and methods. Clearly there are legal constraints on making changes, but then in difficult economic times, this requires innovative thinking. As we have seen throughout this book, one of the key activities of procurement is to obtain acceptable agreements with suppliers. This can be done by using the tendering or by using the negotiating processes.

However, which of these two processes is best and why do some public sector organisations use only tendering, whereas other (commercial) organisations will only negotiate? Obviously tendering is required by legislation in some circumstances, but does it yield the best results? Let's therefore briefly consider the negotiating and tendering processes further in the following sections:

- What is Tendering?

- What is Negotiation?
- Suppliers are one side of the buying process, five questions must be asked by buyers
- What is it fundamentally that Suppliers and Customers want?
- Summary

What is Tendering?

Tendering is defined as:

"The procedure, by which potential suppliers are invited to make a firm unequivocal offer of the price and term which, on acceptance, shall be the basis of the subsequent contract."

Tendering is a formal process involving the following steps:
- identification and selection of suppliers from whom to seek bids for those selected suppliers, the issue of invitation to tender (ITT) documentation that contains the buyers specification or the statement of requirements
- receipt and assessment of tenders
- selection of the preferred tender/supplier

Those tenders received by the nominated date/time, will then be assessed, both technically and commercially, against the required criteria that has been specified in the ITT and at this stage; any offers that do not meet these criteria are eliminated. The objective of the tender assessment is therefore for the purchaser to establish which the best offer is. These assessments will normally cover the following aspects:

Technical assessment	Commercial assessment
Compliance with the specification (either a conformance specification or a performance specification)	Price
The required output parameters will be met	Any other commercial qualifications such as terms of payment
Product/service quality	Perceived risks such as supply lead times
For equipments, the maintenance/repair over the operating life	Value for money

If price is the only selection criterion, then the tender with the lowest price will be awarded the contract; however where price is only one criterion among several others, such as service, lead time, quality etc; then the purchasing organisation will need to decide the most economically advantageous tender (MEAT) or, which one represents the best value for money (VFM).

The result of the assessment is therefore to rank the tenders either by price, or in accordance with assessment criteria and these which could be specified in the ITT. This establishes the lowest assessed tender, which is then recommended for the award of contract. The tender specification in the ITT must therefore be clear, unambiguous and allows suppliers to make an appropriate offer.

In summary, tendering aims in a single round of tendering to obtain compliant tenders from qualified tenderers by allowing for open competition and fairness.

What then are the perceived disadvantages of tenders?

Tendering may not always give the intended open competition and fairness; even though these are the major reasons for its use. Indeed tendering may be merely "going through the motions" as tendering processes can be influenced by those who have power and influence over the eventual selection process. Tenders may also be selectively issued with supplier's responses then being clearly influenced. Additionally, I am reminded of a procurement manager who once said to me, "we are always able to pre-cook the tender board."

The private sector, for example, will usually disregard tendering and after selecting suppliers, moves straight to negotiating. They see the following disadvantages of the tendering process:

- When it is necessary to clarify any technical points in the ITT, this will automatically mean such a question/answer is then passed onto all of the other bidders/suppliers; therefore, any commercial advantages of the supplier are openly revealed.
- The supplier may wish to give better alternatives that can only be found during negotiations; the tender specification can restrict the offering of alternatives.
- Tendering is slow and expensive to administrate.
- Tendering conflicts with "newer" collaboration approaches and working more closely together with suppliers.

- Tendering is irrelevant to monopoly suppliers of for example, OEM spares, brands etc.

Let us explore the negotiation process.

What is Negotiation?

Negotiation can be defined as *"the resolution of conflict through the exchange of concessions"*. This will mean trading concessions, not donating them, and can also only be undertaken with people who have the power to vary the initial terms and are able to give something in return. In other words, all the players have to be prepared to negotiate.

The advantages of negotiations can be seen as follows:
- Relatively expedient
- Unclear requirements can be clarified
- Inexpensive
- Flexible and not prescriptive
- Confidential

Disadvantages of negotiations are seen as below:
- No transparency
- No clear audit trail
- Requires skill and competence
- Viewed as a competition with winners and losers
- Can need a lot of preparation
- Usually only with preferred candidates

Conducting negotiations is a skilled process and whilst there are available some ideal guidelines, it cannot be thought as a strict procedural process; indeed some observers observe there are really few rules involved. As it is a process conducted by people, then, personality and cultural aspects are also involved where for example, negotiating with Koreans is different to negotiating with Germans.

Negotiating is a skill that needs to be learnt and developed. Whilst it is commonly found that supplier's sales people are trained in selling and negotiating, perversely and regrettably, buyers are often not trained to negotiate.

Suppliers are one side of the buying process

In the buying of products/services, the position of the supplier in the marketplace should be considered; this often being something that is not systematically considered by all buyers.

There will often be other buyers for products and this may mean the supplier takes a view of how "attractive" the buyer could be as a customer. Indeed, there may be several reasons why the buyers appear unattractive to suppliers including:

- The buyers standards that need to be met by the suppliers
- The amount of competition for the buyer's business
- The investment that needs to be made
- A low profit level
- The expense of any tendering process

Additionally, the number of available suppliers may be large or small, for example, markets may be expanding or contracting and buyers therefore need to be aware of the expansion or contraction of the supply market from which they are procuring.

It should therefore never be assumed by buyers that every supplier is "desperate" to supply them with products or service. Suppliers have a view of their market and this will affect a suppliers positioning towards buyers; for example the suppliers view may be one of the following:

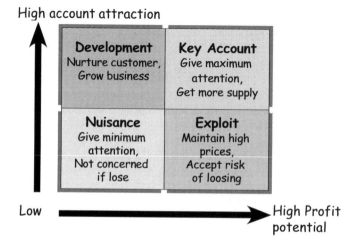

284

Clearly not every purchase has a supplier who views the buyer's business as being a key account for the supplier. In view of these differences then all buyers can usefully consider:

Question 1, just how does my supplier view me?
They may be surprised by the answer and that they are not, universally, going to be seen as being a key account; indeed, they may be seen as a nuisance. The Public sector is seen as being secured for payment, but in many other ways being difficult to do business with and therefore not very attractive.

Additionally, related to this, is the power of each party has, for example:

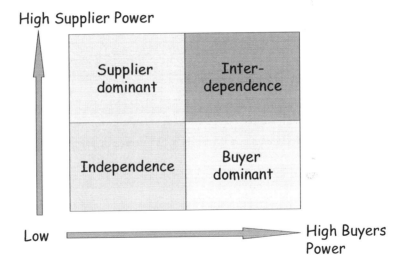

High Supplier Power

| Supplier dominant | Inter-dependence |
| Independence | Buyer dominant |

Low ⟶ High Buyers Power

Where the buyer is dominant there is:
- A small number of big buyers
- Buying of a large percentage of a sellers output
- Ease for buyer to switch
- Many sources of supply
- Low transaction costs
- A "take it or leave it" view from the buyer

Where the seller is dominant there is:
- A small number of big sellers
- Supplying to many buyers
- Difficulty for buyers to switch

- Few sources of supply
- High transaction costs
- An "enforced" view from the supplier

All buyers can therefore usefully consider: **Question 2: what power relationship is there with my supplier?**

The following gives one possible summary from asking and answering the above two questions of the supplier base:

Suppliers name	Q1) Suppliers view of us	Q2) Power relationship
Supplier a	Key account	Independant
Supplier b	Exploit	Supplier dominant
Supplier c	Nuisance	Interdependence
Supplier d	Development	Buyer dominant
Supplier etc.	Etc.	Etc.

This table shows there will be varied responses and whilst some will "match" (e.g. b), others will not (e.g. c). We can ask: **Question 3: What are the implications of these two views?**

Simply here, the answer will reveal that there are varied requirements from buyers and suppliers, some will align, and some may not. We can explore this further by looking at the 5 rights of purchasing related to the well known Kraljic item portfolio. With Kraljic we can see that buyers have a hierarchy of requirements and this is shown below:

The Right	Bottleneck and Critical items Aim: Secure supply and therefore , lower the risk of non supply	Routine and Leverage items Aim: Reduce price by playing the market, possible outsourcing etc.
Quality	Secondary	Secondary
Quantity	Secondary	Secondary
Time	**Number one requirement**	Secondary
Place	Secondary	Secondary
Cost	Secondary , maybe last	**Number one requirement**

From the buyer/customer and demand perspective on the cost/service and the supply balance, then the following ideals are indicated:

- Bottleneck/critical items have service requirements first, (especially the lead time on delivery), with the cost being secondary,
- Routine/leverage items have cost price requirement first and the service aspects are secondary.

The ideal matching response from the suppliers and supply perspective, related to Kraljic, is then going to be as follows:

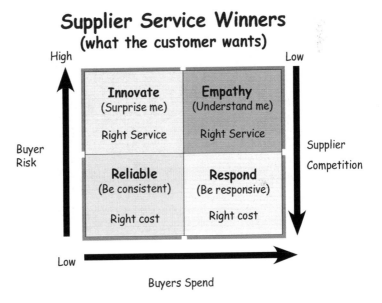

This can be amplified further into an ideal-typical perspective, as follows:

Service winner	Buyers Strategy	Matching Supplier Behaviour	Suppliers Market position
Responsive	Leverage items with Supplier Sourcing "Plays the market"	React rationally with price cuts	Certainty of competition in the short and long term
Reliability	Routine items with Supplier Outsourcing "Organises and lets go"	React by exploring options and "fit"	Certainty of competition, in the short term, followed by stability in the long term
Innovative	Bottleneck items with Supplier Development "Secures supply and attempts to diversify"	Reactive positions when maintaining the monopoly, or, Proactive entrepreneurial behaviour with new product designs	Uncertainties of being able to innovate, high R&D costs, followed by possible monopolistic position
Empathetic	Critical items with Supplier Collaboration "Work collaboratively with suppliers"	Proactive team work and problem solving	Uncertainty initially (forming-storming) followed by norming and long term performing

The question to be asked now is as follows:

Question 4: Will the above mentioned supplier behaviours line up with the buyer's strategy?

Where there is congruence, there is agreement and progress forward will be easier, as both buyer and supplier will have their needs met.

If there is no congruence, then there are possible negotiation options and whilst positions may then be changed, the outcome could be an eventual "no deal." Where however, no negotiation is allowed, then there is really no hope of having a satisfactory relationship and any progress will always be problematic; for example the supplier wants to be innovative and service driven but the buyer is price playing the market and is cost driven.

Indeed with tendering, then it is unlikely the supplier is procedurally able to offer innovative alternatives. May be here therefore, the suppliers only hope of winning a tender is to submit a low price that will "fit the tender" and hope that their alternative can be offered at some later time, once they "in".

Clearly here, it will be the appropriate behaviours by either party that are therefore affecting and driving the supplier/buyer relationship. This should be readily easy to accept with for example, the well know scenarios of "you get what you give" or, "what you give you get", and "what you sow, you will reap". However as we will see with our next question, acceptance of this, does not systematically lead to changing behaviour towards making more optimum buying/supplier selections. So our final question for buyers is as follows:

Question 5: if the buyer's strategy is using tendering 100%, will this give them effective results?

Which is then going to be the best to use, a tendering or a negotiation process? It would seem so far that leverage and routine items may well find a better fit using competitive tendering, whereas bottleneck and critical items are more likely to get better results from with negotiating. Just as in golf where it helps to use the right club for each shot, in procurement it helps to be able to use the appropriate procurement technique for each purchase.

What fundamentally do Suppliers and Customers want?

So now we have seen what fundamentally tendering and negotiations involve and how they relate and vary with each other in a practical way. If we were now to simply view what the supplier and the customer wants, then we can see the following positions:

Source: *The Relationship driven supply chain* Emmett and Crocker (2006)

Criteria	Suppliers want:	Customers want:
Orders	The "business"	Delivered/available goods/services that satisfy a requirement
Information	Clear requirements	Wants clear status information
Performance	Feedback (KPI's that are jointly measured and, benchmarked with other suppliers)	"Feed-forward" (Pre-advice and proactive status/alerts)
Relationship approach	"Fairness" Involvement/"Part of"	Relationships may be a reflection of the procurement portfolio and power positions
Price/Cost	A "fair" to a high price	The "best" total acquisition cost, total cost of ownership, life cycle cost, whole life cost (TAC/ TCO/ LCC/ WLC)
Quality	Clarity on what quality means and what is "valued" by the customer	"Fit for purpose"
Delivery	On time, in full (OTIF)	On time, in full (OTIF)
Quantity	Large regular orders	Smaller, frequent deliveries
Time	Acceptable supplier lead time	Shortest supply lead time
Place	Ex Works (International) or Factory Gate Pricing (Domestic trade)	Delivered domicile duty paid, or Delivered/Carriage paid
Payment time	Prompt	To negotiate

This indicates that there are some very common "wants."

- Orders are the fundamental reason for the relationship as it is the order that drives the supply chain. Customers who are very clear on their specific requirements may generate a response from their suppliers that gives alternative options. Sharing of requirements is useful; after all, suppliers "do not know what they do not know."
- Information is another common objective involving two way communications that gives mutual understanding.
- Performance is another two way process with feedback to suppliers on performance; and feed-forward from suppliers to customers with order status reports and pre-alerts on problems. For example the supplier advising of a delay at least enables the customer to plan; it also builds up trust, understanding and removes uncertainty. Why, for example, should customers need to systematically expedite?
- Relationship; can be combative or collaborative and may reflect the power positions in the buying/selling process
- Price/cost. If total acquisition and total cost of ownership are used in the buyers' evaluation, then there is really little to stop the sharing of the results with suppliers. Again, this can mean that they may be able to better suggest alternatives and options. It will also show "fairness" which after all, is what the supplier looks for.
- Quality. Clarity and understanding will enable the meeting of requirements.
- Delivery has common measures (e.g. on time, in full) for both suppliers and customers and if both parties record these on a per transaction basis and then share such measurements openly on a period basis, they will find this enables better communications and understanding. It also will prevent any "you did/I did not" debates between suppliers/customers, that will eventually lead to mistrust and feelings that "they" are unreliable.
- Quantity; the differences here between the parties are "natural" and will require discussion within the overall negotiations. It may be that allowing supplier's access to demand information and forecasts, will enable the suppliers to better plan their production and so then enable the customer requirements for smaller more frequent deliveries.
- Time; in principle, the supplier lead time can only "kick off" after the buyer's internal process in the total supply lead time. If, therefore, the eventual users within the customer's organisation report continual delays in

supply, it may not be always the "fault" of the supplier. An examination of the lead times will indicate all of the process involved in the lead time "chain" and emphasises the need for such an overall view.

- Place; here the assumption is that the supplier is only interested in producing/ selling a product and that it is the customer's responsibility to "come and get it." Meanwhile, the customers require goods delivered to them including all duties/taxes etc. Of course it is a fact that to enable full comparisons, goods need to be costed at the place where they are to be consumed/used. Again a negotiation point and one possible area is where some buyers find advantage in purchasing on ex works or factory gate terms as they then get clearer lead time visibility and control of both the transit lead times and freight/ logistics cost prices.

- Payment time. A clear negotiation aspect. Indeed most suppliers are more than willing to discuss this and for example, offer discounts for earlier payment.

By exploring the above common wants, then this facilitates potential mutual benefits and gains. The point here is, will these benefits and gains, come from a tendering, or from, a negotiating process?

Summary

Let us now summarise the relative advantages and disadvantages of tendering and negotiating:

Advantages of tendering

Aspect	Tendering	Whereas Negotiations
Openness	Open to all suppliers (in theory) and often with some visibility of results	Open to those approached only and this is usually confidential
Supplier Competition	Competitive between those suppliers invited/ submitted	Competitive between those suppliers negotiated with
Auditable	Auditable	Not easy to audit
Procedures	Procedural and routine , therefore it is more of a rational process	Non procedural and needs skilled trained people. It is an emotional process with some rational judgements
Outcomes	The lowest price or best value for money, and this is "fixed" for the prescribed specification	Easily allows for joint working on solutions for the best deal possible, (for both parties)
Kraljic best fit	Leverage and routine items	Bottleneck and critical items
Power relationship	Buyer is dominant or is independant from supplier	Supplier may be dominant or there is interdependency of buyer and suppliers
Cost/service balance	Cost is usually the prime requirement with possible "value for money" service aspects, (providing these are in included in the specification)	Service supply is prime but allows for cost/ service trade offs in the negotiation

Disadvantages of tendering

Aspect	Tendering	Whereas Negotiations
Clarifications	Cannot always clarify technical points	Can more easily clarify technical points
Specifications	Fixed specification is given, therefore the supplier cannot easily suggest any better alternatives	Supplier can give better alternatives and jointly work on solutions with buyers
Limited usage	No use at all with a "monopoly"	Can use with a monopoly
Cost and time	Slow and expensive	Expedient and cheap
Approach	Conflicts with "newer" collaboration approaches as is a prescriptive approach	Skilled and varied approach can be used
Suppliers invited	In theory is open but can be "fixed" e.g. only certain suppliers are invited. Additionally, suppliers may refuse to be involved in tendering	Can also be "fixed" but most suppliers are prepared to talk/negotiate
Supplier's view	Supplier has "one shot" to get it right	Many opportunities and meetings are possible

Conclusion

This raises the final question for all buyers to consider: Which is best, tendering or negotiating? The answer is in the above discussion; it will depend on the circumstances, however it will be seen that the "one size fits all" approach of tendering is just not going to be the most effective.

Whilst the advantages of tendering, in theory, do seem to be rational; tendering remains questionable in practice, for example:

- Buyers are not able to look at suppliers alternatives that could actually offer improvements against the given/prescribed/closed specification
- The open "for everyone" tender approach is only the theory and the practice is so often closed, as some suppliers are not invited, resulting in the same "recurrent club" of suppliers being used
- Suppliers may feel that the award decision has already been made, so "why bother?"
- Suppliers may choose not to be involved in the perceived bureaucratic and expensive tendering process

Of course, mixed tendering and negotiating may be used, for example some organisations use tender procedures to cover the technical assessment/compliance, and they will then negotiate on the commercial aspects.

However, if we can assume that we will be using honest and ethical negotiators, then it seems very clear that it is negotiating that can offer the overall best approach.

This is further supported by observing that public/ government organisations will generally only tender whereas, the private commercial sector rarely tender and systematically use negotiating. Which of these two sectors is the most commercially efficient?

The UK Government has successively moved activities such as utilities into the private sector in recent decades and more recently, placed much of the NHS procurement into the private sector; (all this being done of course whilst retaining regulatory powers). One driver for this was so that they can become more commercially competitive. Does this also include better procurement practices?

This is not to say that we cannot use both negotiating and tendering as for example, tendering may be useful for the purchase of leverage standard items. However even here, tendering has been replaced by reverse e-auctions in some leading edge organisations; reverse auctions being a classic application for leverage items and also simplify the award process to the benefit of both parties. In conclusion, as argued above, given a free choice between tendering and negotiating, then tendering is just not going to be the single best practice.

By adopting tendering as the sole acceptable solution for public procurement, the EU procurement directives have tackled one set of problems (the openness and fairness of the procurement process) but have then created a system that is both inefficient and bureaucratic, and does little to create innovation, competitiveness and value for money. In the economic crisis from 2008, creating a cash poor public sector environment, then it must be correct that whilst rightly retaining the open and fair movement of goods and services across the European Union, then the member states should look to make procurement more effective by being less (rather than more) prescriptive about the approaches mandated by procurement directives.

As far the UK is concerned, the sooner the government release the talent of procurement people, the better for the tax payer. Indeed in the words of Sir John Egan in "Rethinking Construction" (1998):

"Industry must replace competitive tendering with long-term relationships based on clear measurement of performance and sustained improvements in quality and efficiency."

The same can be said for the Public Sector. Clearly this involves replacing tendering with sitting down and talking and negotiating.

It has to be the right thing to do.

Appendices

Whilst the approaches and practices identified in this book should have applicability in many, if not most countries, there are some aspects to be considered when moving out of English or EU contexts, and we therefore indicate some of these here.

Public Procurement in Scotland

The overriding role of the European legislation means that many of the principles outlined in this book are applicable regardless of country. However, there are some specific approaches developed in Scotland that are worth noting as being different from England.

Public procurement in Scotland takes place within the framework of European, UK and Scottish legislation. It is well understood in Scotland, but less well understood in England, that not only are some powers developed to the Scottish Parliament, but the legal system in Scotland can differ significantly from that in England.

Often laws enacted in England will have an equivalent in Scotland, but these are not necessarily identical in scope or practice.

Scottish public sector procurement policy is based on five key principles of equal treatment, transparency, proportionality, mutual recognition and confidentiality, as laid down in:

- EU Treaty Obligations
- EC Procurement Directives
- Public Contracts (Scotland) Regulations 2006, and
- Utilities Contracts (Scotland) Regulations 2006.

As a geographically diverse country, with a smaller market than England, the Scottish Parliament has different challenges to England in ensuring engagement in the public sector, and in establishing Value for Money. They have therefore established the Scottish Procurement Directive (SPD) to develop and advised on public sector procurement policy. A range of information is available on their website at www.scotland.gov.uk/procurement.

The SPD co-ordinates a Public Procurement Reform Programme to improve practices and to encourage collaboration between the many organisations that procures goods, services and works. At the national level Procurement Scotland are responsible for developing and implementing strategies for Category A commodities such as office supplies on behalf of all Scottish public bodies.

Centres of Expertise have established to manage procurement of Category B goods and services, including the Central Government Centre of Procurement Excellence (CGCoPE), the Advanced Procurement for Universities and Colleges (APUC), Scotland Excel for local authorities and NHS National Procurement for health goods and services for NHS Scotland, with, Fire Scotland Procurement being the proposed centre of expertise for Fire Sector Category B contracts.

Contract opportunities are published at www.publiccontractsscotland.gov.uk and is funded by the Scottish government. As well as the website, this site also sends e-mail notification of appropriate tenders to registered users (whether based in Scotland or elsewhere), and has an innovative iphone application to facilitate easy notification of opportunities.

The aims of the SPD are to:
- Improve collaboration in procurement across public bodies in Scotland
- Ensure Value for Money
- Support better and more consistent practices
- Implement effective policy, regulation and clear guidance
- Provide a point of enquiry for suppliers
- Improve access to contract opportunities
- Recognise whole-life costs and sustainable procurement, and
- Adopt a common, innovative and advanced e-procurement platform across public bodies in Scotland.

Public Procurement in Wales and Northern Ireland

The Central Procurement Directorate in Northern Ireland provides information and public contract opportunities for the public sector at www.cpdni.gov.uk/index/current-opportunities.asp

Sell2Wales provides information on public contract opportunities in Wales at www.sell2wales.co.uk/index/html and also provides e-mail notification of appropriate tenders to registered users.

International Public Procurement challenges

The challenges faced by Public sector procurement in the UK are not unique. All countries face the problems of how to spend public funds in the most effective manner, and as different approaches to best practice have been adopted in different countries, there is therefore no readily identifiable single best practice.

Indeed the UK, although not perfect, is generally spared the consequences of poor practices endemic in some countries from the "hidden" impacts of corruption and political interference.

The International Research Study of Public Procurement (IRSPP), a comparative study based around case studies of major public procurement reforms in a range of nations, has run a number of workshops since 2002 and identified some common issues and insights (full details will be found at www.irspp.com).

Firstly, in most cases compliance with rules is the principal way in which performance is evaluated, rather than from the outcomes of the purchasing decision. The acceptance or irritation with these rules seems to vary from country to country by culture. In all cases, sanctions for failure to comply with rules will affect civil servants more than politicians, though politicians are often identified in the media as being accountable for procurement failures.

Secondly, consortia are usually formed for short term and operational savings and only those long lasting consortia, move onto to be more strategic collaborations.

Thirdly, there are substantial skills shortages in public sector procurement, and there are considerable challenges in addressing these shortages. These shortages are even more problematic, because, in some ways, public sector procurement, is seen as more demanding than private sector procurement due to the need for regulative compliance, and the pressures of public scrutiny.

Public sector procurement is seen as following a seven stage framework:
1) Sourcing goods and services
2) Compliance with legislation/regulation
3) Efficient use of public funds
4) Accountability

5) Value for money

6) Support of broader government policy objectives

7) Delivery of broader government policy objectives

Within this framework, the ability of Procurement to directly influence spending decisions is often limited; as an example from the UK shows, a 2003/4 review of the NHS identified that only 34% of non-pay revenue expenditure was directly controlled by purchasing departments. The remainder was controlled by other departments.

Oversight of the Procurement process is often identified as being a complex system of interacting bodies and agencies, which increases the regulatory and auditing requirement, without necessarily improving the quality of the decision making.

Determining appropriate specifications is seen as consequently problematic; as an example, the US military specification for hot drinking chocolate is some 20 pages in length.

A major paradox for public sector bodies is the balance between red tape and the potential for fraud and corruption. A good balance is hard to achieve, and generally the international public sector is towards increased red tape, with the intention, of reducing the potential for fraud. Improvements in public procurement processes and efficiency is seen as a priority in many places, but in practice, there is a reluctance to move away from a heavily regulated environment even though this has not stopped fraud and corruption having a negative impact, on some procurement processes, in even the most advanced countries.

Although there has been little quantitative comparison between public sector procurement in different countries and regions, the challenges identified are very recognisable to practitioners in the UK public sector.

Bibliography

Armstrong. (2001). *NHS Selects DHL* in **Supply Management** 6 September

Crocker B, Moore, D and Emmett, S. (2010). *Excellence in Services Procurement.* Cambridge: Cambridge Academic.

Emmett, S. (2005). *Excellence in Warehouse Management.* London: John Wiley & Sons.

Emmett, S. (2005). *Supply Chain in 90 minutes.* London: Management Books 2000 Ltd.

Emmett, S and Crocker, B. (2006). *The Relationship Driven Supply Chain.* London: Ashgate Publishing Limited.

Emmett, S and Crocker, B. (2008) *Excellence in Procurement.* Cambridge: Cambridge Academic.

Emmett, S and Crocker, B. (2009) *Excellence in Supplier Management.* Cambridge: Cambridge Academic.

Emmett, S and Granville, D. (2007) *Excellence in Inventory Management.* Cambridge: Cambridge Academic.

Emmett, S and Sood, V. (2010) *Green Supply Chains.* London: John Wiley & Sons.

Gilbert, H. (2008). *A Clean Bill of Health* in **Supply Management** 8 May.

OGC. (2006). *Supply Chain Management in Public Sector Procurement Partnering Works* (2003). London: The Housing Forum.

Parsons, A. (2000). *NHS Supplies* in **Supply Management** 15 June.

Supply Management, 29 June 2000, *Secrets of Outsourcing*

Supply Management, 5 July 2007, NHS *Supply Chain*

Supply Management, 2 September 2010, *Selecting the Procurement Procedure*

Index

43975773R00182

Made in the USA
San Bernardino, CA
03 January 2017